FOREWORD 1

To ensure the completion of the "Fourteenth Five-Year Plan," focusing on the development approach of "promoting advantages, shoring up our weak spots, improving quality, boosting strength, and seeking rejuvenation," the company has established the strategic plan of the "Fourteenth Five-Year Plan" and the 2030 Vision, namely: One-three-six Strategy. The "one" development goal is to return to the "top three" of the Chinese baijiu industry. The "three" development principles include promoting brand leadership, building a quality foundation, and developing culture. The "six" means to build Luzhou Laojiao the model of "six-in-one," which includes "brand," "quality," "culture," "innovation," "digital intelligence," and "harmony." It asks us to inherit and carry forward the company's cultural resources. By taking the lead and focusing on publicity, we are working hard to improve the cultural leadership, enrich the cultural connotation, create cultural icon, develop the artistic style, and take the lead in establishing the cultural image of Luzhou Laojiao as a "700-year-old enterprise" and "24 generations of famous liquor makers."

Li Bin and Yang Jianhui's book *Luzhou Laojiao: Chinese Baijiu in Comics* covers the history of Luzhou baijiu, which contains a professional explanation of the seven significant resources of Luzhou Laojiao, such as land, cellar, technique, fermentation, water, grain and storage, and drinking health. While humorous and interesting, it also systematically and thoughtfully introduced the historical culture, brand culture, craft culture, and health culture of Luzhou Laojiao. It seems like 20 lectures on Luzhou Laojiao liquor culture.

We hope that every employee and friend of the company, including the supply chain system and distribution customer system, can read it and become a "storyteller" who can tell the cultural story of Luzhou Laojiao. It should be the responsibility and mission of everyone who works for Luzhou Laojiao to jointly speak about the brand story and forge the brand monument in the new era.

LIU MIAO
Master of Chinese Baijiu Distilling, Chairman of the Board,
Luzhou Laojiao Co., Ltd.
August 18, 2021

FOREWORD 2

The development of a brand in ten years depends on marketing, but in hundreds of years, it should rely on the quality, while in thousands of years, on culture.

Liquor is a carrier of communication and the medium of emotional communication between adults. Therefore, if the mission of internet enterprises is to "link everything," liquor is also to "link everything." However, one depends on technology, the other on emotion, spirit, and culture. More accurately, liquor aims to "integrate everything."

In 1873, after Zhang Zhidong drank Wenyongsheng baijiu in Yinggoutou, Luzhou, he said that "the good baijiu is not afraid of the deep lane." However, with the improvement of the brand of the baijiu industry in recent years and increasingly fierce competition, we can no longer stick to the concept of "baijiu is not afraid of the deep lane" in the market. We should tell its story to consumers, including the long history of Luzhou Laojiao baijiu culture and Luzhou Laojiao's craft quality culture with living samples awarded as "The First Batch of National Intangible Cultural Heritage Representative Projects," and Luzhou Laojiao's excellent poetry and culture. When speaking to consumers, we should talk bravely, invariably, and skillfully so that the corporate and baijiu cultures can be spread and deeply impact the public in their daily work and life.

Li Bin and Yang Jianhui's book *Luzhou Laojiao: Chinese Baijiu in Comics* is a collection of some of the best articles from *The Cellar Master Speaks* series published over the past two years. And they have been collected into a book once again, which provides a model for reference and study. They can also be used as a tool for distinguished visitors and VIPs to read: using baijiu as a medium and meeting friends with literature.

LIN FENG
General Manager,
Luzhou Laojiao Co., Ltd.
August 18, 2021

Luzhou Laojiao

Chinese Baijiu in Comics

LI BIN and YANG JIANHUI

Books Beyond Boundaries
ROYAL COLLINS

Luzhou Laojiao: Chinese Baijiu in Comics

By Li Bin and Yang Jianhui
Translated by Feng Lei, He Li, and Wu Rina

First published in 2023 by Royal Collins Publishing Group Inc.
Groupe Publication Royal Collins Inc.

Headquarters: 550-555 boul. René-Lévesque O Montréal (Québec) H2Z1B1 Canada

ISBN: 978-1-4878-1039-9

To find out more about our publications, please visit www.royalcollins.com.

Preface 1 Tell the Story of Chinese Baijiu Well

Liquor can also be a typical "language" globally and one of the best mediums for domestic and foreign cultural communication. First, drinking has the broadest mass base. Although the language is different among people in most countries, as long as they hold up the liquor glass, "everything is in the liquor." The psychological distance becomes close and promotes cultural communication in the process of drinking. Second, liquor culture is also an important part of Chinese traditional culture. When it comes to liquor, there are many stories in the 5,000-year inheritance of Chinese civilization, including the changes in the nation, the details of people's lives, reform and changes in politics and the economy, and the inspiration of literature and art. Because the liquor culture includes all aspects of Chinese traditional culture, as long as foreigners fall in love with Chinese liquor, they will understand the Chinese character, customs, history, and even the whole Chinese civilization.

Baijiu is one of the important mediums of Chinese culture. Its traditional distilling techniques are outstanding achievements of conventional Chinese distilling techniques. They are the fruits of the "harmony between man and nature" of farming formed by the Chinese laboring people who adapted to nature and made use of nature for a long time. In recent years, with the guidance of national cultural confidence, we first promoted that the Chinese word "baijiu" should be translated into English by transliteration. No English ready-made vocabulary can accurately express the rich connotation of Chinese baijiu. Meanwhile, in the development and production of baijiu, we should follow the development concept of "both flavor and health." All sectors of society have widely recognized these practices.

Of course, there are also a few backward areas left in China's traditional liquor culture. We should absorb the beat of the culture and keep pace with the times. China's traditional liquor culture includes respect for elders, etiquette, courtesy, hospitality, modesty, and the artistic works of calligraphy, painting, poems, and songs linked to liquor tasting. We hope every consumer can become a "preacher" of China's excellent liquor culture, spread the concept of healthy rational drinking and Chinese baijiu's remarkable history and culture, craft heritage, and abandon some dross culture. Start with how to taste a cup of liquor in our life to present compelling Chinese stories and propose Chinese cultural self-confidence.

For a long time, due to the traditional distilling techniques of "harmony between man and nature," Chinese baijiu has been divided into three prominent aromas, namely, strong aroma, light aroma, and soya-sauce aroma. It has formed the dominant Chinese baijiu-producing areas in Sichuan-Guizhou, Jianghuai, Shanxi-Hebei-Henan, and other regions. Chinese baijiu is rapidly developing in the chief producing regions and has excellent brands. Meanwhile, with the upgrading of consumption, consumers worldwide gradually praise the high-quality baijiu produced in the relevant, advantageous areas and hope to understand the history, distilling techniques, and drinking habits of baijiu.

Color, aroma, and taste are ways for people to directly feel the quality of a glass of liquor. What everyone cares about most is whether the liquor tastes good. How about the quality? How do you feel after drinking? At a daily party, when you pick up a glass of liquor, through the process of observing its color, smelling its fragrance, and tasting its taste, you can explain to everyone what kind of liquor it is, whether it is good to drink and how you feel after drinking, which will make people look at you in a new way. However, ordinary consumers cannot have the opportunity to receive professional training in distilling and tasting knowledge. The published books on professional distilling and tasting are difficult and suitable for experienced practitioners, not ordinary consumers. Therefore, we need to make consumers understand the basic knowledge of baijiu distilling and evaluation in a relaxed and enjoyable way so that consumers can easily read and understand it.

Luzhou Laojiao partly writes about this in the book *Luzhou Laojiao: Chinese Baijiu in Comics*. It tells consumers about the core elements of Luzhou baijiu by comics, including the geographical climate of the distilling industry, the old cellar pond, the raw materials and water used for distilling liquor, microbial fermentation, and the distilling process, and the storage of liquor. The book combines liquor-distilling history with science, pictures, and texts humorously. It tells the story of Luzhou Laojiao liquor, which is worth reading.

In the future, it will be an important direction for Chinese baijiu to upgrade and spread worldwide to tell consumers the history, distilling techniques, product style, and the story of Chinese baijiu in plain language.

SUN BAOGUO
Academician of the Chinese Academy of Engineering,
President of Beijing Technology and Business University
December 18, 2019

Preface 2 A Better Life and the Pursuit of Better Liquor

At first, liquor was distilled naturally and fermented from grain. Then it was distilled artificially with superior manufacture. Chinese baijiu stands towering among the world's liquors. China's baijiu culture is spread worldwide, including the liquor culture inherited for thousands of years. However, Chinese baijiu culture should find a new form of communication. With the help of new media and platforms, it will make young consumers understand Chinese baijiu better. We should make them fall in love with Chinese baijiu with the concepts which are more open, more avant-garde, more fashionable, and more internationalized, and realize consumption concepts that are healthier, more rational, more elegant, and more refined.

At the same time, we should use Chinese baijiu as the medium to tell the world the liquor story of China's culture. Therefore, our professional workers should take the responsibility of "everyone is responsible" and "spread Chinese baijiu to the world" and do well in the popular science and story of baijiu. Chinese baijiu distilling technique has been developed since the 1950s and is significantly involved in grain processing, microbial fermentation, distillation, and storage technology. Under the guidance of the baijiu "169 plan," "158 plan," and "Chinese baijiu 3C plan," the Chinese baijiu industry has entered a further field since 2007. Our purpose is to let the Chinese people truly understand the scientific, technological, and cultural values of Chinese baijiu and to establish cultural self-confidence and scientific and technical self-confidence. At the same time, the popular science service of baijiu must be continuously promoted with industrial strength. During the "Fourteenth Five-Year Plan" period, the China Alcoholic Drinks Association plans to pursue the national liquor science popularization plan and strive to attract more consumers.

Baijiu consumption is upgrading continuously, and our better life is seeking better liquor. Therefore, baijiu quality is boosted, and good liquor becomes the pursuit. The widespread consumption of the baijiu market frequently changes with the requirements in supply and demand, the concept of rational consumption, the pursuit of personalized consumption, and the fierce competition in the baijiu market. Undoubtedly, improving the quality of baijiu will lead to better consumption for consumers. Under the guidance of famous brands, the quality of Chinese baijiu will improve and show more wonderful aspects to consumers.

While improving the quality, the baijiu industry should pay more attention to different expressions of category and the grade of quality. Although many creative brands have had many concept expressions in recent years, there are also many hidden dangers. We encourage personalized quality expression but firmly oppose the implicit expression of quality through conceptual creativity. Through the systematic construction of a product quality grade expression system and the systematic establishment of classification, typing, and grading standards, consumers can understand the raw materials, technology, varieties, storage, and quality grade of liquor. Consumers can know what good liquor is.

We should also create new consumption reasons for liquor and make liquor spread into people's better life with rapid changes. Therefore, we should firmly grasp the opportunity of consumption upgrading and gradual improvement of consumption capacity, help quality upgrading and market upgrading with quality consumption, and comprehensively improve the proportion of famous and high-quality liquor products. We should pay more attention to the changes in consumption patterns, psychology, concepts, environment, and scenes, develop marketable products carefully, attach importance to product differentiation innovation, and build a product structure suitable for the market and self-development.

The inheritance of traditional industries is the most important, the innovation of traditional industries is equally important, and the culture of traditional industries is more important. Therefore, inheritance, innovation, and culture all go further.

Inheritance goes further. Chinese baijiu, Huangjiu, and Lujiu are typical traditional industries with a long history. They are distinctive Intangible Cultural Heritage Inheritance industries, taught by teachers and handed down from generation to generation. They are specific industries dominated by manual distilling, and they are the only naturally distilled liquor in the world. Its micro ecological environment cannot be copied or migrated. Therefore, inheritance is the core of the traditional distilling of Chinese liquor.

Therefore, the traditional distilling industry must respect the tradition, adhere to the tradition, carefully cultivate the talents of traditional distilling techniques, and adhere to the original intention of Chinese liquor distilling: awe of heaven and earth, grain, time, sages, and consumers.

Innovation goes further. Only through continuous innovation can the industry be stable and far-reaching. During the "Fourteenth Five-Year Plan" period, China's distilling industry's scientific and technological innovation direction is to comprehensively improve the ecological distilling level, strengthen the research on distilling micro-ecosystem, and comprehensively improve the personalized distilling level of famous liquor flavor. Each famous liquor has its taste and is based on studying the complex composition of multi-flavor substances from personalized liquor distilling. Secondly, comprehensively improve the research on healthy drinking, the health attributes of famous liquors with multiple active substances, and the research on moderate and scientific drinking attitudes and behavior. Thirdly, comprehensively enhance the scientific and technological value of Chinese liquor distilling, deeply reveal the fermentation mechanism of microbial diversity, study the complex system of flavor and active substances of famous liquors, and research the distillation and storage mechanism of famous liquors, to enhance the scientific and technological confidence of Chinese famous liquor distilling. Finally, comprehensively improve the transformation from traditional distilling to intelligent distilling and deeply study micro ecological reproduction, optimization technology, liquor-making engineering, and sensory flavor of the liquor.

Culture goes further. Culture is the soul of the industry. The liquor will contribute to the inheritance of Chinese culture and the expression of Chinese culture. Sharing Chinese liquor with people who love life worldwide requires higher cultural confidence in China's liquor industry.

Chinese liquor culture is rich in connotation. We not only have a long history of baijiu origin but also have the invention of the artificial distillery, the invention of liquor distilling techniques, and distilled spirits. We also have liquor etiquette, liquor virtue, fun of drinking liquor, drinking vessels, liquor culture, literature, art, sharing, and expression from public life. We also have the auto fermentation mechanism of baijiu, the complex flavor of baijiu and study of the complex composition of multi-active substances, and the modern biotechnology culture of the research on the microbial diversity of baijiu.

Chinese distillers fulfill their mission only by inheriting and protecting our long and splendid liquor culture and by carrying forward and innovating the new liquor culture for a better life. We should innovate the liquor culture and make the new rational, healthy and happy drinking culture a new form of a better life. According to the consumption habits of modern people, we should innovate the consumption culture, lead a healthy drinking culture, and create new consumption rituals, scenes, and experiences. We will create an expression system of Chinese liquor culture through the development and inheritance of Chinese liquor culture that inherits tradition and contains modern elements.

With the continuous progress of human society, liquor quality is improved by people's higher quality of life. The progress of liquor distilling techniques contributes to biological fermentation technology, food flavor science, and life and health. Only with the continuous improvement of liquor culture can the liquor industry move towards a different future.

In recent years, Luzhou Laojiao has been a pioneer and an executor of the popular science of baijiu. They have created an animation and popular science video account for baijiu in the new media, "Jiao Xiao Er Bu Er (bartender never in a daze)." They have about 2,000,000 fans and have accumulated 150 million people's playbacks. Li Bin and Yang Jianhui's book *The Cellar Master Speaks* has been published in its third popular science series. They invited me to write a preface. I will write some observations on Chinese baijiu recently to arouse further thinking. Chinese baijiu is the essence of the national brand and the best material medium to tell the world the Chinese traditional culture. I hope more and more liquor companies and related media organizations can stand at the height of the industry and take a concrete step in the Chinese baijiu popular science road like Luzhou Laojiao, which still has "heavy responsibilities and a long way to go."

SONG SHUYU
President of China Alcoholic Drinks Association
June 30, 2021

宋書玉

Contents

景阳冈

舒聚源

CHAPTER 1

What Is Unique in This City That Refines Much Happiness?

When it comes to drinking, it is recognized that Henan people can drink more. Henan people have a unique custom of drinking: no fish, no liquor, no banquet. The liquor can be drunk with a fish like this:

If the master of the table picks the fish's eyes for anyone, he must drink three cups,
it means "attaching great importance to you."

If the master picks the fish face (i.e., cheek cover) to anyone, he must drink two cups,
it means "saving face."

If the master picks the fish's dorsal fin for anyone, he must drink three cups,
it means "everything will go smoothly."

If the master picks the shark fin under the fish belly to anyone, he must drink three more cups,
it means "going higher."

...

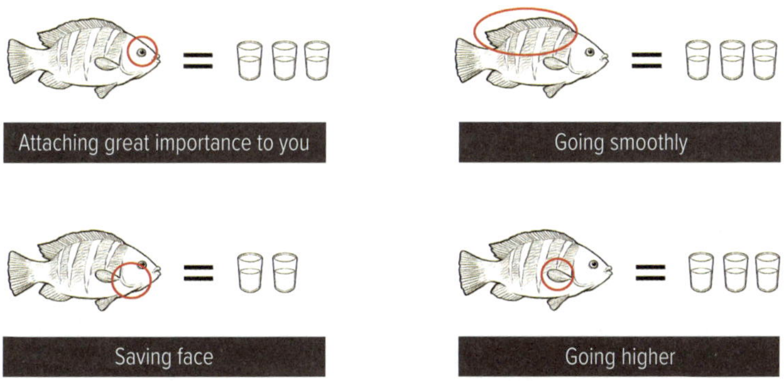

Of course, some cannot drink but are pointed by the fish head, and they can make a unique move to put a leaf to cover the fish's eyes, called "cover everything."

Shandong men do not think so. It can be said that there is no lack of a harmonious liquor party behind anything successful.

There is no doubt that people in **Shandong** drink more liquor than in any other city in China.

Men in Shandong are all good at drinking.

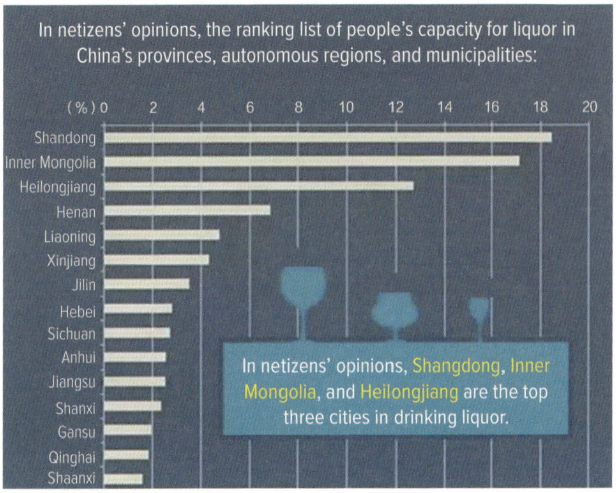

But the women here can drink more than men.

In Shangdong, women do not drink too often, but they will become unusual once drunk.

People in Luzhou of Sichuan are more respectful. In other cities, when people hear the word “Luzhou,” they will have an impression such as:

There is a song in my mind which sings:

We drink liquor like drinking soup, and boys and girls are open ...

Wait! What! Are they drinking liquor like drinking soup? Where is Luzhou?

Duang~

Many people may don't know where Luzhou is. They only know that there is a Luzhou Laojiao that produces liquor. Next, the cellar master will popularize Luzhou. Luzhou also has a nickname called the "**City of Liquor**." Marshal Zhu De personally "registered" and named it a hundred years ago.

In March 2019, at the opening ceremony of the China International Alcoholic Drinks Expo, Zhang Chonghe, the President of the China Light Industry Federation, officially awarded Luzhou the title of the "City of Liquor in China."

So far, this is the first and only city named the "City of Liquor" in China.

The Geographical Location of Luzhou

Luzhou is located in the southeast corner of Sichuan, bordering Chongqing and Guizhou in the East, Guizhou in the South, and Yunnan in the West. It is a central regional city at the junction of Sichuan, Yunnan, Guizhou, and Chongqing. It was called Jiangyang in ancient times, located at the intersection of the Yangtze River and Tuojiang River. It has a long history, rich products, and a developed liquor industry.

People called the north of water Yang and the south of water Yin in ancient times, so Luzhou is also called Jiangyang. There is another city in Jiangsu called Jiangyin.

Luzhou is the largest port in Sichuan in the upper reaches of the Yangtze River. Since ancient times, Sichuan's products and resources, copper in Yunnan and lead in Guizhou have been transported to Luzhou first by land, then along the water to the middle and lower areas of the Yangtze River.

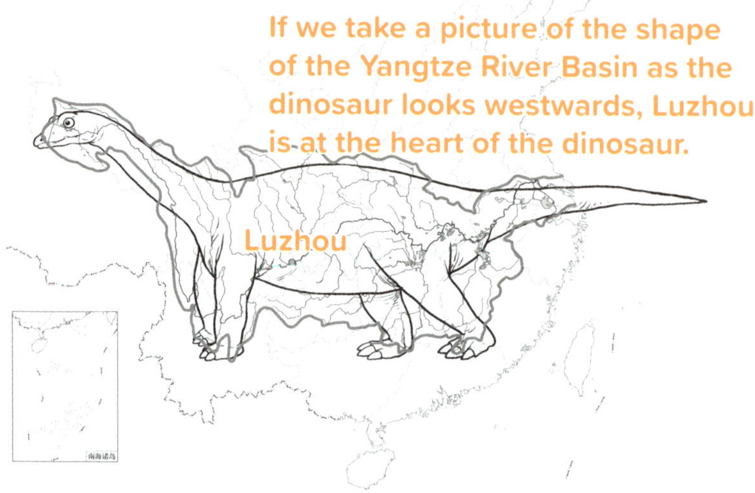

If we compare the Yangtze River to a dragon: Shanghai, as the head of the dragon, has a traction effect; Nanjing, Wuhan, and Chongqing, as the body of the dragon, play a supporting role; Chengdu, as the tail of the dragon, has a balancing effect; Luzhou is located in the center position, which is also the position of the golden section: the navel, that is, shenque acupoint.

So far, Luzhou has won the honorary titles of National Civilized City, National Famous Historical and Cultural City, National Sanitary City, National Water Ecological Civilized city, National Double Support Model City, National Forest City, Excellent Tour City, and so on.

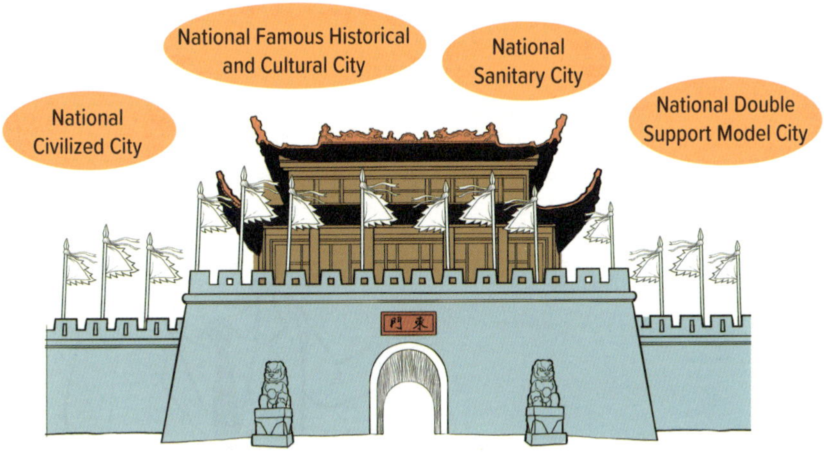

Luzhou is located in the union of Sichuan, Yunnan, Guizhou, and Chongqing, so Luzhou has convenient transportation. It is close to the Qinghai-Tibetan plateau in the west, the Yunnan-Guizhou plateau in the south, the Qinling Mountains in the north, and the Daba Mountains in the east. It is also near Chongqing in the east, Kunming in the west, and Guiyang in the south. So Luzhou has the climate characteristics of all three cities:

It's warm in spring and autumn,

hot and cool in summer,

and not too cold in winter.

Luzhou is the core of the Chinese Baijiu Golden Triangle. The FAO (Food and Agriculture Organization) experts have evaluated it:

"On the same latitude of the earth, only the Luzhou along the Yangtze River can produce pure strong-aroma flavor baijiu."

Convenient transportation brings a prosperous economy and a diversified liquor industry. In addition, Luzhou is also a place rich in subtropical fruits.

Hejiang County of Luzhou is a late-maturing litchi base in China. There are dozens of litchi varieties. The standard types are dailv, tuoti, feizixiao, etc. It is said that the last litchi and longan in China must be eaten by the Luzhou people every year.

It is the origin of the poem written by Du Mu in the Tang Dynasty that says, "the cavalryman rode a horse to deliver for the empress, no one know he brought litchis and fresh fruits." It is said that the litchis eaten by Lady Yang were produced in Luzhou.

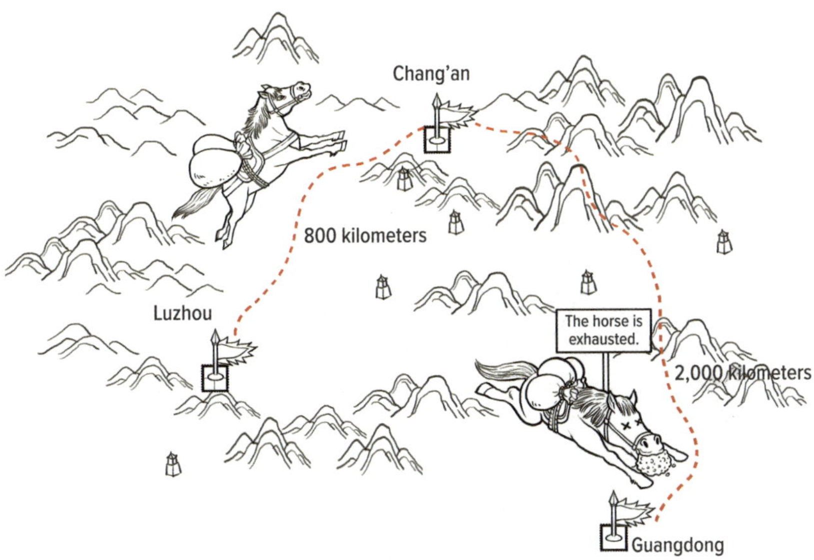

It is more than 2,000 kilometers from Guangdong to Chang'an, which is Xi'an now. With the transportation mode of old post stations, either the horses were too tired, or the litchi had been fermented into liquor. In the Tang Dynasty, there was an ancient litchi post road from Sichuan to Chang'an, which could reach Chang'an in three days, and the color and flavor of litchi remained unchanged.

It is recorded in Luo Dajing's works *He Lin Yu Lu* of the Southern Song Dynasty: "In the reign of the Emperor Ming of the Tang Dynasty, the cavalryman rode a horse to deliver for the empress, it was litchi produced in Hejiang County of Luzhou."

In 2008, the litchi eaten at the Beijing Olympic Games came from Hejiang County of Luzhou.

Historical Changes in Luzhou

Luzhou belonged to Liangzhou in the Xia and Shang Dynasties.

It belonged to the State of Ba in the Zhou Dynasty.

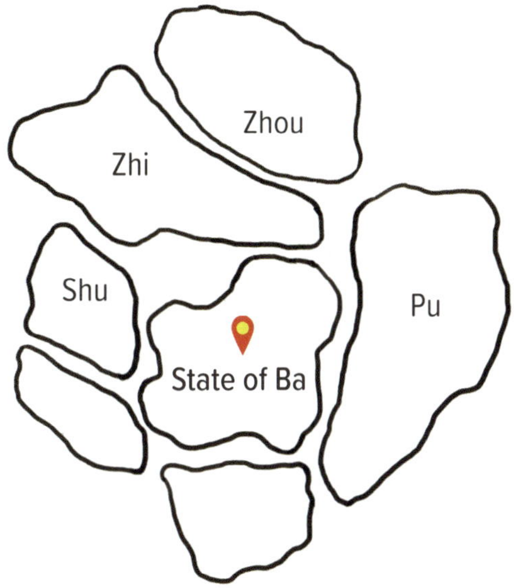

King Jing of Zhou established Ba County.

Emperor Jing of the Western Han Dynasty appointed Su Jia as the Marquis of Jiangyang. You may not be familiar with Su Jia. He was the brother of Su Wu, a shepherd who was exiled to Baikal Lake after being sent to the Huns (an ancient ethnic group in the north of China).

In the period of Emperor Wu of the Western Han Dynasty, Tang Meng was promoted to Zhonglang general to develop the southwest region. Starting from Hejiang County in Luzhou, he went up the Chishui River into Guizhou to conduct economic and cultural exchanges.

He entered Northern Guizhou and persuaded Yelang, Qielan, and other kingdoms to submit to the Han Dynasty.

The scene seemed a little familiar. Ancient people liked to take an oath as soon as they were happy:

The plot continued like this, and something would happen after the oath. Later, Tang Meng set up Qianwei County by marking out a part of the territory of the Ba and Shu Counties.

The origin of the word "Luzhou" can be traced back to the Southern Dynasties. Jiangyang County was established during the Song and Qi Dynasties. Emperor Xiao Yan of the Liang Dynasty took the name of Lushui and built Luzhou, and it governed one prefecture and three counties in Jiangyang.

An emperor who cannot name is not good enough.

In the Song Dynasty, Luzhou was one of the 26 major national commercial cities and a large taxpayer of the imperial court, which had a developed economy and convenient ports. It was important as Chengdu and Chongqing in Sichuan.

Emperor Huizong of Song

On May 2, the first year of Xuanhe (1119), Emperor Huizong of Song issued an imperial edict: Luzhou was an important city in the southwest. It is also a critical border area. So, I decided to upgrade Luzhou to a military governorship and name the army Luchuan.

The key area of Southwest China

In the autumn of 1236, Mongolian soldiers attacked the Song Dynasty on three routes, and the West Route Army, led by Kuo Duan, a strategist of the Mongol Empire, invaded Sichuan from Qinzhou and Gongzhou.

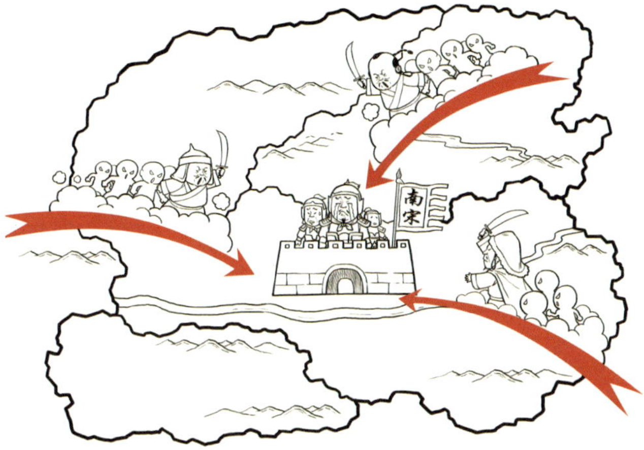

In 1242, Yu Jie, a famous anti-Mongolian general, was appointed as an official of Sichuan. Because of uncertainty about the Mongolian cavalry, and the fact that it was difficult to defend in the Western Sichuan plain, Yu Jie was inspired by the stockade village in the mountain, moved the city to the mountains, and established a mountain city defense system.

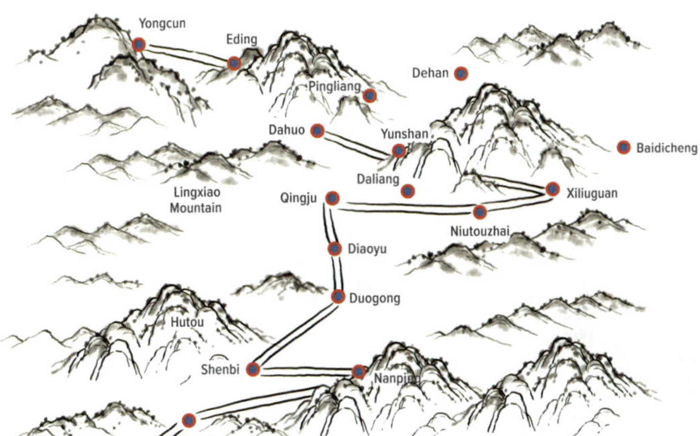

Luzhou Shenbi City and Hechuan Diaoyu City were close to each other, fought against Mongolia together. The war among them lasted more than 30 years and safeguarded the rule of the Southern Song Dynasty. In 1259, Mongke Khan died in Diaoyu City. Since then, the "golden family" has been broken apart.

To compete for the Khan's position and stabilize the rear battle line, Kublai Khan signed a short peace treaty with the Southern Song Dynasty.

After becoming a Khan, Kublai Khan continued to attack the Southern Song Dynasty. The sovereignty of Shenbi City repeatedly changed, with five gains and five losses. Due to the betrayal of traitors, it was occupied by the Yuan army in 1277. Therefore, it is said that "Chongqing is a natural fortress, and Luzhou is as impregnable as iron."

When the Song Dynasty perished, a significant person was born. He was Guo Huaiyu.

(He will be introduced in detail in the next chapter—"Momently Know about the History of Luzhou Baijiu.")

In 1573, after ten years of imperial examination, Shu Chengzong abandoned literature and took the martial arts examination. After that, he left his official position and returned to his hometown. He founded the prosperity of Jiangyang liquor city. Combined with the features of liquor-distilling workshops and liquor shops, he built cellars in 1573.

In the Qing Dynasty, the liquor industry of Luzhou was prosperous. Zhang Zhidong, one of the four important officials of the Late Qing Dynasty, passed Luzhou when he was appointed to the official in charge of culture and education in Sichuan.

Zhang Zhidong was impatient. He waited for a long time to see the servant come back. He was about to get angry. The servant quickly explained:

In 1916, Zhu De set out with Cai E to fight with Zhang Jingyao and Xiong Xiangsheng of the northern army in Mianhuapo of Luzhou. Finally, he defeated the northern army with fewer soldiers and drove them away. This war is also known as the "**Mianhuapo War**."

In 1926, the Lushun uprising led by Liu Bocheng started in Luzhou, known as the precursor of the Nanchang uprising.

Luzhou was liberated in December 1949, and the southern Sichuan administrative office was established in 1950, which governed cities and counties. In 1983, the State Council agreed to change Luzhou City from local to provincial jurisdiction, with four counties and three districts under its jurisdiction.

Administrative division map of Luzhou

Luzhou Economic Construction

Approved by the Sichuan Provincial Bureau of Statistics, Luzhou achieved a regional GDP of RMB 215.72 billion yuan in 2020, to which the liquor industry contributed strongly.

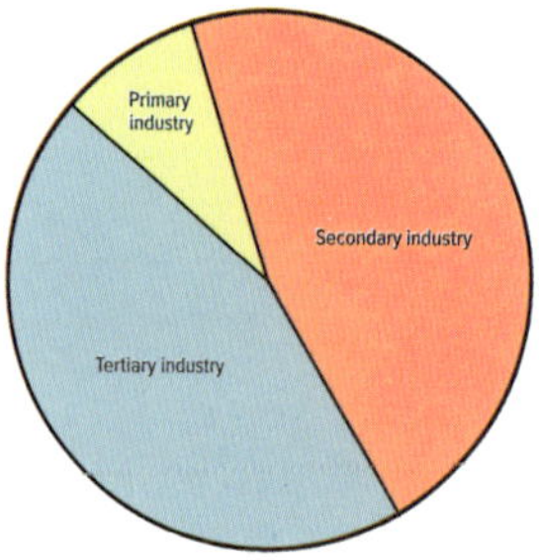

The GDP of Luzhou is RMB 215.72 billion yuan in 2020.

Baijiu enterprises jointly achieved revenue of RMB 100.84 billion yuan in the main business.

In addition to liquor, Luzhou has many developed industries. With the development of the economy and the vigorous growth of emerging industries, traditional industries need to be transformed and upgraded and gradually form three hundred-billion industries.

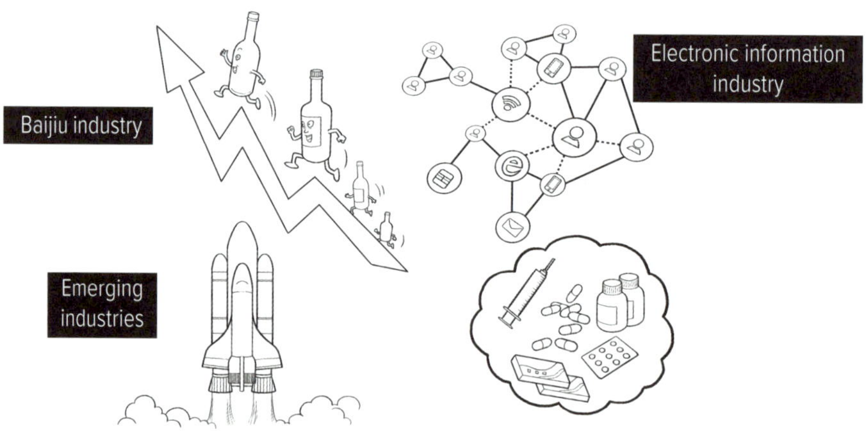

"Three hundred-billion industries" include the 100 billion baijiu industry; the 100 billion electronic information industry; and 100 billion emerging industries with equipment manufacturing, aerospace, new energy, new materials, modern medicine, and other emerging industries.

It is believed that with the joint efforts of five million Luzhou people, Luzhou will strive to become a sub-provincial economic center and promote high-quality economic development.

CHAPTER 2

Momently Know about the History of Luzhou Baijiu (I)

Many people in Luzhou will meet such a situation:

When we refer to the history of Luzhou liquor, we can generalize it in one sentence: Luzhou liquor has a long history, which originated in remote antiquity, started in the Qin and Han Dynasties, grew in the Tang and Song Dynasties, flourished in the Ming and Qing Dynasties, and developed in the New China.

If we want to tell a good story, we must remember the key points.

Let's focus on the following:

1. Pre-Qin Period

During the pre-Qin period, Luzhou had always been a dependency of Ba. The King of Ba often brought the leader of Luzhou to the Zhou Dynasty. The leader of Luzhou was not only rich in liquor but also had an excellent voice:

When Marquis of Han, living in Duling, set out to worship his ancestors, Xianfu gave a banquet to see Marquis off and prepared many pots of sweet and clear liquor.
—Recorded in *The Book of Songs, Greater Odes, Han Yi*

When referring to the customs of ancient Sichuan Province in ancient times, *The Book of Record of Huayang Kingdom* introduced:

The cliff is flat, and its crops are abundant. The liquor distilled from it can nourish the father.

In the field of Fuqiu, there are many cereal crops. The liquor distilled from it can nourish the mother.

Later, the Zhou Dynasty was continuously defeated. King Huiwen of Qin ordered Zhang Yi, Sima Cuo, and Duwei Mo to attack Shu from the Shiniu Road. They destroyed Shu and Ba, and successively established two counties in the same year. Since then, Ba and Shu have been included in the scope of the State of Qin.

2. Qin and Han Dynasties

Although Bashu was included in the scope of the State of Qin, they often fought with each other. After a long time, both sides were tired. Then Qin and Bashu signed an agreement:

> If Qin invades Bashu, they lose a pair of huanglong jade;
> if Bashu invades Qin, they lose 128 kilograms of liquor.
> —*Record of Huayang Kingdom*

Huanglong means huanglong jade, and liquor means Ba liquor. Change liquor with jade, and we can know how precious liquor is.

In addition, a pottery horn cup was used for drinking at that time. It has a unique design: a tapered bottom that cannot be put down until it is finished.

The pottery horn cup in Han Dynasty
Collected in Luzhou Laojiao Museum

However, with the tyranny and demise of the Qin Dynasty, Liu Bang, who worked in the grass-roots civil service system, finally became the emperor and reached the peak of his life after several years of hard work. From then on, it entered the Han Dynasty.

Grain is an important raw material for liquor distilling. In the Han Dynasty, Luzhou was governed by the Marquis of Jiangyang. He brought prosperity to the nation and security to the people, and food was abundant, which made the liquor shops in Jiangyang City very prosperous.

Sima Xiangru, a famous poet of the Han Dynasty, wrote a poem about Luzhou liquor when he passed Luzhou: In the distance of Wu, clouds are blowing; Liquor in southern Sichuan, full of aroma; Heating liquor on the stove, and drinking it to warm my heart, which made me happy, so I wrote this poem.

Liquor in southern Sichuan, full of aroma.

When we refer to Sima Xiangru, I have some gossip to share.

Sima Xiangru, formerly known as Sima Changqing, was renamed because he admired Lin Xiangru. In the sixth year of the Zhongyuan reign of Emperor Jing (144 BC), Sima Xiangru returned to Shu. Zhuo Wangsun, the vulgar local tycoon, invited the county magistrates Wang Ji and Sima Xiangru to attend his banquet.

Due to Sima Xiangru's handsome appearance and elegant demeanor, he immediately became the center of attention and attracted many fans.

It seems that the "appearance" association has existed in ancient times.

It was said that Sima Xiangru had a handsome appearance and played the *guqin* well. He immediately won the heart of Zhuo Wenjun, the daughter of Zhuo Wangsun.

Zhuo Wenjun's husband had just died. Zhuo Wenjun became a widow and returned to her family's home. She enjoyed Sima Xiangru's *guqin* and liked his good-looking appearance, so she fell in love at first sight.

One night, Zhuo Wenjun ran off with Sima Xiangru to Chengdu and obtained a marriage license without telling her father.

While Sima Xiangru and Zhuo Wenjun were on their honeymoon, Zhuo Wangsun was very angry when he knew it and determined not to pay for Wenjun's living expenses. As a result, Wenjun and Xiangru were so poor that they had to go back to Qionglai and open a distillery in the street. Wenjun sat at the counter and sold drinks, and Xiangru worked with the workers. It is the famous story of "Wenjun sold drinks."

Some days later, with the advice of his friends, Zhuo Wangsun finally calmed down and gave Wenjun a lot of money and servants. This story has a perfect ending.

Luzhou people thought "liquor was to complete etiquette" for more than 2,000 years. Here is another piece of evidence.

In 1983, a Han Dynasty sarcophagus was unearthed in Maliuwan, Luzhou's new area. The sarcophagus was engraved with a "magic prayer picture" of a wizard holding a liquor cup to pray to the gods.

In ancient times, liquor had low alcohol content. It was dry and cold in winter, and it tasted terrible. A warm liquor apparatus was invented to solve the problem.

National first-class cultural relic—Kylin Liquor Warmer
(now stored in Luzhou Museum)

When it comes to liquor warmer, it is a hard-core technology.

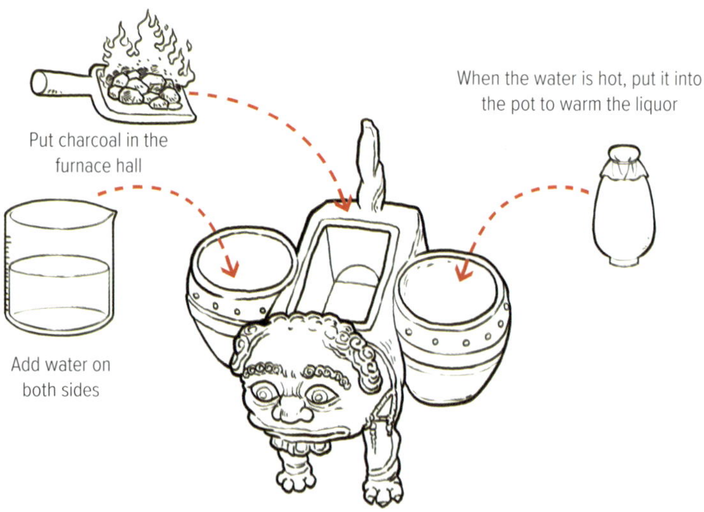

Its abdomen is the furnace hall, and its tail is the furnace door. When drinking, open the furnace door at the tail, put charcoal in the furnace hall, then put the cup into the round drum containing water on both sides of Kylin's abdomen to warm the liquor. The water temperature rises and heats the liquor. The front chest and hips are connected, and the water vapor can be recycled and ejected from the mouth.

When the liquor is hot, the Kylin liquor warmer will eject white gas from its mouth, indicating that the liquor has been warmed.

At present, there is another way to use the Kylin liquor warmer:

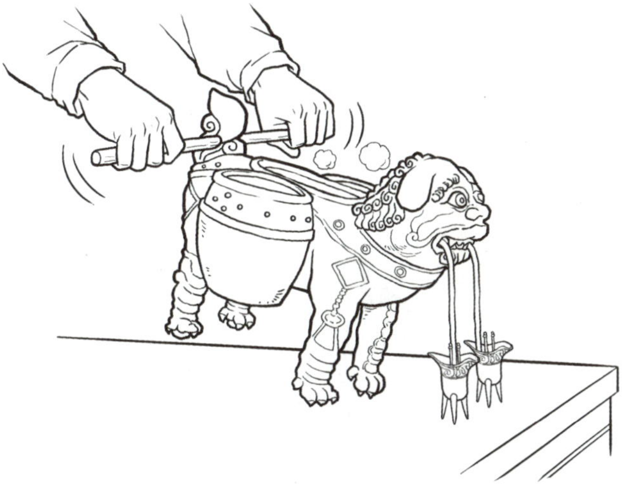

Directly pour the liquor into the drums on both sides of the warmer, add charcoal in the middle, and when the liquor is hot, lift it from the tail, and the liquor will naturally flow out of the Kylin's mouth.

Due to the uniqueness of the Kylin liquor warmer, it has become the treasure of the Luzhou Museum and the symbol of the city of liquor. Therefore:

3. Sui, Tang, and Five Dynasties

When it comes to the Sui and Tang Dynasties, we may be familiar with Cheng Yaojin with two axes in the *Legend of the Heroes of the Sui and Tang Dynasties*. In the first year of the Zhenguan reign in the Tang Dynasty (627), Cheng Yaojin served as the left leading general of Luzhou governor.

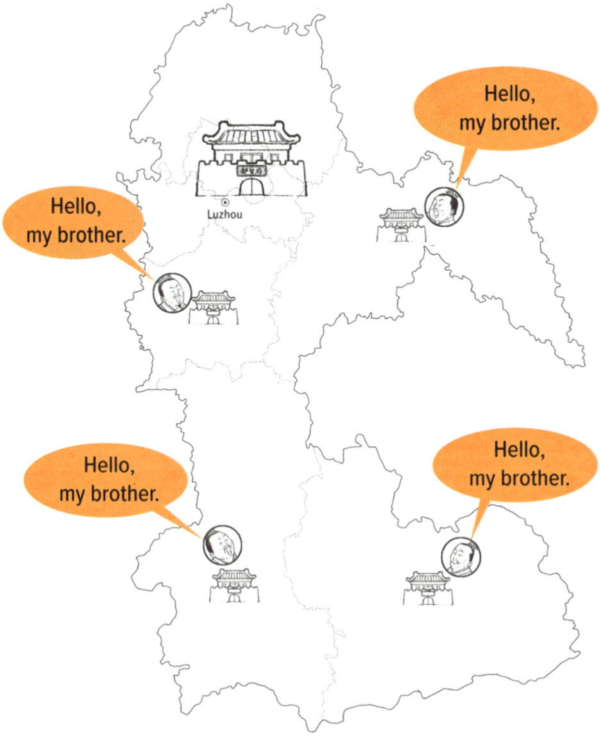

Since then, Luzhou had been promoted from a small county to the military commander's office, which governed the 14 surrounding states.

There were many ethnic minorities, such as Bo, Liao, Yi, Miao, etc. The folk customs were unique. They always drink when they dispute with each other.

The people here are good at drinking and like to make their liquor. Luzhou is rich in litchi, longan, and other fruits. Local people also use litchi to make wine. The wine is called "litchichun wine."

I went further south, away from my teacher,
litchis are ripe in Chongqing and Luzhou.

—"The two poems of 'I was recording stories on my trip to Luzhou when I met Pei Wu, an official who was relegated to Suizhou,'" were written by Zheng Gu, a poet of the Tang Dynasty.

Zheng Gu

Here's another story: Emperor Xuanzong of Tang, the husband of Lady Yang, specially built a litchi post road to let her eat fresh litchi. This "litchi expressway" is in the south of the Qinling Mountains. Today, there are some relics, which take a shortcut called "Ziwu Road" to Chang'an.

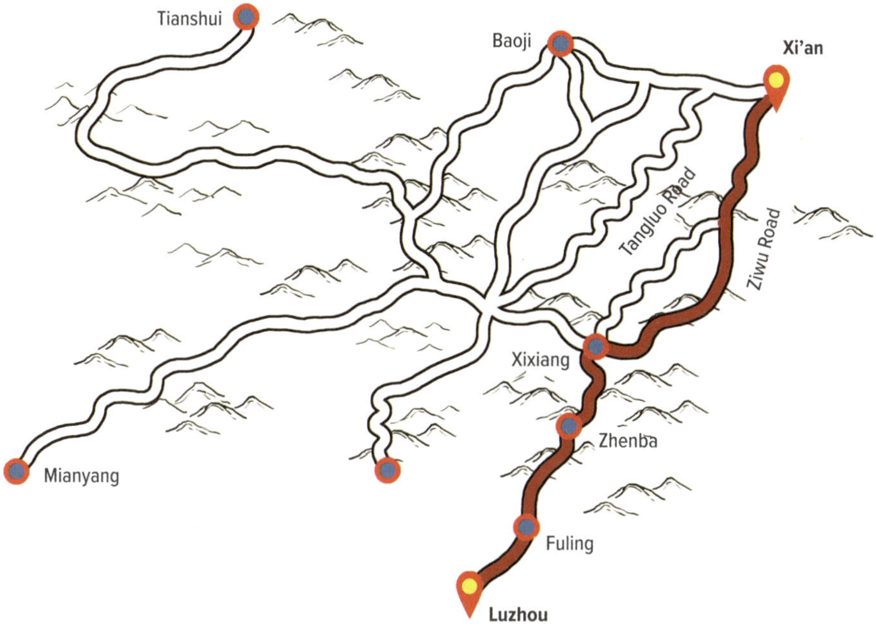

Some people may ask:

(1) Although the scale of litchi in Luzhou of Sichuan is not as large as that in Guangdong and Guangxi, it is said that Lady Yang was born in Sichuan, and she liked the taste of litchi in her hometown.

(2) In ancient China, transportation was very inconvenient. For thousands of years, the way of transportation in China was horse riding, and the fastest speed was 400 kilometers per day, almost reaching the extreme. The preservation of litchi transported from Huizhou to Dongguan was the biggest problem. The Ziwu Road was more than 1,000 kilometers closer than the post road from Guangdong and Guangxi.

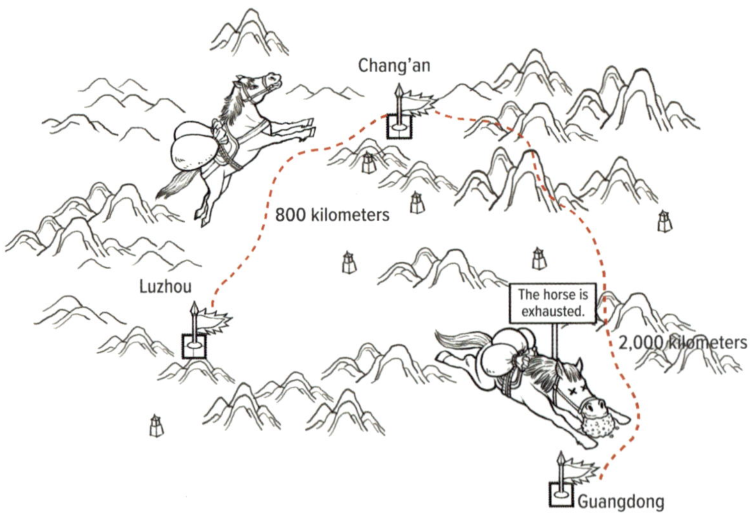

Ancient Shu-Chang'an litchi post road not only sent litchi but also sent Luzhou liquor.

During the Five Dynasties and Ten Kingdoms period, former Shu General Wang Zongruan served as an official in Luzhou and held God-worshipping activities in the ancient temple of Shanyunfeng Mountain. The activities were grand and provided great presents and liquor.

From the pre-Qin to the Five Dynasties and Ten Kingdoms, Chinese baijiu was mainly made of low alcohol rice liquor because of its short distilling time and low alcohol content. And its color was white, so it was called unstrained liquor. After filtration, strained liquor removes impurities, which is higher-grade rice liquor.

Strained liquor symbolizes a wise man, and unstrained liquor represents a virtuous man.
Qingsheng and Zhuoxian have become the elegant name of liquor.

Since the Song and Yuan Dynasties, rice liquor has constantly developed, but it no longer dominates the liquor-distilling industry. As for the new technology after the Song and Yuan Dynasties, why don't we talk about it next time?

CHAPTER 3

Momently Know about the History of Luzhou Baijiu (II)

We have talked about the Five Dynasties and Ten Kingdoms before. Now let's continue.

4. Song and Yuan Dynasties

People could drink much in the past. In the Han Dynasty, they could drink one *dan*, which was 18 kilograms; people in the Tang Dynasty could drink eighteen *sheng*, which was 9 kilograms; in the Song Dynasty, the maximum was ten *sheng*, which was 5 kilograms.

Confucius　　Li Bai　　Su Dongpo

The container is getting smaller and smaller, and the alcohol content is increasing.

The liquor was fermented before the Song Dynasty, often called fermented glutinous liquor, and the degree was 3%–6% vol. From the Song Dynasty, China began to have "big liquor." Its raw material selection, process operation, and fermentation methods were close to today's distilled spirit. However, with the limited production technology and equipment, the alcohol content of baijiu was lower than that of today.

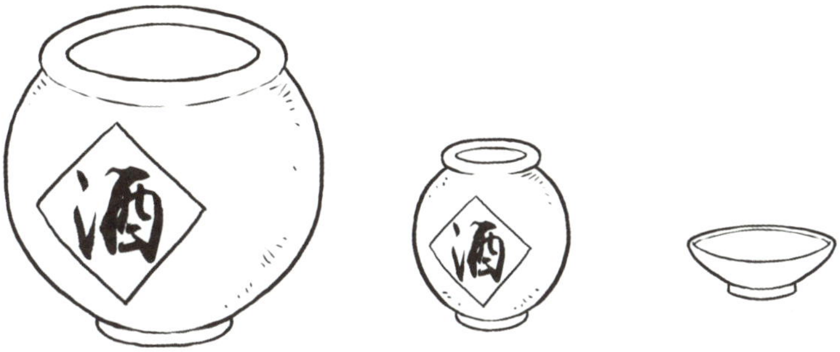

3%–4% vol　　5%–6% vol　　8%–9% vol

It was recorded in Tian Xi's works *Herbs of Liquor* in the Northern Song Dynasty: "The Xianluo liquor is heated twice by the Chinese spirit. Those who are good at drinking can only drink three or four cups, and the amount of alcohol is ten times higher than ordinary liquor."

Tian Xi

In *Monograph on Food and Currency of the History of Song*, it recorded that the liquor was distilled from spring to autumn and sold immediately, which was called small liquor. The price was divided into twenty-six levels between 0.5 taels and 3 taels. Big liquor refers to the liquor prepared in the twelfth lunar month and stored until the following summer after distilling and steaming. The price was divided into twenty-three levels between 0.8 taels and 4.8 taels. So, we can find that "small and big liquor" existed in ancient Luzhou.

Small liquor is a kind of rice liquor. Its raw material is glutinous rice or millet, fermented in hot weather.

The fermentation and aging cycles of "small liquor" are very short. It does not need storage, so it is sold after distilling, and its alcohol content is relatively low. There was a hero in Shandong who drank 18 bowls and killed a tiger.

"Big liquor" is a distilled spirit that uses sorghum as its raw material and adopts a distillation process, which adds jiuqu to ferment after sorghum gelatinization.

New liquor needs to be stored for half a year. It can be sold after it is volatilized and aged naturally. Generally, the alcohol content is relatively high.

So, the distilling process is the biggest difference between small and big liquor.

A famous poet was demoted to Rongzhou. He passed Luzhou and traveled with the public expense for half a year.

He found that Luzhou had developed agriculture and prosperous restaurants, and the glutinous red sorghum planted everywhere was used to make liquor. But in Jiang'an, it was poor, and many people didn't have enough food to eat. Huang Tingjian wrote the poem:

Jiang'an is short of food, Jiangyang has a surplus of liquor.

—"Ode to Shi Yingzhi," written by Huang Tingjian in Song Dynasty

At the end of the Song Dynasty and the beginning of the Yuan Dynasty, the Mongolian army attacked the Eurasian continent from the east and west, indirectly promoting communication between the people of both sides.

Then the European distilled vessels were transported to Central China with the Mongolian cavalry.

People brought new equipment and new technology. The distillation technology of Chinese baijiu was becoming more mature, and the liquor alcohol content was higher and higher.

Guo Huaiyu, a native of Luzhou, learned how to make liquor. In 1324, he created a new jiuqu named "ganchunqu," which was used to make liquor. It had a strong fragrance, mellow and delicious taste, and persistence.

Why is it that the invention of ganchunqu opened the era of Daqu liquor?

Before the invention of "ganchunqu," they used the nie and xiaoqu for distilling. After the invention of ganchunqu, it produced three varieties according to different fermentation temperatures, covering the whole series of baijiu.

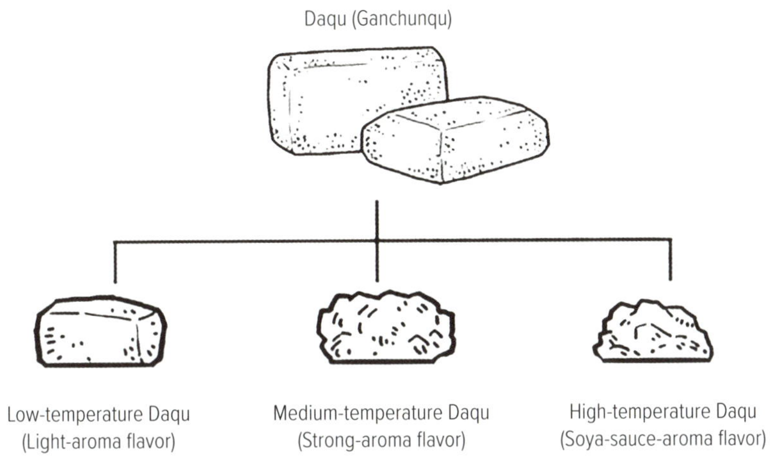

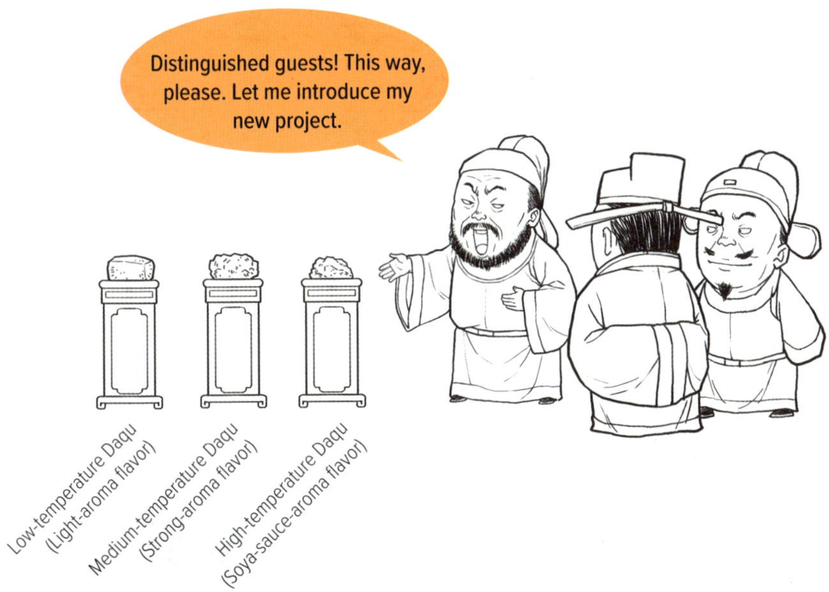

Therefore, Guo Huaiyu is honored as the father of Chinese jiuqu-making, creating the history of Chinese Daqu making. He is also celebrated as the first-generation inheritor of Luzhou Laojiao baijiu's traditional distilling technology.

Guo Huaiyu

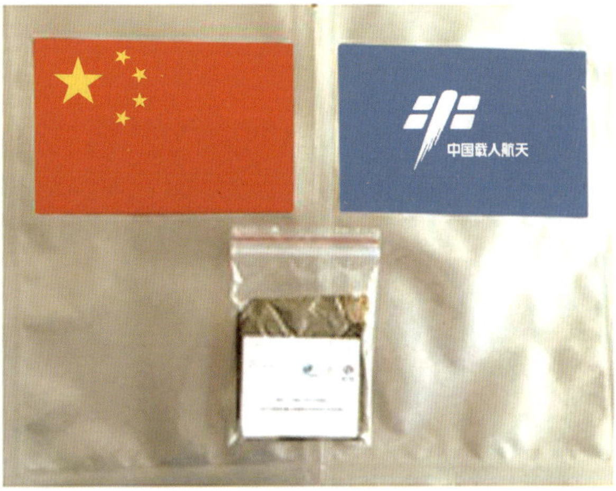

In 2016, Luzhou Laojiao jiuqu entered space with the "Shenzhou-11" manned spaceship, opening a new advance for the space scientific research of distilling microorganisms.

"Shenzhou-11" manned spaceship

Many people think distilling is a fermentation process, just like making noodles. It is correct, but it is not accurate and comprehensive.

Comprehensively, the distilling process is a complex biochemical reaction process. In short, there are two steps:

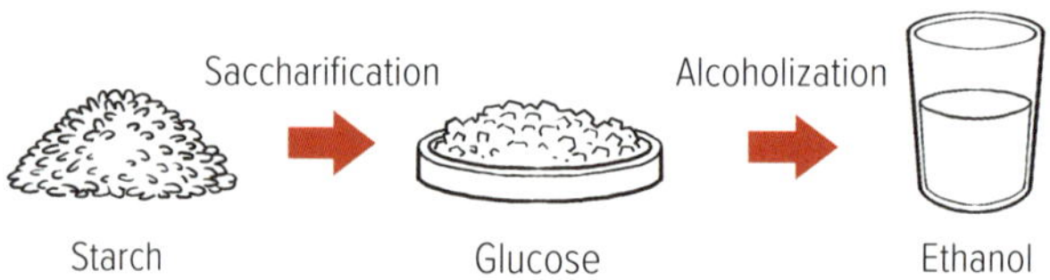

The above two steps, however, cannot be taken out of thin air; they must be done with the help of enzymes. The first step of the saccharification process requires the participation of starch hydrolase; the second step of the alcoholization process requires the addition of alcoholase.

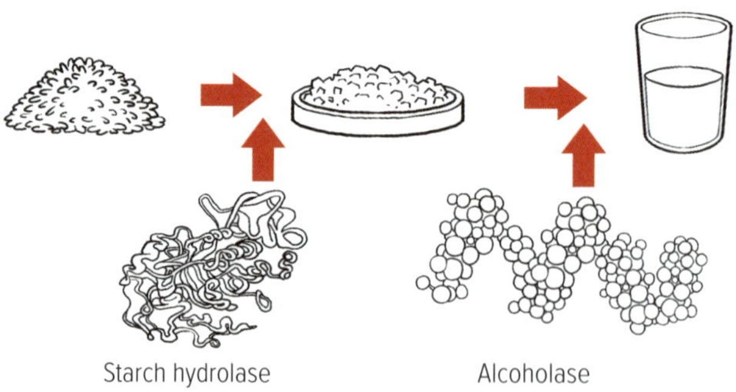

Microorganisms mainly produce the two enzymes. Starch hydrolases are produced by molds (Rhizopus, Mucor, etc.), and yeast is used to provide alcoholase.

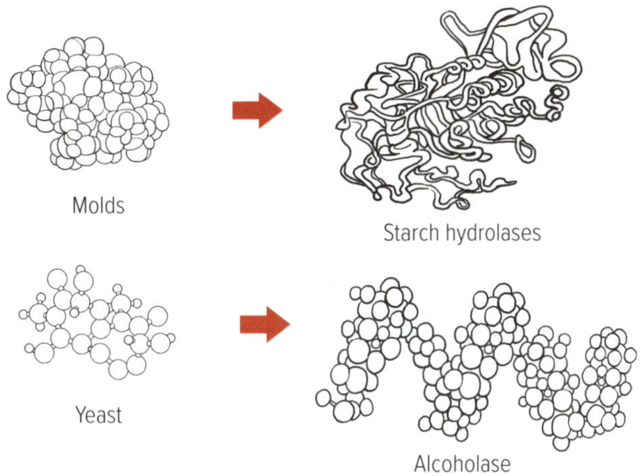

Jiuqu is a fermentation flavoring agent, and qu base is a hotbed or a solid medium for cultivating many microorganisms such as molds and yeasts. It is the basic structure diagram:

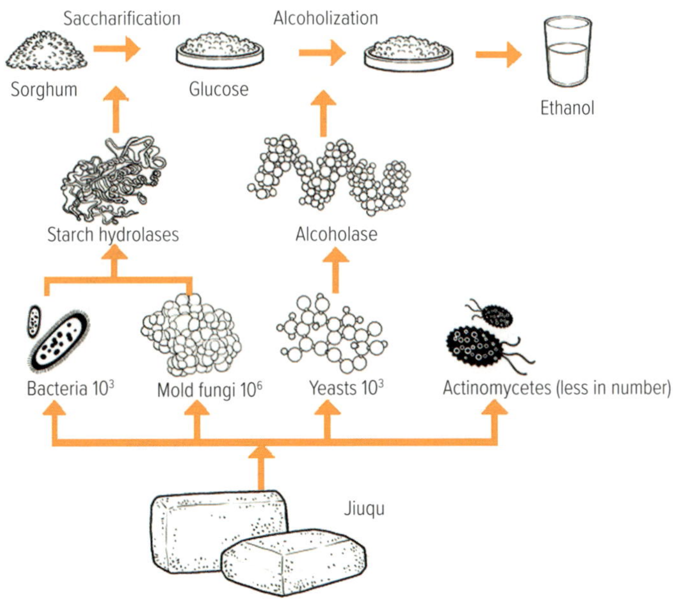

Let's look at the birthplace of liquor:

Two River Basins in the Middle East: Wine

South Coast of the Mediterranean: Malt beer

Yellow River and Yangtze River Basins: Baijiu

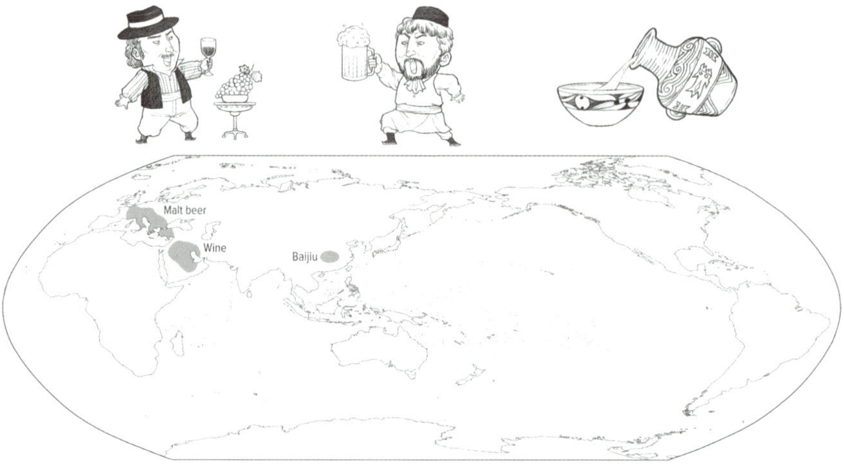

Daqu liquor was invented in the Yuan Dynasty of China. It was not until the end of the 17th century that Italian expert Rady put forward the theory of natural microbial fermentation. It was not until the end of the 19th century that Calmette of France established the amylo process to make alcohol.

Therefore, Joseph Needham, a British historian of science and technology, rewarded “distilling liquor with qu” as the“fifth great invention” in ancient China.

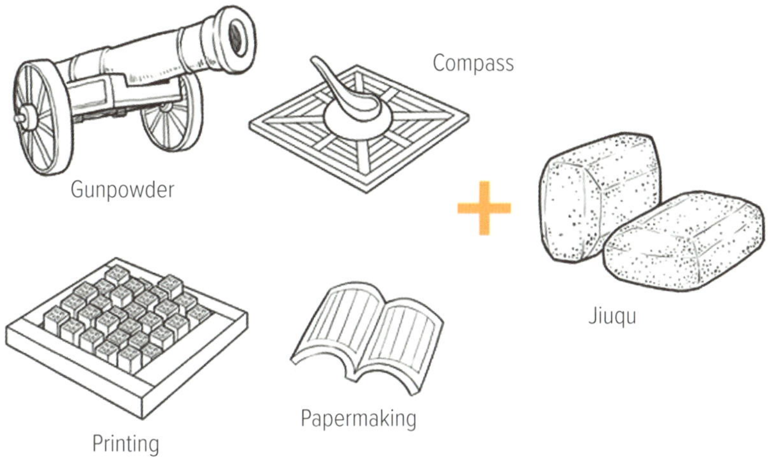

5. Ming and Qing Dynasties

After the mid-Ming Dynasty, capitalism sprouted in China, and there was no need to bring a lot of cash when going shopping and traveling.

Jiaozi, the earliest paper money globally, was first issued in Sichuan during the Northern Song Dynasty.

As the central passageway for Sichuan to sail, Luzhou has unique port resources, and the pillar liquor industry has developed rapidly.

During the Jiajing period of the Ming Dynasty, the talented man Yang Shen angered the emperor because of the "Great Ritual Controversy" and was demoted to Yunnan. When passing through Luzhou, he was impressed by the high-quality liquor and beautiful scenery, so he lived in Jiangyang for more than ten years.

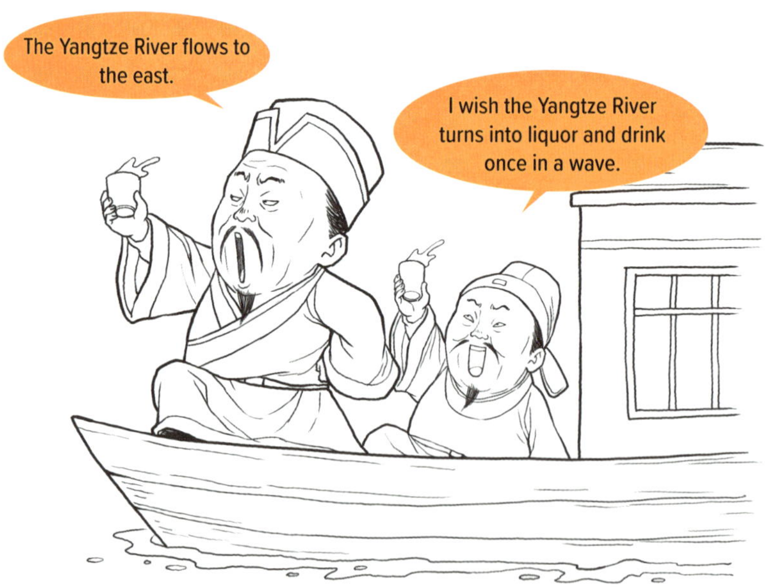

As the saying goes, poets can write many poems when the country is in trouble. Only after experiencing major setbacks can they write high-quality poetry. The opening word of *Romance of the Three Kingdoms*, "Linjiangxian · Rolling Water Flowing East of the Yangtze River," was written by Yang Shen in Luzhou.

In the first year of the Wanli reign of the Ming Dynasty (1573), after ten years of imperial examinations, Shu Chengzong abandoned the brush for the sword and passed the martial arts examination. After that, he left his official position and returned to his hometown. Combined with the features of distilling workshops and restaurants, he built mud cellars in 1573.

The general structure of the mud cellar was built as follows:

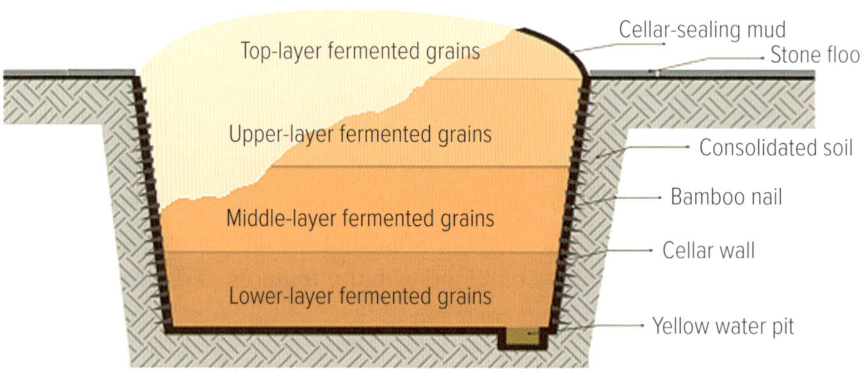

The most significant difference between the mud cellar and other cellars was that the body was built of yellow mud, and the bottom and four walls of the cellar were pasted with a thick layer of mud. The mud provides a living environment for microorganisms.

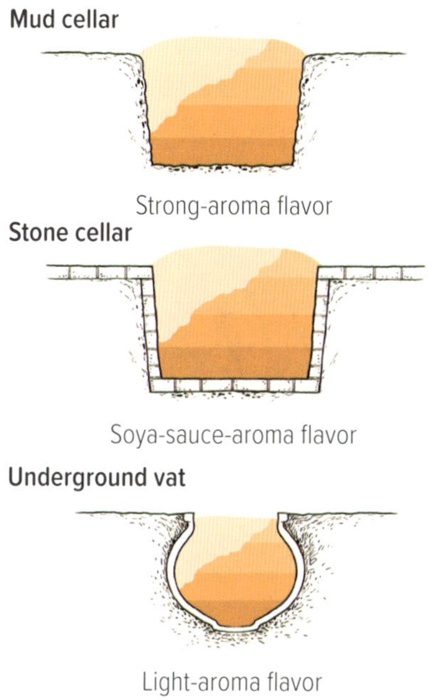

In grain fermentation, the beneficial components and nutrients in the fermented grains could nourish many microorganisms which produce aroma in the cellar mud. When used longer, more microorganisms were involved in fermentation and aroma produced in the cellar mud. And it could make better liquor in the older cellar with fragrant perfume.

Microorganisms convert starch, protein, and other components in the grain into various esters, acids, alcohols, aldehydes, and other trace components, to form a unique flavor.

After fermentation, the active microbial communities would increase and stabilize, producing more fragrant and high-quality baijiu. Just like human development: they are getting smarter and wiser in evolution.

Shu Chengzong was a great master of China's strong-aroma flavor baijiu and opened the new era of Chinese baijiu, described as a "mud cellar that produces fragrance."

After the Shu managed the liquor industry for several generations, the descendants did not manage it well and sold it to the Rao. Later, the Rao sold it to the Du. Finally, they sold it to Wen, who moved to Luzhou from Guangdong.

Shu Xingwen Rao Tiansheng Du En Wen Xuanyu

Initially, the Wen family, whose ancestors made vinegar, came from Guangdong. They heard that Sichuan had favorable policies and social welfare, so they began to drift north with their family and finally settled in Luzhou.

In the eighth year of the Tongzhi reign of the Qing Dynasty (1869), Wen Xuanyu, the ninth ancestor of the Wen family, bought the Shujuyuan workshop and changed its name to"Yuji Wenyongsheng Distillery."

In the Qing Dynasty, the Luzhou liquor industry was prosperous. One of the four essential officials of the Late Qing Dynasty, Zhang Zhidong, passed Luzhou when he was appointed as an official in Sichuan. He heard Luzhou was famous for producing liquor, so he ordered people to buy it. Zhang Zhidong was an impatient person. He waited for a long time to see the servant come back. He was about to be angry, and the servant quickly explained:

This is the story's origin: "Good liquor is not afraid of deep lanes!"

In 1915, Wen Xiaoquan teamed up to take Wenyongsheng Daqu Liquor across the ocean to participate in the Panama Pacific World Expo held in San Francisco.

Foreigners are always curious but dismissive of local specialties from the East. However, they were conquered by a jar of Wenyongsheng liquor from China (the predecessor of Luzhou Laojiao Daqu) and finally awarded the gold medal for the liquor.

In 1915, Wen Yongsheng liquor (the predecessor of Luzhou Laojiao Daqu) participated in the World Expo and won gold. It was the first time Chinese baijiu had gone out of the country and conquered the world with its strong fragrance.

So, a good master of qu-making, a good master of distilling, and a good master of marketing can be described as the highest-level combination.

Three famous people of liquor city: Guo Huaiyu, Shu Chengzong, and Wen Xiaoquan.

The history of ancient baijiu is finished. As for modern baijiu, it's getting late! Why don't we talk next time?

CHAPTER 4

Momently Know about the History of Luzhou Baijiu (III)

I have finished talking about ancient baijiu. Now let's continue.

When it comes to liquor, many people have this misunderstanding:

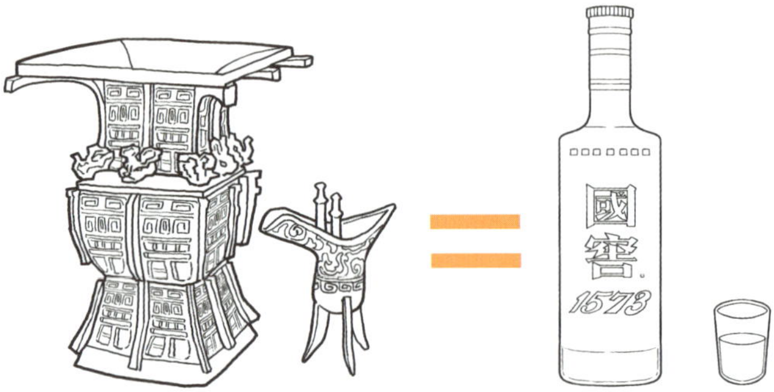

Ancient baijiu Modern baijiu

There are significant differences between ancient baijiu and modern baijiu: Most ancient baijiu refers to rice liquor, a relatively low alcohol content fermentation liquor, including strained and unstrained liquor.

Han Dynasty

After the Song and Yuan Dynasties, most baijiu refers to spirits: as Huojiu, Jiulu, Shaodaozi, and Baigan.

Therefore, the time of liquor is divided as follows:

Chinese people always like to name things by color. For example:

Black tea

Green tea

White tea

Mahogany (red)

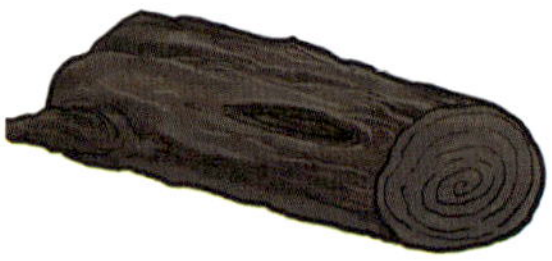
Ebony (black)

Rhodiola (red)

Cloisonné (blue)

So liquor is no exception. Baijiu had many local names in the past, which can be described as messy. It was standardized after the founding of the People's Republic of China:

Baijiu

Wine

Huangjiu

Beer

Since the foundation of the People's Republic of China, all trades and professions have carried out public-private partnerships, as has the Luzhou liquor industry. Thirty-six distilling workshops founded in the Ming and Qing Dynasties cooperated in establishing a public-private Luzhou Qujiu Factory, the predecessor of Luzhou Laojiao.

At the beginning of 1950, with the support of the government, thirty-six old workshops founded in the Ming and Qing Dynasties, including Wen Yongsheng, Chunherong, Yongxingcheng, Dingji, and Dingfengheng, established the Luzhou Qujiu Factory.

Luzhou Laojiao has experienced a long process from the public-private partnership of old workshops to large enterprise groups:

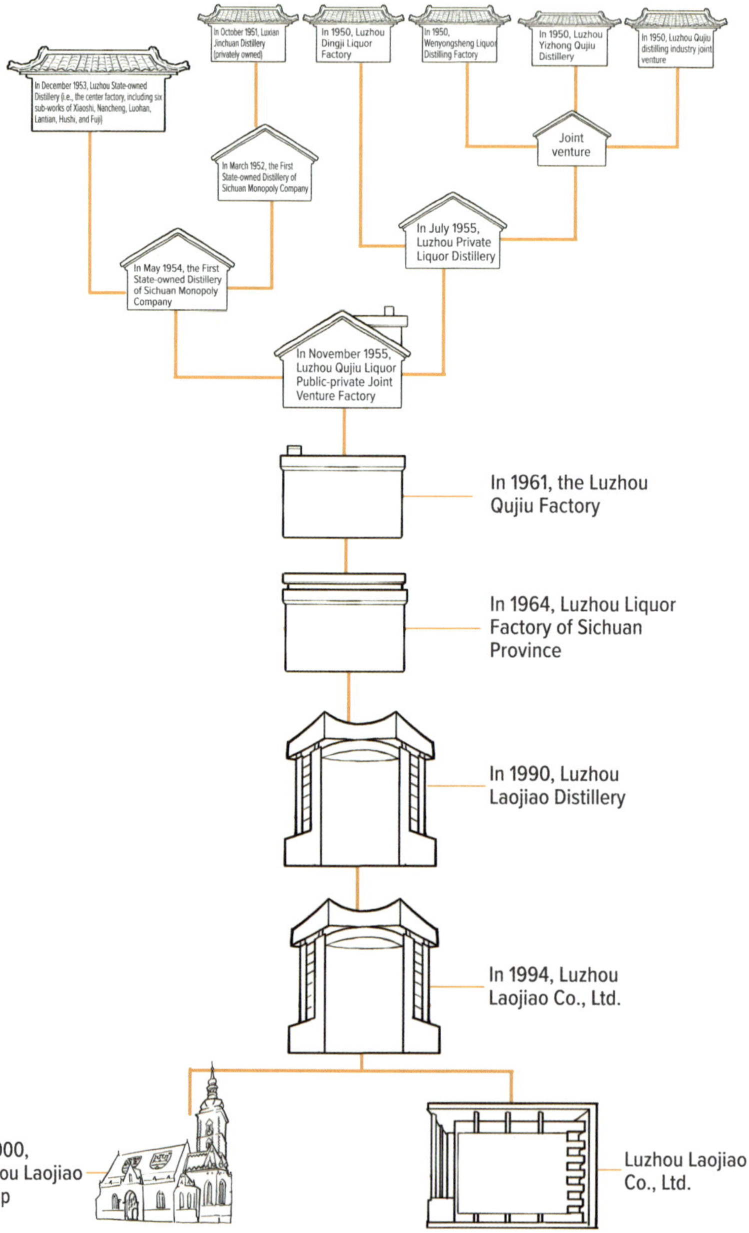

In 1952, to promote the recovery and development of China's baijiu industry, the First National Liquor Evaluation Conference was held in Beijing under the personal intervention of Premier Zhou Enlai. More than 100 kinds of liquor participated in the contest, and the selection criteria were also stringent.

It has a long history and sells well all over the country.

It is recognized by the masses and welcomed by consumers.

High quality is in line with high-grade liquor standards.

The manufacturing method is unique and cannot be imitated by other regions.

Luzhou Laojiao Maotai Xifeng Fenjiu

After fierce competition, the earliest four famous baijiu in China was selected.

Luzhou Laojiao always won the gold medal in the subsequent famous liquor selection meetings. As strong-aroma flavor baijiu, Luzhou Laojiao is the only national famous liquor rewarded five times.

Later, Luzhou Laojiao was served at the state banquet in Zhongnanhai to entertain international guests. In 1966, Luzhou Laojiao changed the original trademark "Baita brand" to the "Gongnong brand," and came into the era of the "Gongnong brand." At that time, it belonged to the planned economy. Baijiu was supplied by ticket, not money. People found it hard to get a ticket. Only leaders at or above the county level could get the planned quota, also it was also called the "Old County Magistrate."

At that time, the domestic economy was still in a recovered period, and the government paid more attention to daily necessities. So baijiu was included in the long-term plan for scientific and technological development of the State Council.

Therefore, in October 1957, the Sichuan Sugar and Wine Industry Research Office (now Sichuan Food Fermentation Industry Research and Design Institute), the Sichuan Monopoly Company, and the Food Industry Bureau of the Sichuan Provincial Department of Industry, began the investigation and summary of the Luzhou Laojiao distilling process.

He Qirui, deputy general manager of the Sichuan Monopoly Company, is responsible for leading the overall work. Chen Maochun, deputy director of the Sichuan Sugar and Wine Technology Research Office, served as the team leader, and Xiong Zishu served as the deputy team leader. Sixteen organizations and sixty-two people participated in the experimental investigation.

It is the Luzhou Laojiao experiment.

In this way, it took more than half a year to research. It formed a complete scientific theory according to the research data and materials. And *Luzhou Laojiao Daqu Liquor*, the first baijiu distilling textbook in China, was printed and published by the Light Industry Press in 1959.

Spoiler Alert: This book has influenced the development of Chinese baijiu and laid a foundation for the supermarket pattern in which strong-aroma flavor baijiu is the king of Chinese baijiu.

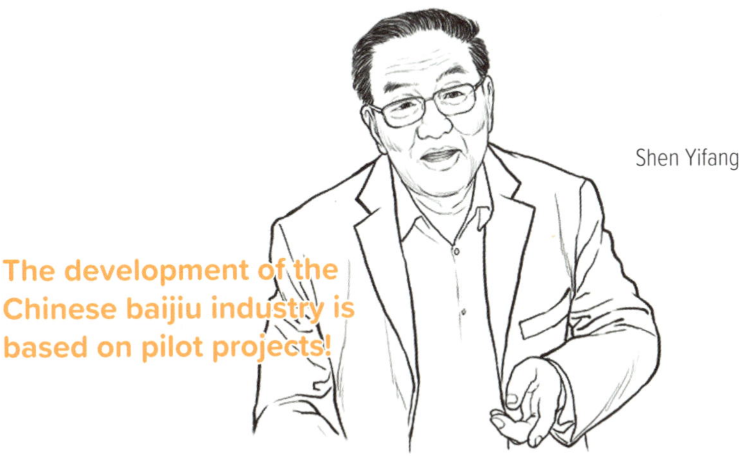

Shen Yifang: a famous baijiu expert, presided over the 5th National Baijiu Evaluation Expert Group

Since the pilot of Luzhou Laojiao, the strong-aroma flavor baijiu industry has developed quickly. After that, other baijiu flavors have also carried out pilot projects.

"Three pilot projects" of Chinese baijiu

The pilot project of Luzhou Laojiao has made outstanding pioneering contributions to the pilot projects of Chinese baijiu.

Xiong Zishu: a famous baijiu expert and senior engineer

Under limited production capacity, continuous experiment, and experience promotion, baijiu enterprises, especially strong-aroma flavor baijiu enterprises, have developed rapidly.

List of previous famous brands of liquor

First session	1952	Stand alone	Maotai; Luzhou Daqu; Fenjiu; Xifeng Liquor	Famous Brands of Liquor
Second session	1963	Half of the industry	Maotai; Luzhou Laojiao Tequ; Fenjiu; Quanxing Daqu; Wuliangye; Gujing Gongjiu; Xifeng Liquor; Dongjiu;	Eight Famous Brands of Liquor
Third session	1979	Strong aroma is the Lu-aroma flavor.	Maotai; Luzhou Laojiao Tequ; Fenjiu; Wuliangye; Jiannanchun; Gujing Gongjiu; Yanghe Daqu; Dongjiu	Eight Famous Brands of Liquor
Fourth session	1984	More than half are strong-aroma flavors.	Maotai; Luzhou Laojiao Tequ; Fenjiu; Wuliangye; Yanghe Daqu; Jiannanchun; Gujing Gongjiu; Quanxing Daqu; Shuanggou Daqu; Special-made Huanghelou Liquor; Langjiu; Dongjiu; Xifeng Liquor	Thirteen Famous Brands of Liquor
Fifth session	1989	More than half are strong-aroma flavors.	Maotai; Luzhou Laojiao Tequ; Fenjiu; Wuliangye; Yanghe Daqu; Jiannanchun; Gujing Gongjiu; Dongjiu; Xifeng Liquor; Quanxing Daqu; Shuanggou Daqu; Special-made Huanghelou Liquor; Langjiu; Wulingjiu; Baofengjiu; Songhe Liangye; Tuopai Qujiu	Seventeen Famous Brands of Liquor

(Note: The brand marked red is strong-aroma flavor baijiu.)

Now, the sales volume of strong-aroma flavor baijiu accounts for 75% of the national market share.

Luzhou Laojiao has been officially certified as the national famous liquor for five consecutive times. More importantly, strong-aroma flavor is also known as the "Lu-aroma flavor." So, Luzhou Laojiao deserved number one at that time.

Chen Qiyu, the 18th generation inheritor of Luzhou Laojiao's traditional distilling technology, mixed the remaining liquor in different batches, accidentally tasted it, and was surprised to find:

After repeated experiments, an idea came to his mind. Then, he quickly organized scientific researchers to develop and apply the tasting, evaluating, and blending technology of strong-aroma flavor baijiu.

After more than ten years of exploration, blending has been officially proposed as technology and widely used in production. It dramatically improves the yield of high-quality liquor and endows Luzhou Laojiao with a unique style.

Later, driven by Lai Gaohuai, Luzhou Laojiao held a training course on distilling technology to spread technical talents to the national distilling industry. To be honest, the development of many famous liquor enterprises has benefited from the support of Luzhou Laojiao, which has created the world of strong aroma.

Luzhou Laojiao is also known as the Huangpu Military Academy in the liquor industry.

In 1983, President Hu Yaobang visited Luzhou and inspected Luzhou Laojiao, naming it "the wind passing through Luzhou bringing the fragrance of liquor."

In the same year, under the province's jurisdiction, the newly-built Luzhou City decided to take liquor-distilling as one of the "three pillar industries" of the city. Luzhou liquor, represented by Luzhou Laojiao, moved towards the road of reform and opening up. By the end of the 1980s, the production and sales volume of Luzhou Laojiao was the sum of the other five Sichuan liquors.

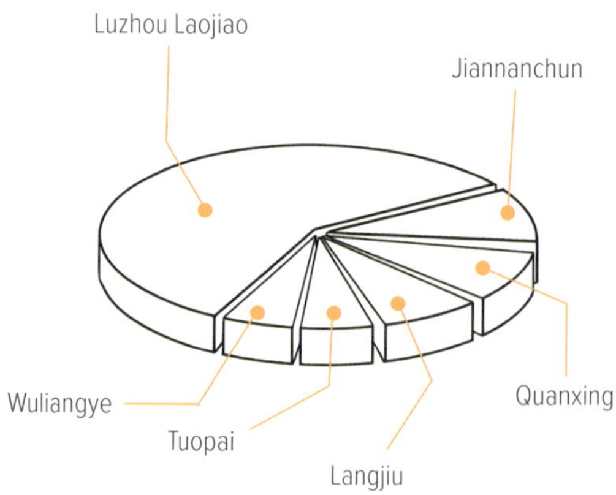

In the late 1980s, Sichuan liquor had six famous liquors, and Luzhou Laojiao was unique.

In 1987, the first Internationally Famous Liquor Festival was held in Luzhou.

The Internationally Famous Liquor Festival attracted more than 7,000 guests from all walks of life, and the commodity turnover reached RMB 853 million yuan.

In 1994, Luzhou Laojiao stock (000568) was the first baijiu enterprise listed on the Shenzhen Stock Exchange in China. So far, the stock of Luzhou Laojiao has increased more than 400 times. On September 6, 2020, the return rate ranked first in 3,000 companies.

No.	Corporate name	Increase multiple	Industry types
1	Luzhou Laojiao	425	Daily consumption
2	Guizhou Maotai	352	Daily consumption
3	Yili Shares	317	Daily consumption
4	Vanke A	285	Real estate
5	Yunnan Baiyao	183	Medical care
6	Hengrui Medicine	177	Medical care
7	Changchun High-tech	176	Medical care
8	Gree Electric Appliance	171	Optional consumption
9	Founder Technology	169	Industry
10	Hundsun Technology	125	Information technology
11	HASCO Automotive	117	Optional consumption
12	Shanxi Fenjiu	112	Daily consumption

The content of the chart from research on Guotai Junan Securities.

In 1996, the State Council approved the "1573 National Cellars" as the first "Important Heritage Site under State Protection."

Luo Zhewen: a Chinese ancient architect and head of the ancient architecture expert group of the National Cultural Heritage Administration

In 1999, at the Ninth International Famous Liquor Festival, Luzhou Laojiao national treasure liquor held the "grand ceremony of liquor production and tasting." The liquor was divided into 1,999 bottles. Each one was 1,999 ml, and numbered one by one.

Two bottles of national treasure liquor numbered 0002 and 0003 were presented to former chief executive Dong Jianhua of Hong Kong and former chief executive He Houhua of Macao, respectively. The liquor numbered 0001 is still stored in Luzhou Laojiao Museum and will be given to Taiwan compatriots when the time is ripe.

Yuan Xiuping

It is the culture that rules alcohol consumption!

Yuan Xiuping: then chairman and general manager of Luzhou Laojiao Co., Ltd.

As time goes by, the brand is upgrading. Just after 2000, Guojiao 1573 was officially launched. Once the product was launched, it was praised by all parties.

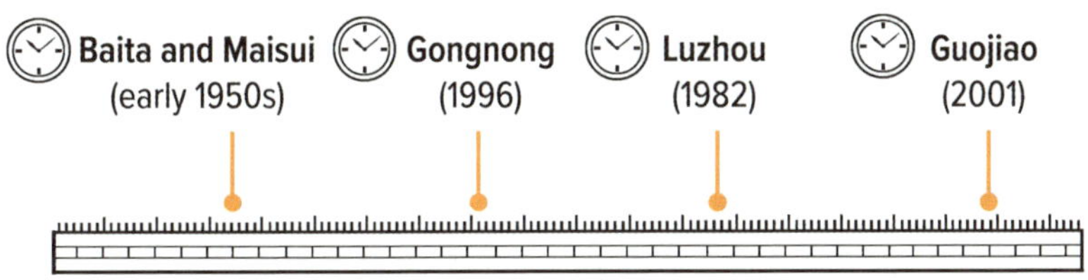

Zhou Henggang

Guojiao 1573 is like a beauty. One extra point is excessive, and one less point is a pity. It's just perfect and impeccable!

Zhou Henggang: a leader in the liquor industry, presided over the 2nd, 3rd, and 4th National Liquor Evaluation Conference

In 2006, "the traditional baijiu-distilling techniques of Luzhou Laojiao" were included in the first group of "State-Level Non-Material Cultural Heritage List." Since then, they have had national treasure technologies and national treasure cellars.

The living "double national treasures" has become the biggest trump card of Luzhou Laojiao.

In 2007, Luzhou successfully held the first China International Alcoholic Drinks Expo. So far, it has been successfully held 13 times. Since 2014, China International Alcoholic Drinks Expo has been permanently settled in Luzhou.

In 2008, the Luzhou Municipal Party Committee and the government proposed developing competitive industries and supporting local industries.

The Guojiao 1573 sealing ceremony was opened in the same year, creating a precedent for the industry to seal and worship ancestors.

Zhang Liang: Party secretary and chairman of Luzhou Laojiao Group, then Party secretary and general manager of Luzhou Laojiao Co., Ltd.

In the same year, Guojiao 1573 was certified as an organic baijiu.

Yuan Longping: an expert in hybrid rice breeding and a pioneer in the research and development of hybrid rice in China

In 2010, Luzhou Laojiao Jiaoling Baijiu was born, creating the Chinese Jiaoling Baijiu era.

In 2013, Luzhou Laojiao's 1619 old cellars of more than one hundred years of history, the 16 ancient baijiu workshops, and the three major baijiu preservation caves were announced to be the "Important Heritage Sites under State Protection."

Since then, Luzhou Laojiao has become a national treasure unit on an enormous scale, with complete categories, and the highest protection specifications in the liquor industry.

Xie Ming: then chairman of Luzhou Laojiao Co., Ltd.

In 2013, the activity of "the jar of liquor in life" moved the whole country, which paid tribute to the most important people.

In 2015, Luzhou Laojiao formed the "Five Single Product Strategy."

Liu Miao: Party secretary and chairman of Luzhou Laojiao Co., Ltd.

Lin Feng: deputy secretary of the Party Committee and general manager of Luzhou Laojiao Co., Ltd.

In 2017, they held "a global cultural tour to let the world taste China." The event has traveled through Brussels, Paris, Hong Kong, China, Moscow, etc. Luzhou Laojiao has been exported to more than 50 countries and regions worldwide.

In 2018, with the support of the municipal Party committee and the municipal government, Luzhou Laojiao's distilling technology transformation project had formed.

After completing the project, it will form a modern distilling base with an annual output of 100,000 tons of high-quality crude liquor, 100,000 tons of jiuqu, and 380,000 tons of liquor storage capacity.

OK! The history of Luzhou liquor has come to an end.

CHAPTER 5

Why Is the Strong-Aroma Flavor Baijiu Peerless in Smell? (I)

Recently, a significant event happened in the Chinese baijiu industry.

Led by the soya-sauce-aroma flavor craze, some companies have entered the soya-sauce-aroma flavor baijiu industry.

Some brands try their best marketing to expand the market.

It is easy to spread a rumor but refuting it is hard. It hurts the industry and distorts consumers' understanding of baijiu.

To make consumers understand baijiu and consume it clearly. Today, let's figure out what the flavor of baijiu is.

1. Three Baijiu Flavors

Chinese baijiu has three basic flavors. According to different distilling equipment and techniques, those using underground vats as fermentation equipment are called light aroma, and those using stone cellars as fermentation equipment are called soya-sauce aroma ...

There is no need to explain strong-aroma flavor, which is using a mud cellar as fermentation equipment.

The three techniques represented by the three baijiu flavors also represent the climatic and agricultural civilization characteristics of the Yellow River Basin, the Yangtze River Basin, and the Chishui River Basin. For example:

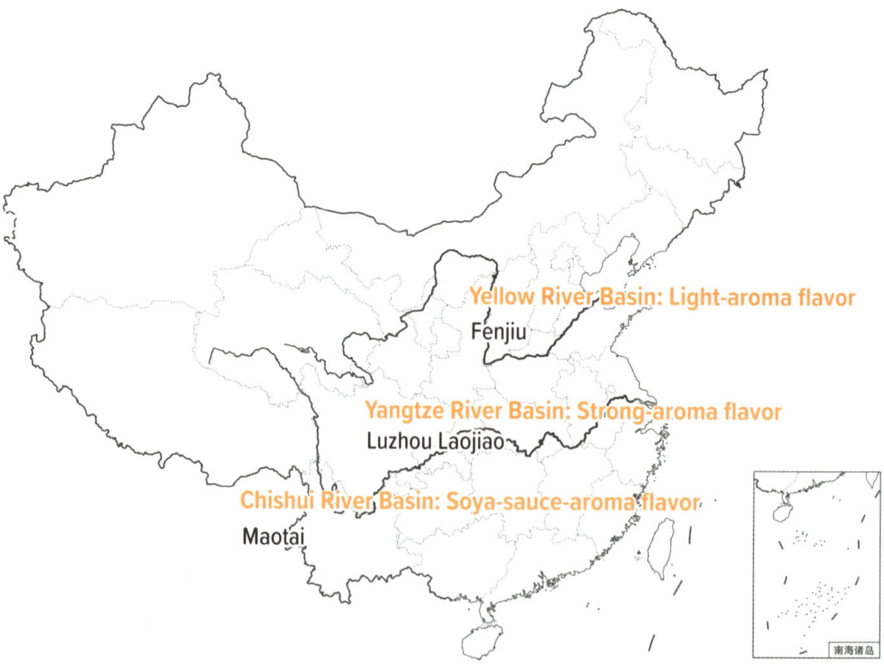

Like the three primary colors, the twelve flavors are derived from the three basic flavors.

Oh no! The twelve flavors of baijiu developed in this way.

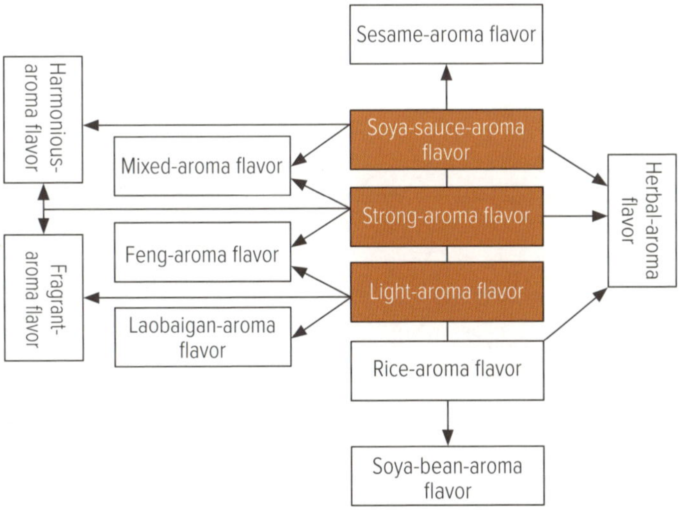

Firstly, let's talk about the strong-aroma flavor of baijiu culture in the Yangtze River Basin.

The cellar is built with yellow mud. Because the cellar mud is soft, it is easy to control the fermentation temperature and convenient for microorganisms to reproduce. The longer the time is, the richer the microorganisms are. Therefore, it is known as the "thousand-year cellar."

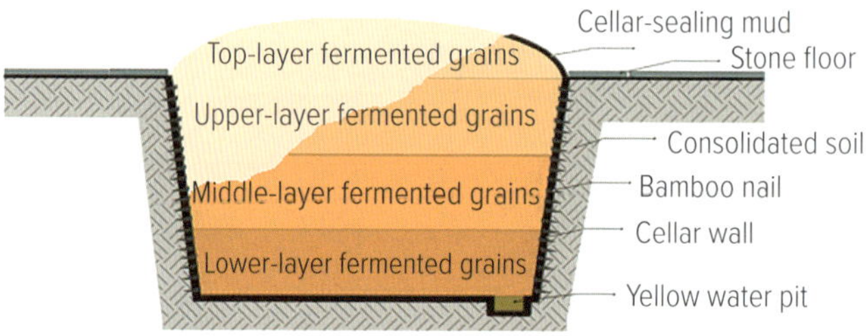

At the same time, with the method of "adding more materials to fermented grains," the flavor substances become rich, forming the unique process characteristics of the "ten thousand-year fermented grains" of strong-aroma flavor baijiu.

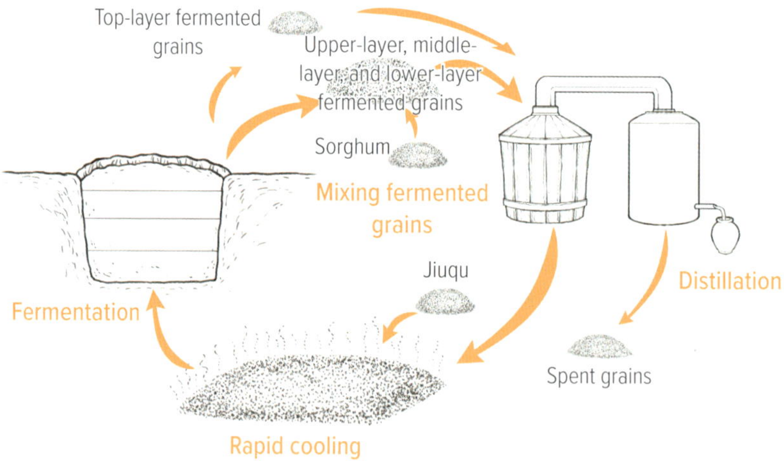

Thus, the taste characteristics of strong-aroma flavor baijiu are formed with "an intense aroma, smooth and mellow, and harmonious flavor."

Light-aroma is the result of conforming to the climate characteristics of the Yellow River Basin.

The pottery jar is used as the cellar to keep warm and avoid water leakage.

Light-aroma baijiu is "firstly fermenting in the underground vat, then steaming grains and distilling liquor separately, finally separate steaming in two rounds."

It has created the taste characteristics of "pure fragrance, mellow and soft, and a refreshing" aftertaste of light-aroma flavor baijiu.

Soya-sauce aroma is the fruit of the microecological effect in the Chishui River Basin.

Soya-sauce aroma takes the stone cellar as the cellar and adopts high-temperature accumulation fermentation.

Soya-sauce-aroma flavor baijiu adopts the techniques of grain feeding twice, steaming nine times, fermenting eight times, taking out baijiu seven times, and fermenting for one month.

It has created the taste characteristics of "an outstanding soya-sauce aroma, elegant and delicate, leaving fragrance in the empty cup."

On the whole, the three flavors have their advantages and characteristics.

Due to the hard texture of underground vats and stone cellars, microorganisms cannot survive.

It's the same as an hourly worker, who is changed after working in someone's house.

The mud cellar emphasizes "thousand-year cellars and ten thousand-year fermented grains." The older the mud cellar is, the more microorganisms and the richer the species are.

From the perspective of the inheritance of fermentation containers, the mud cellar of strong-aroma flavor baijiu is good for the proliferation of microorganisms, which significantly impacts the distilling quality and has more historical, economic, and cultural values.

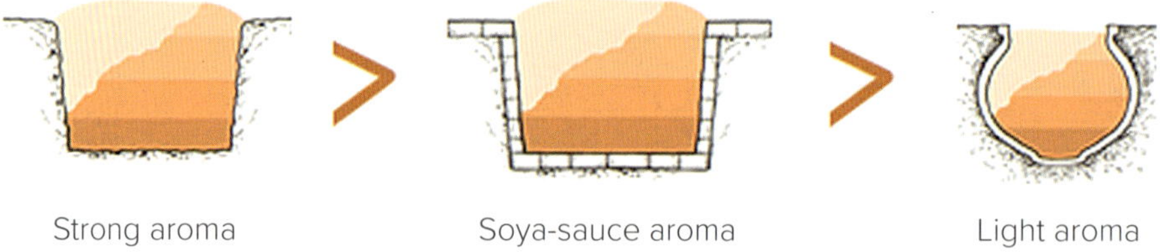

Tips: So far, among the eleven important heritage sites under state protection in the alcohol industry announced by National Cultural Heritage Administration, eight are strong-aroma flavor baijiu, one is soya-sauce-aroma flavor baijiu, one is light-aroma flavor baijiu, and one is qingkejiu.

The strong-aroma flavor mud cellar has living cultural relics' economic and historical value.

2. Strong Aroma Spread to the World

Generally speaking, when it comes to the three basic flavors of baijiu, the sequence is as follows:

Strong-aroma flavor, light-aroma flavor, and soya-sauce flavor

In 1952, to promote the recovery and development of China's baijiu industry, the First National Liquor Evaluation Conference was held in Beijing under the personal intervention of Premier Zhou Enlai. More than 100 kinds of liquor participated in the contest, and the selection criteria were also stringent.

It has a long history and sells well all over the country.

It is recognized by the masses and welcomed by consumers.

High quality is in line with high-grade liquor standards.

The manufacturing method is unique and cannot be imitated by other regions.

After fierce competition, the earliest "four famous baijiu" in China were selected.

Luzhou Laojiao Maotai Xifeng Fenjiu

Then, according to flavor and technique similarity, baijiu was divided into four major flavors.

At this time, they have a vague understanding of the concept of flavor, which is only referred to as "Mao-aroma," "Lu-aroma," and "Fen-aroma."

Strictly speaking, at this time, not until more than 20 years later, in 1979, at the third famous liquor selection hosted by Zhou Henggang, the leader of the liquor industry, were there the professional terms "strong aroma," "light aroma," and "soya-sauce aroma."

After the selection, to improve the quality and production of baijiu, the state-organized experts investigated and piloted the three representative processes of Luzhou Laojiao, Maotai, and Fenjiu, respectively, and scientifically summarized the works for popularization.

It is the Luzhou Laojiao experiment.

In this way, it took more than half a year to research. It formed a complete scientific theory according to the research data and materials. And *Luzhou Laojiao Daqu Liquor*, the first baijiu distilling textbook in China, was printed and published by the Light Industry Press in 1959.

Tips: This book has promoted the development of Chinese baijiu and the technology of strong-aroma flavor spread to the whole country.

After the pilot of Luzhou Laojiao, the strong-aroma flavor baijiu industry developed quickly. Then, other baijiu flavors have also carried out pilot projects.

"Three pilot projects" of Chinese Baijiu

The first time: 1957–1958 Luzhou Laojiao pilot
The second time: 1964–1966

The first time: 1959–1960 Maotai pilot
The second time: 1964–1966

The first time: 1963 Fenjiu pilot
The second time: 1965

The theoretical and practical achievements of the three pilot projects have been rapidly popularized to enterprises across the country. Luzhou Laojiao, Maotai, and Fenjiu enterprises have sent theoretical knowledge, operation technology, and expert team to major liquor factories on behalf of strong-aroma flavor, soya-sauce-aroma flavor, and light-aroma flavor.

They also sent the brand ...

As a result, “Baoshan Maotai” is distilled in Baoshan, Dongguan in Guangdong, “Mulan Fenjiu,” and “Longbin Fenjiu” are distilled in Heilongjiang, “Fengcheng Laojiao” is distilled in Fengcheng, Liaoning, and “Hetao Laojiao” is distilled in Inner Mongolia.

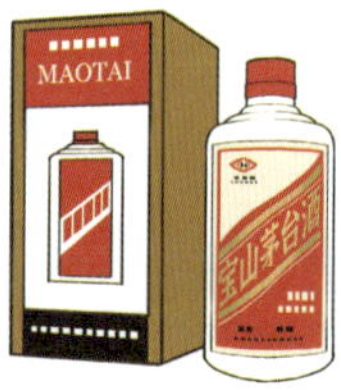

Baoshan Maotai

Mulan Fenjiu

Ningcheng Laojiao

Hetao Laojiao

Tips: “Laojiao” is the abbreviation of “Luzhou Laojiao.”
Today, many wineries still use this name.

We can find that “Maotai,” “Fenjiu,” and “Laojiao” were not brand concepts but category or flavor concepts.

In other words

Those named "* * Laojiao" adopt Lu-aroma flavor technology;

Those called "* * Fenjiu" adopt Fen-aroma flavor technology;

Where it is called "* * Maotai," it adopts Mao-aroma flavor technology.

It is no exaggeration to say that Luzhou Laojiao is at the forefront when popularizing strong-aroma flavor baijiu throughout the country, with the most significant number of students and the most outstanding contribution.

Lai Gaohuai: a representative inheritor of national intangible cultural heritage and the 19th generation inheritor of Luzhou Laojiao traditional distilling technology

Tips: Since the 1960s, Luzhou Laojiao has held more than 20 training courses for the national distilling industry on distilling technology, tasting and blending, physical and chemical inspection, and factory director and enterprise management. They have trained thousands of distilling technology and management personnel, and the strong-aroma flavor baijiu process has spread throughout the country.

Since then, in 1979, 1984, and 1989, at the three National Liquor Evaluation Conferences, strong-aroma flavor baijiu has occupied no less than 50% of the famous liquor.

At the Third National Liquor Evaluation Conference, experts formally established the concept of "strong aroma," "light aroma," and "soya-sauce aroma," according to the process and flavor characteristics of several famous liquors. In addition, the "rice-aroma flavor" is represented by Guilin Sanhuajiu with rice as raw material. It resulted in the "four major flavors" of the earliest Chinese baijiu.

Strong-aroma flavor

Soya-sauce-aroma flavor

Light-aroma flavor

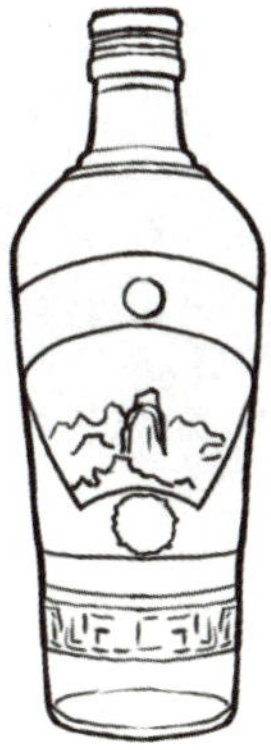

Rice-aroma flavor

In 1989, at the Fifth National Liquor Evaluation Conference, Luzhou Laojiao was rewarded as a famous Chinese liquor again and was also awarded the title of "Famous Chinese Liquor" five consecutive times. To reflect on the meaning of the "strong-aroma flavor standard," Luzhou Laojiao Tequ changed the "square bottle" to a "knife-shaped coin type" bottle.

Tips: Luzhou Laojiao Tequ expresses the "standard" through the appearance and liquor label of "knife-shaped coins and cloth-shaped coins" used in the Qin and Han Dynasties.

Zhou Henggang, the leader of the liquor industry, personally wrote the four characters "Nong Xiang Zheng Zong (authentic strong-aroma flavor)" for Luzhou Laojiao to correct some communication chaos in the industry. The four characters mean the strong-aroma flavor is orthodox in the baijiu industry.

Zhou Henggang, the leader of the liquor industry, personally wrote the four characters "Nong Xiang Zheng Zong (authentic strong-aroma flavor baijiu)" for Luzhou Laojiao.

In 2019, among the three main flavors of "strong aroma, light aroma, and soya-sauce aroma" Chinese baijiu, the market share of strong-aroma flavor baijiu was more than twice that of the sum of light-aroma flavor and soya-sauce-aroma flavor baijiu.

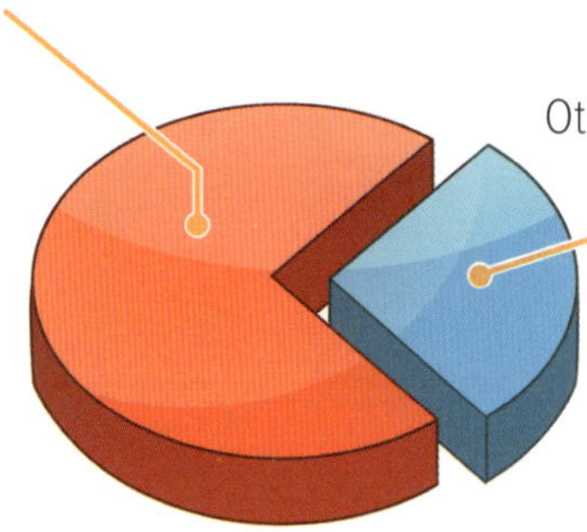

Through the efforts of Luzhou Laojiao distillers from generation to generation, the strong aroma technique has been popularized throughout the country, forming a pattern of the "strong-aroma flavor world."

You see, strong-aroma flavor is number one in the baijiu industry.

It's late. Let's talk about it next time!

For more excellent content, please pay attention to the next chapter—"Why Is the Strong-Aroma Flavor Baijiu Peerless in Smell? (II)."

CHAPTER 6

Why Is the Strong-Aroma Flavor Baijiu Peerless in Smell? (II)

Many people have an understanding of today's baijiu industry:

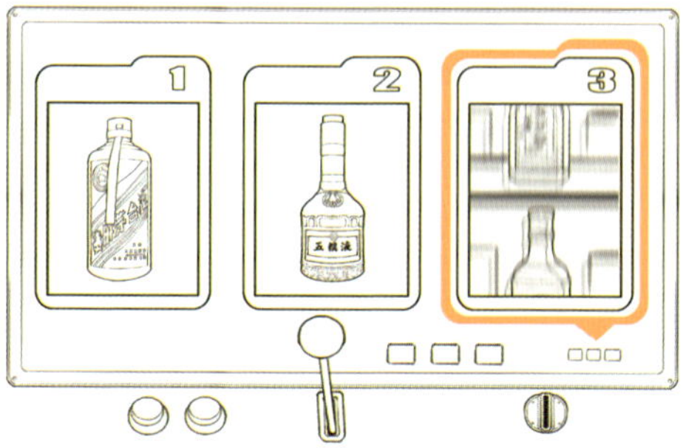

Maowuguo (including Maotai, Wuliangye, and Guojiao 1573) or Maowulu (including Maotai, Wuliangye, and Luzhou Laojiao)

It's not true! Experienced people will tell you:

The Chinese baijiu industry has experienced great changes since the foundation of the People's Republic of China in 1949.

3. Baijiu Billboard

Where there are people, there is competition, and so it is in the baijiu industry ...

Tips: In 1949, industries were waiting to be taken up after the founding of the People's Republic of China. As a national industry, the baijiu industry worked together.

Luzhou Laojiao is outstanding in cooperation and offers help selflessly. Luzhou Laojiao has popularized technology to all who need help.

In its production capacity, Luzhou Laojiao built the first garden-factory-type Luohan distilling ecological park in China in 1988, with an output of more than 10,000 tons.

It was five times more than Maotai!

Tips: In 1992, the output of Maotai exceeded 2,000 tons, and it was not until 2004 that the scale of Maotai reached 10,000 tons.

In sales and profit taxation, Luzhou Laojiao achieved profits and taxes of RMB 100 million yuan in 1988, ranking first.

It was more than the sum of the five Sichuan liquors!

Tips: In 1988, Wuliangye realized profits and taxes of RMB 22.088 million yuan, and Maotai realized profits and taxes of RMB 13.91 million yuan.

From the 1950s to the late 1980s, Luzhou Laojiao was undoubtedly the first-generation navigator of Chinese baijiu.

At the beginning of 1988, the market liberalized the price of baijiu, and baijiu competition became competitive.

However, a few months later, the state issued a policy restricting public consumption and giving price reduction guidelines to famous liquors.

In 1989, Fenjiu became the number one in the industry with an advantageous production capacity and was called the "boss."

In 1994, Wuliangye, a strong-aroma flavor baijiu, took over "number one in the industry" from Fenjiu and became the third-generation navigator.

In 1998, the case of adulterated liquor in Shanxi Shuozhou hindered the development of Fenjiu.

Tips: The case of adulterated liquor in Shuozhou has nothing to do with Fenjiu. Fenjiu was a scapegoat.

The 1990s belonged to Wuliangye in China's baijiu industry.

In 1998, Wuliangye's operating income and net profit were four times more than Maotai.

Until 2012, Maotai surpassed Wuliangye in operating income and net profit, and the overlord of China's liquor industry changed again.

Therefore, the baijiu charts are as follows:

4. The Value Secret of Strong Aroma

As we all know, soya-sauce-aroma flavor baijiu stresses the "12987" process.

Strong-aroma flavor baijiu formed a unique "516" digital password because of its unique process of "producing aroma in a mud cellar and adding more materials to fermented grains."

"5": Five kinds of "four"

Five 4 in English

Abbreviation: F4

"F4" refers to a cycle of one year, including grain feeding, steaming, qu feeding, and taking out liquor all four times. It ferments all the year (spring distilling, summer distilling, autumn distilling, and winter distilling). Then it formed thousand-year cellars and ten thousand-year fermented grains, which is recycled and used year after year.

Soya-sauce aroma

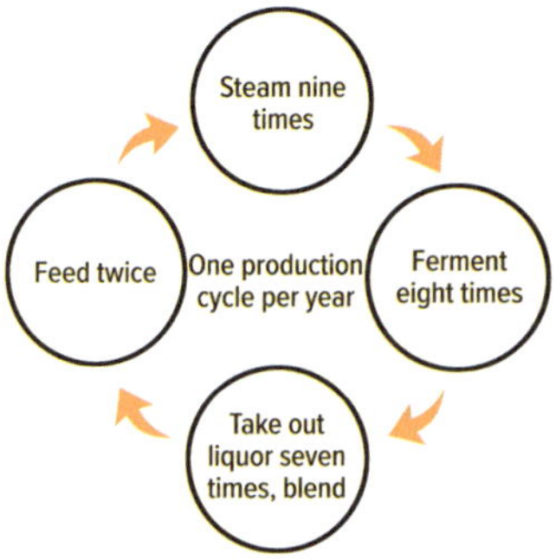

Strong aroma

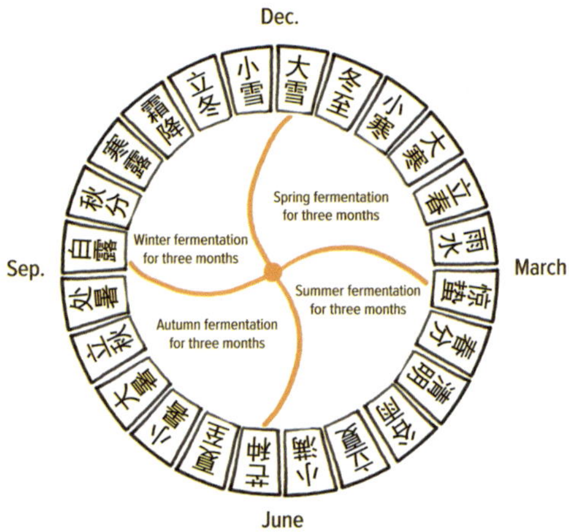

Tips: The strong-aroma flavor process is complex and can be divided into large-scale and small-scale conversions. The large-scale conversion starts in September every year, one cycle a year, and the small-scale conversion begins in June every year, four cycles a year.

For understanding, let's talk about the small-scale conversion.

Soya-sauce aroma | Strong aroma

Feeding

Feeding twice

Feeding four times

Steaming

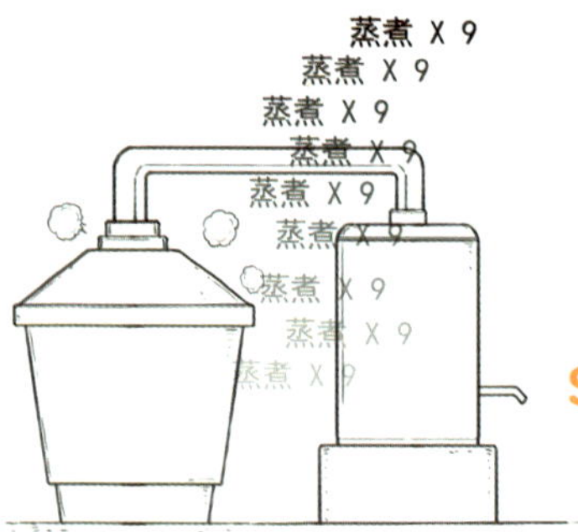

Steaming nine times

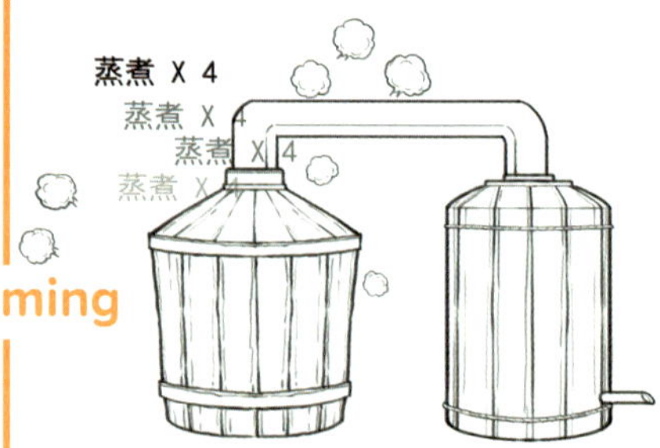

Steaming four times

Soya-sauce aroma

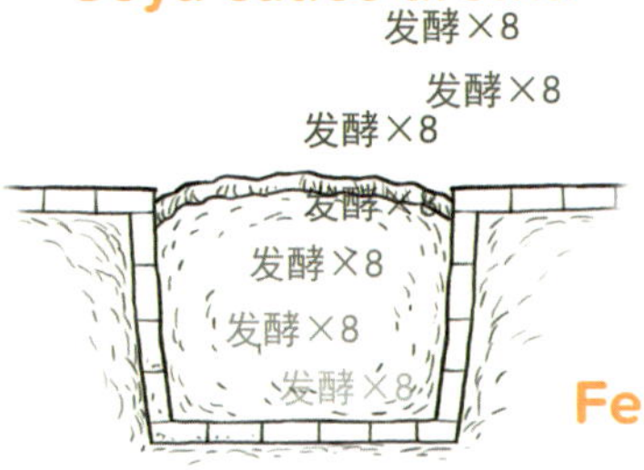

Fermenting eight times
(30 days for each fermentation)

Strong aroma

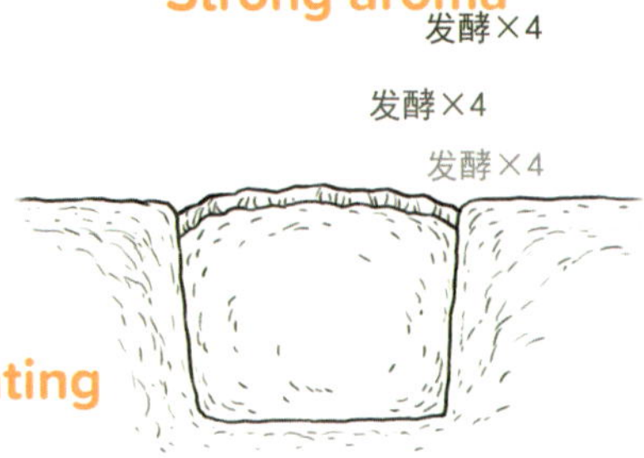

Fermenting four times
(90 days for each fermentation)

Fermenting

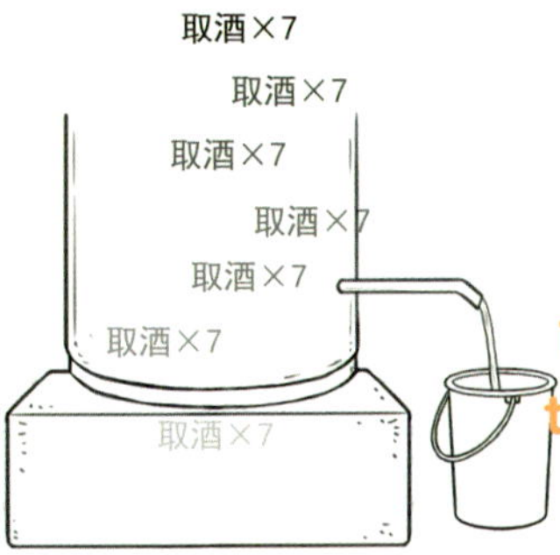

Take out the liquor seven times and blend

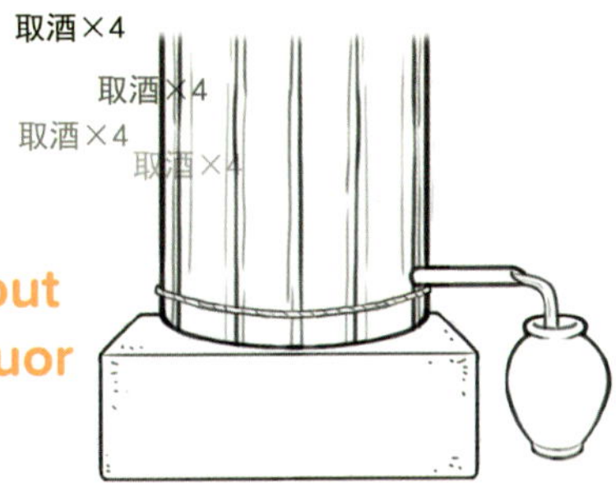

Take out the liquor four times: spring distilling liquor, summer distilling liquor, autumn distilling liquor, and winter distilling liquor, which have different styles.

Take out the liquor

"1": one "infinite loop"

Abbreviation: "3 / 4 ∞"

Strong-aroma flavor baijiu adopts the unique process of "adding more materials to fermented grains." After a fermentation period, a quarter of vinasse will be taken out from the cellar cap and replenished with fresh sorghum so that the new grains and old vinasse can be recycled from generation to generation and repeated year by year.

One foot-long whip, take half of it every day, inexhaustible for ten thousand years.

—Zhuangzi, *Zhuangzi · The World*

$$3/4 \times 3/4 \times 3/4 \times 3/4 \times \infty$$

Tips: "∞" means an infinite loop.

Before the next cycle of fermentation of other flavors of baijiu, all the previous cellars' grains will be discarded, and there is no inheritance between flavor substances and microorganisms. The secret of strong-aroma flavor lies in the inheritance contained in the processes such as "mud cellar producing fragrance, adding more materials to fermented grains," and "thousand-year cellars and ten thousand-year fermented grains."

The relationship between cellar age, the age of fermented grains, and crude baijiu quality can be shown as a diagram as follows:

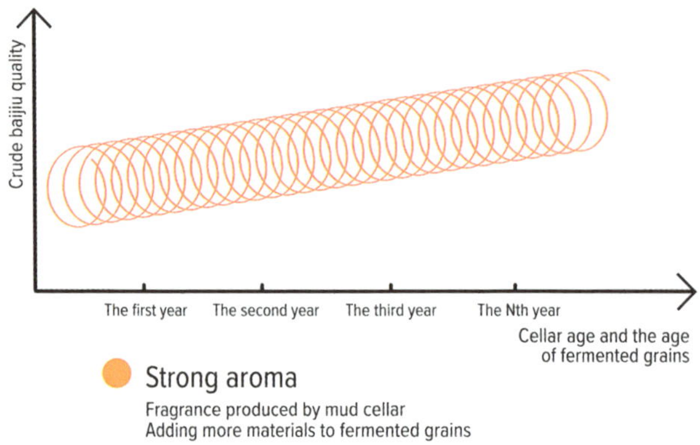

Tips: As the cellar and lank get older, the quality of the strong-aroma flavor crude baijiu increases year by year. So Luzhou Laojiao's mud cellar was named "Important Heritage Site under State Protection."

"Six": the six-phase method

The method includes layered feeding grains, layered fermentation, layered scattering fermentation agent, layered stacking fermented grains, picking liquor by stage, and storing liquor by grade.

It depends on the number of distilled alcoholic fermentative materials in the mud cellar, and let's look at the cellar structure:

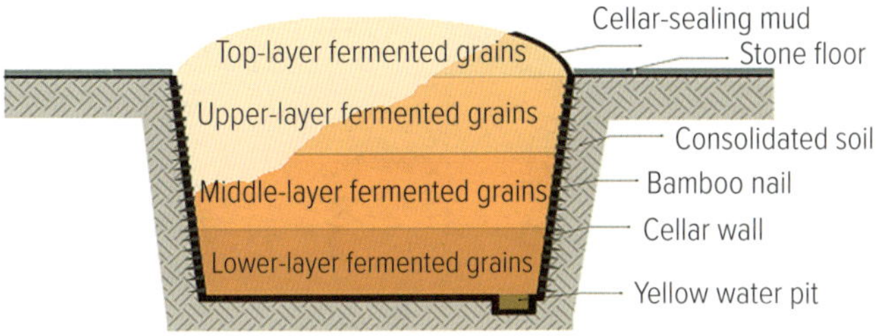

To ensure the fermented quality, every session must be "layered" due to the different fermented states of each layer, which include:

Grain feeding

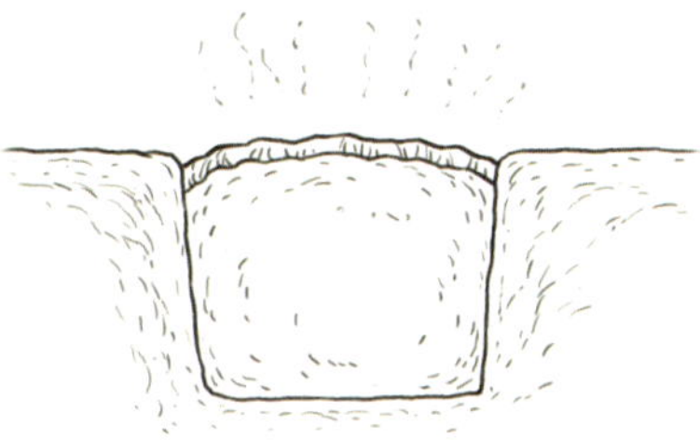

Fermentation

Stack fermented grains

Scatter fermentation agent

Distilled alcoholic fermentative material should be layered, and so should pick the liquor

Soya-sauce aroma pays attention to the blending, which is about to collect the liquor-taking seven times.

Strong aroma separated from each other.

The proportion of soya-sauce aroma and strong aroma is different in selecting high-quality liquor.

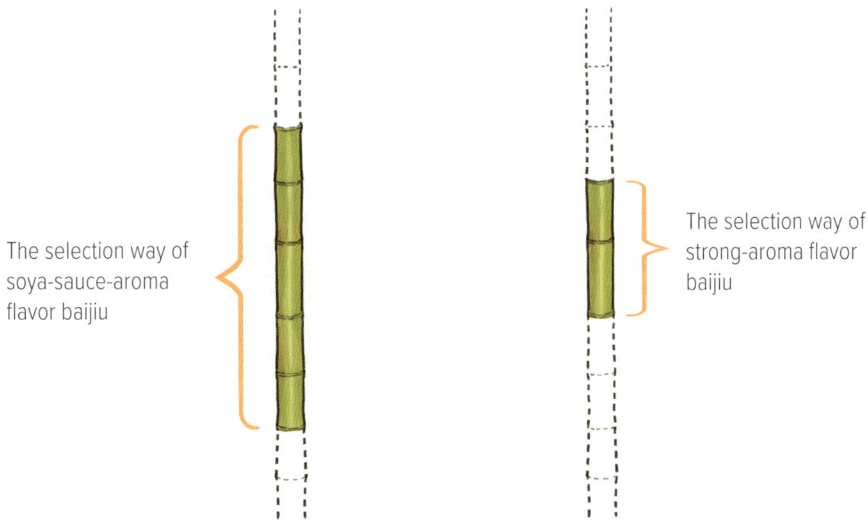

The principle of taking strong-aroma flavor baijiu is referred to as “P×%”:

High-quality liquor = Σ × X%

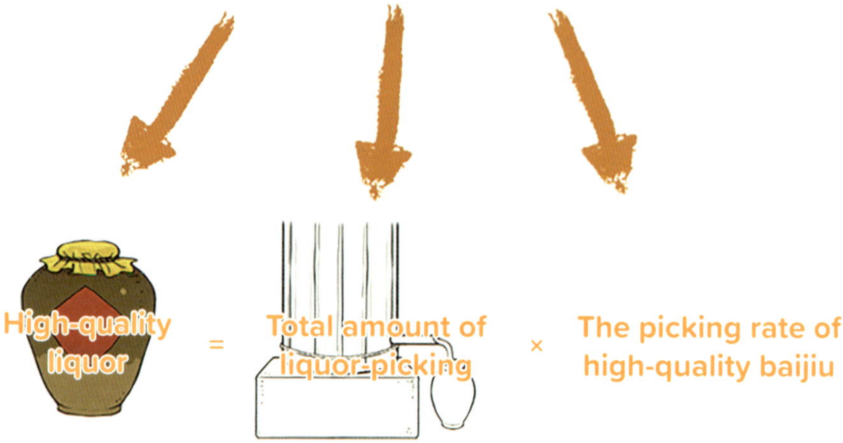

How can we understand? We regard it as a mathematical formula.

High-quality liquor = Σ × X%

Variable (quality level)

Quantitative (total amount of liquor-picking)

The value of “X” depends on the quality level of the crude baijiu, the age of old cellars, and the technological operation level of the workers.

Tips:

1. The level of high-quality liquor is inversely proportional to the value of “X”;
2. The age of the old cellar is proportional to the value of “X”;
3. The process operation level of workers is proportional to the value of “X.”

Look! Distilling is not only a craft but also an arithmetical problem.

Storage is also very particular.

As early as the 1960s, Luzhou Laojiao began to adopt graded storage and pricing. It has high quality, and the old and young all trusted it.

In 1983, President Hu Yaobang visited Luzhou to inspect Luzhou Laojiao and praised Luzhou Laojiao for its high quality, and the old and young all trusted it.

Different levels of liquor have different standards.

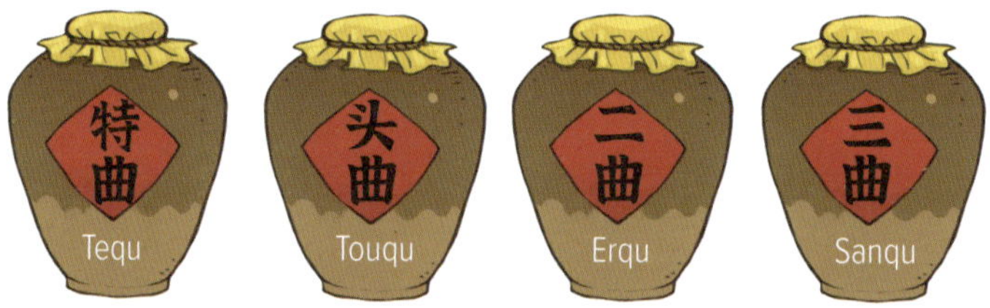

National quality liquor

Provincial quality liquor

Therefore, compared with other baijiu, strong-aroma flavor baijiu can rarely produce high-quality liquor or high-end baijiu.

Xiong Zishu

The rate of liquor production in the thirty-year cellar is 20%, and in the fifty-year cellar is 40%. (It refers to the liquor that can reach the same quality as famous liquor.) The rate of famous liquor production in the one-hundred year cellar reached 60%.

—Xiong Zishu, "Origin and Development of Chinese First Fermentation Pit," *Liquor-Making Science and Technology*, no. 2 (2001).

Finally, the three basic flavors of solid-state distilling Chinese baijiu are only different in style, not means one is superior to another.

Some people love carrots while others love green vegetables. Consumers can choose it confidently after knowing the truth about technique and flavor.

CHAPTER 7

Each Place Is Unique in Fostering Its Inhabitants, While Each Cereal Is Distinct in Distilling Liquor

Some historians say that humans evolved from Africa.

Archaeological studies have proved that ancient homo sapiens overcame physical geographical obstacles, walked out of the African continent from the African Grand Canyon, and then migrated to the world.

Because of the differences in the duration and intensity of direct sunlight on the seven continents, the skin color of humans is also different.

Black Yellow White

After about two hundred thousand years of migration, human beings occupied the earth, so they began studying gravity and preparing to get rid of the planet.

A long time ago Ming Dynasty 19th century 20th century

Then, they want to get rid of the solar system.

Since we have to leave sooner or later, before leaving ...

Let's talk about the land under our feet.

28° Latitude North: An Extraordinary Place

During 4.6 billion years of historical changes, the earth has formed unique geological and geomorphic features.

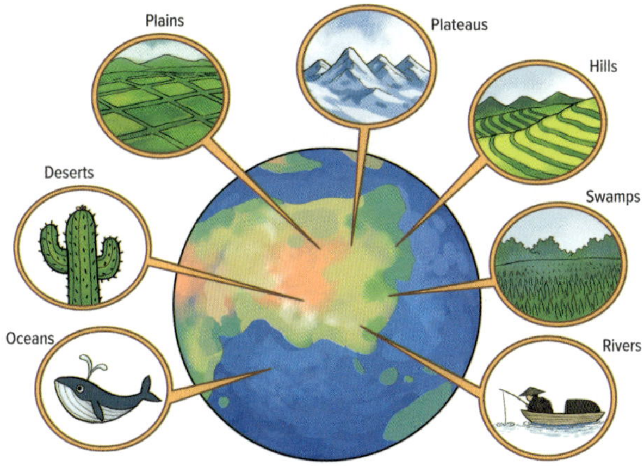

However, there is a mysterious and strange weft across the four ancient civilizations.

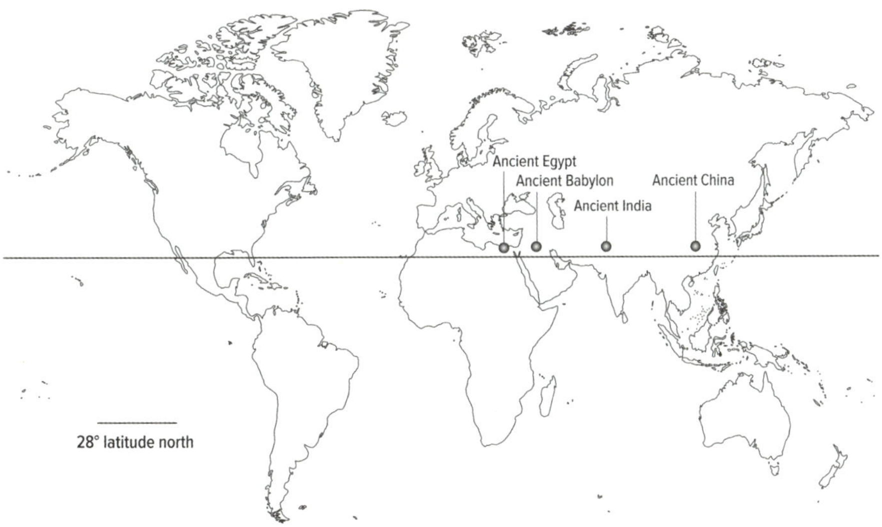

What is stranger are the countless secrets where the 28° latitude north line passes.

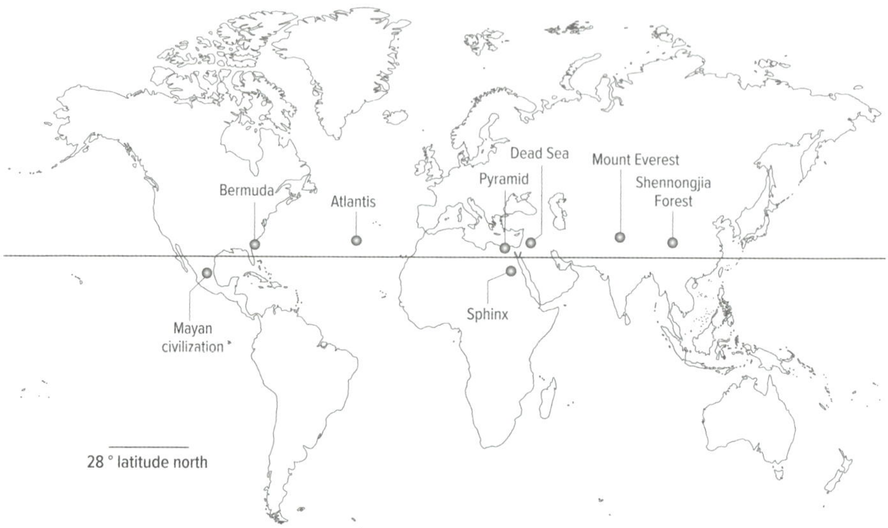

They are mysterious because their mysteries have not yet been solved.

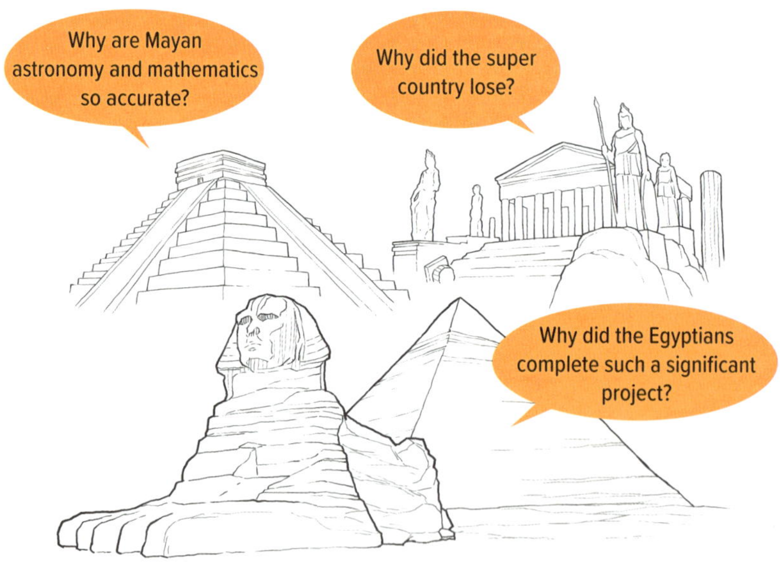

The latitude zone is the most suitable for human survival and reproduction. As soon as there were many people, they began to change the world.

Over time, the family property becomes a legacy.

Sichuan Basin: Natural Cellar

The Eurasian plate collided with the Indian Ocean plate about sixty million years ago. With the continuous rise of the Qinghai-Tibet Plateau, the Sichuan Basin gradually surfaced and tilted from west to east. Since then, the Sichuan Basin was born.

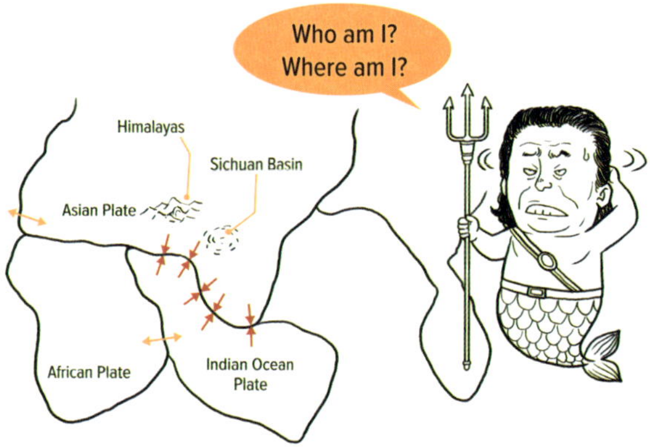

Mountains on all sides surround the Sichuan Basin. The Qinghai-Tibet Plateau is on the west, known as "the roof of the world." To the south is the Yunnan-Guizhou Plateau, with undulating terrain and typical karst landform. To the north are the Qinling Mountains. To the east are the Daba Mountains. It is like:

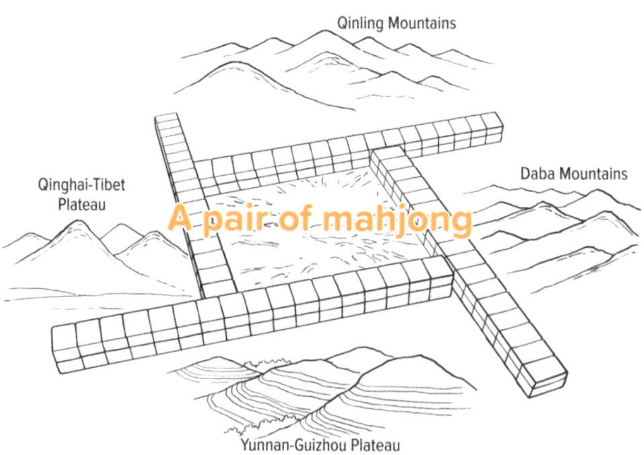

Now you know why Sichuan people like playing mahjong.

The cold air from Siberia intersects with the warm and humid air that flows from the Pacific and Indian oceans. The three air flows have mixed and adjusted in the basin for ten thousand years. As a result, the Sichuan Basin is warmer and wetter than other places at the same latitude, and the temperature is higher than zero all the year. Then it formed a subtropical climate.

Even if you use a measuring cup, you cannot make the three air flows mix more appropriately than now.

The temperature is higher than zero all the year, so it is not cold in winter, and there is no frozen soil. Then, it formed the unique strong-aroma flavor liquor-distilling process of "mud cellar producing fragrance." The humid climate all the year ensures the microenvironment of medium-temperature fermentation in the cellar.

Compared with the Yellow River Plain, there is no excessive drought in Sichuan Basin. Compared with the Jiangsu-Zhejiang Plain, there is no humidity. Compared with the Guangdong Plain, there is no water shortage, and compared with the fertile Songliao Plain, there is no disaster of frost and snow.
—Ren Naiqiang

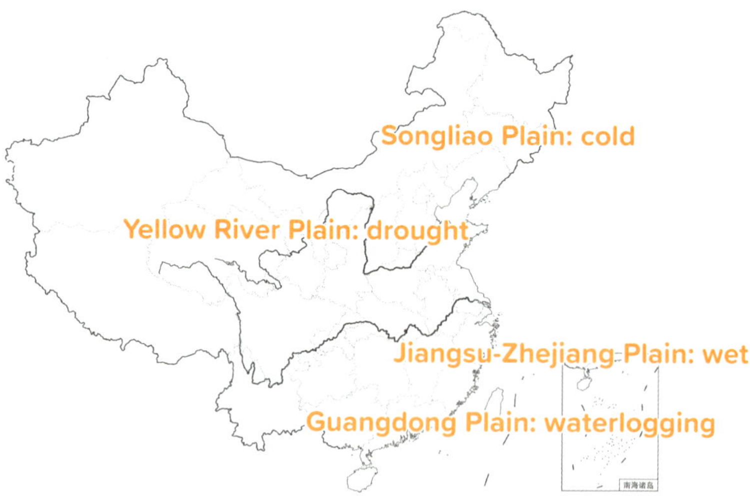

Ren Naiqiang: a famous national historian, one of the pioneers of Tibetan studies in modern China.

From the north to the south, the north of the Sichuan Basin is a cold and dry Shaanxi-Gansu region, and the south is a warm and humid Yunnan-Guizhou region. From the east to the west, the west is the Qinghai-Tibet Plateau, where nomadic people live, and the east is the Jianghan Plain, where farming is the main production way.
—Yuan Tingdong

Yuan Tingdong: a famous scholar of Bashu culture.

Therefore, it formed a U-shaped famous liquor belt with many liquors around the Sichuan Basin.

When it comes to baijiu distribution, Chinese baijiu has a characteristic. In the north of the Yellow River Basin, it is chiefly used the underground vat fermentation process, and mud cellar fermentation is widely used in the Yangtze River Basin. And the stone cellar fermentation process is used further south. It is related to the local climate, soil, microorganisms, and temperature.

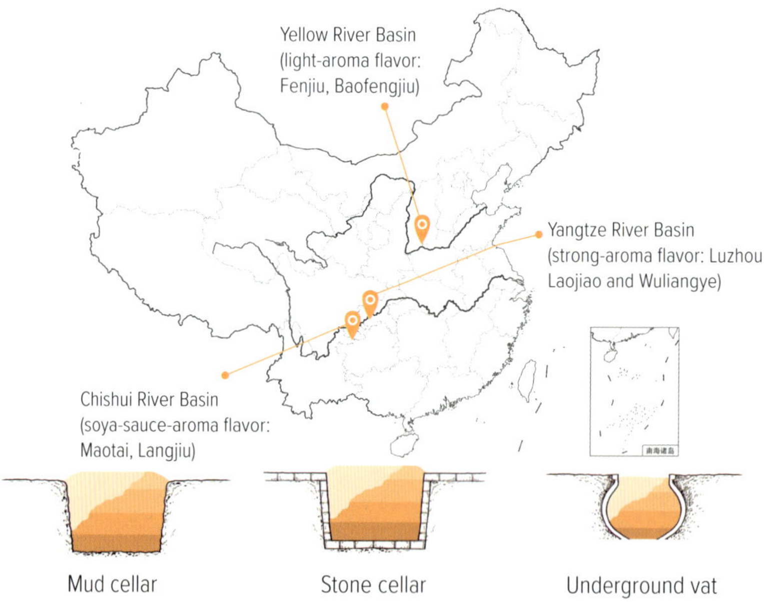

It is like fruit. Different fruits can only grow in the right place. The taste, acidity, and sweetness of the fruit will be affected by rain, sunshine, and different temperature between day and night.

Because of the unique local geographical environment, it formed the production area. The "production area" is a gold signboard on the world liquor industry map.

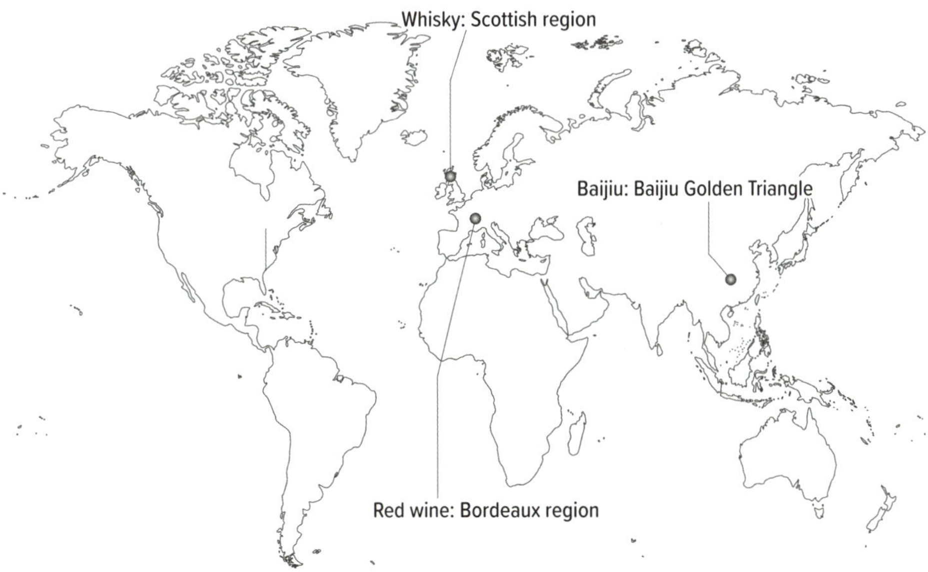

Luzhou, the Liquor City: The Golden Triangle of Chinese Baijiu

Just as there is only one Bordeaux in the world, there is only one place suitable for distilling high-quality and top baijiu—the golden triangle of Chinese baijiu. At present, three famous high-end Chinese liquors are all produced here.

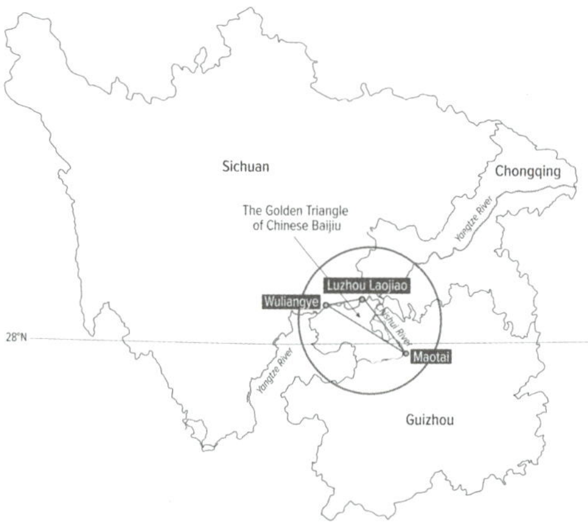

Maotai Guojiao 1573 Wuliangye

Its output share of the liquor-distilling industry occupied more than 40% of the whole industry, and the profit contribution accounts for more than 60% of the industry, which is half of the Chinese baijiu industry.

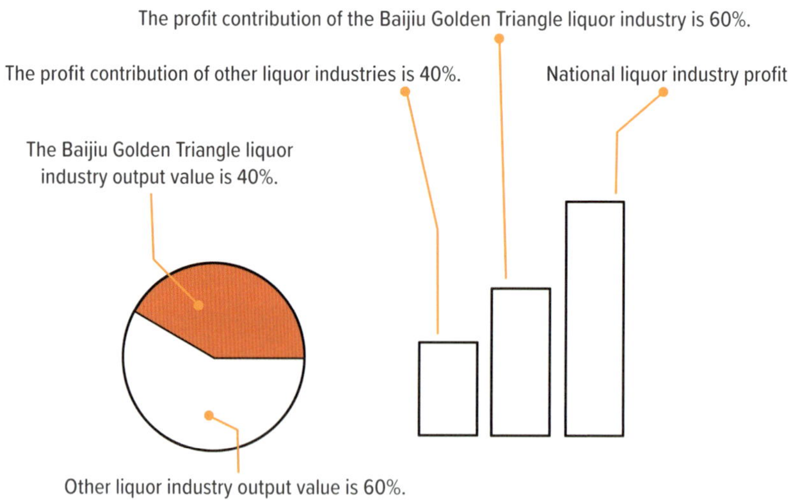

A bottle of baijiu looks very simple.

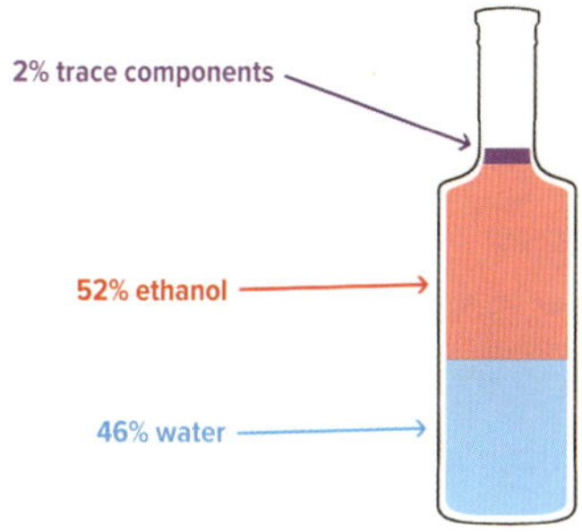

But It's complex. It contains 2% trace components, 52% ethanol, and 46% water.

The critical 2% is the main component that leads to the difference in flavor and taste of baijiu.

The aroma of traditional Chinese baijiu is mainly formed by fermentation or heating. The key to determining the aroma is microorganisms. The factors that determine microorganisms are environment, temperature, humidity, and soil nutrients.

Simply, it's the geographical environment of baijiu.

Yu Qiao: a senior engineer, chairman of the Expert Committee of the International Famous Liquor Federation

Luzhou is located in the center of China's three-level geographical classification. Chengdu is the fertile land in the north. Guiyang is a warm and humid forest city in the south. In the west of Luzhou is Kunming, the spring city, and Chongqing, the fire city, is in the east of Luzhou. And Luzhou is among them, which has the climate characteristics of the four cities.

With four distinct seasons and a moderate climate, Luzhou has the most suitable warmth and moisture, warm in spring and cool in autumn, and rain in the hot season.

The average annual temperature in Luzhou is 17.1°C–18.5°C, and the annual temperature difference is no more than 20°C.

Luzhou has abundant rainfall, with an average of 748–1184 mm. The Yangtze River and Tuojiang River converge at Luzhou, making Luzhou rich in water resources.

Luzhou has annual sunshine of 1,200–1,400 hours and a frost-free period of 300–358 days.

After investigating Luzhou, the officials and experts of UNFAO (United Nations Food and Agriculture Organization) praised it:

"As a city spanning the Yangtze River and located at the same latitude, Luzhou is the best place for distilling high-quality strong-aroma flavor baijiu."

It has been proved that only with the unique and unduplicated geographic conditions, like the climate, soil, water resource and raw materials, microorganisms, and baijiu-distilling techniques, can Luzhou make this protected eco-origin product with legendary quality: Luzhou Laojiao and Guojiao 1573.

瀘字趣解

卜 Bu: It means "people" in Oracle Bone Inscriptions. So people should make liquor sincerely. The traditional distilling techniques of Luzhou Laojiao have been inherited for 23 generations and taught from mouth to mouth.

厂 Chang (Workshop): Luzhou is full of aroma because of the traditional production mode with "shops in front and workshops in back." Sixteen ancient liquor-distilling workshops have been selected as "Important Heritage Sites under State Protection."

氵 Water: Luzhou is the intersection of the Yangtze River, Tuojiang River, Yongning River, Chishui River, etc., with rich underground water resources and the unique water of Longquan Well.

七 Seven: "Seven" is the unique core resources of liquor distilling: location, cellar, technique, yeast, water, grain, and cave. Also implied are: the sun, moon, metal, wood, water, fire, and earth. Put "seven elements" into the liquor, distill the liquor with heaven and land, and the human world exists forever.

田 Field: The unique "red soil" that produces grain in southern Sichuan is rich in producing organic red glutinous sorghum, commonly known as "red grain" in Luzhou.

皿 Utensil: The baijiu is stored in unique liquor-distilling utensils. It adopts unique liquor storage techniques in pottery jars and exquisite packaging utensils.

CHAPTER 8

What Is the Cellar? Is There Liquor in It?

People visiting the national treasure cellar for the first time will have a question. They feel illiterate if they ask, and feel confused if they do not.

What is the cellar? Is it just a mud cellar? Why can the precious 1573 National Cellars of Luzhou Laojiao be awarded the title of "National Living Cultural Relics"?

Today, let's talk about the "cellar."

In short, the cellar is a container for storing and fermenting grains, which was first uesd 4,800 years ago.

Up to now, the cellar has various styles.

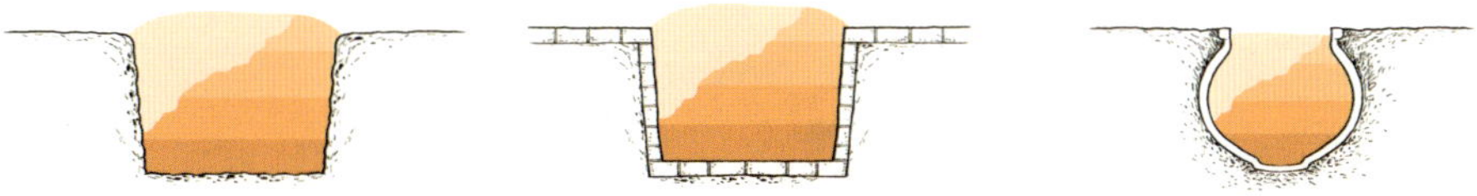

Mud cellar (strong aroma)   Stone cellar (soya-sauce aroma)   Underground vat (light aroma)

Due to different climates, it formed unique fermentation types.

- In the north of the Yellow River Basin, it is chiefly used the underground vat as fermentation equipment.
- In the Yangtze River Basin, it is widely used mud cellar as fermentation equipment.
- In the Chishui River Basin, it is chiefly used stone cellar as fermentation equipment.

The liquor is different in different places, even with the same ingredients, technique, and cellar. It has proved that the origin is essential.

Luzhou is located in the south of the Sichuan Basin, and the cold air from Siberia intersects with the warm and humid air flowing from the Pacific and Indian oceans. As a result, the Sichuan Basin is warmer and wetter than other places at the same latitude, and the temperature is higher than zero all the year. Thus it forms a subtropical climate.

The temperature is higher than zero all the year, so it is not cold in winter, and there is no frozen soil. Therefore, the microorganisms that can "produce fragrance in aging cellars" exist from generation to generation. The warm climate all the year provides excellent environmental conditions for the fermentation in the open operation mode with grain as raw materials.

Even during the little ice age of the Ming and Qing Dynasties, the local climate of Luzhou did not change.

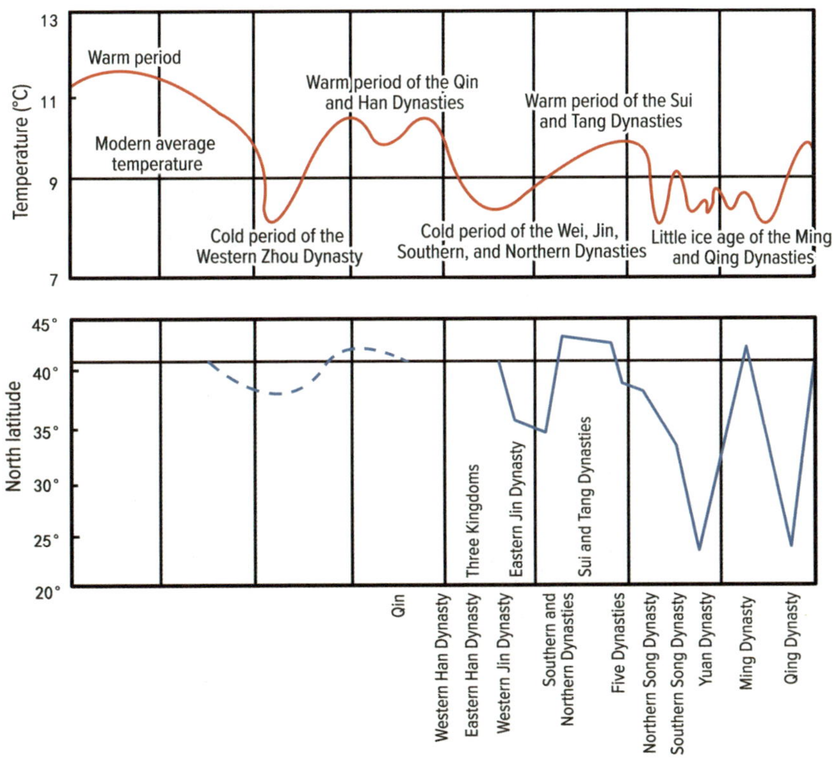

Tang Dynasty

Ming Dynasty

In the first year of the Wanli reign of the Ming Dynasty (1573), Zhu Yijun, the Emperor of the Ming Dynasty, changed the reign title to Wanli and became the 13th Emperor of the Ming Dynasty.

Zhu Yijun

In the same year, Shu Chengzong took off his armor and returned home. He decided to abandon his official position and engage in business. He returned to his hometown and built mud cellars.

Shu Chengzong selected Luzhou's unique viscous yellow mud to build the cellar, which opened the new mode of strong-aroma flavor baijiu so that the aging cellar produced a strong fragrance. The general structure of the mud cellar was built as follows:

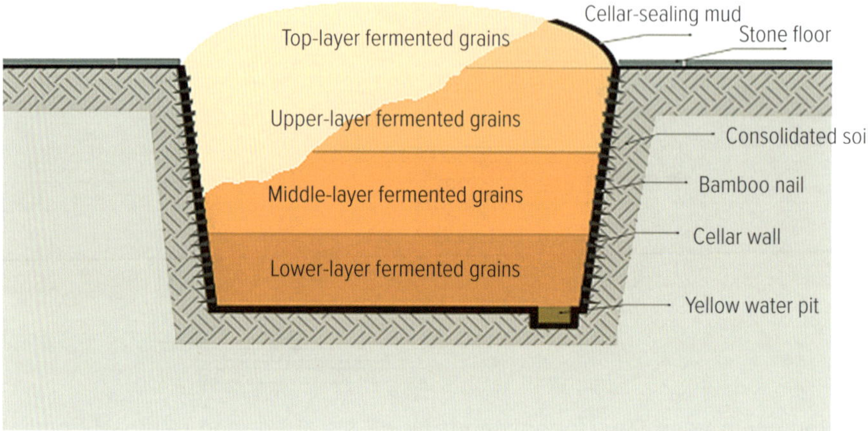

The biggest difference between the mud cellar and other cellars is that the mud cellar is built with viscous yellow mud, and it pasted a thick layer of cellar mud rich in microorganisms on the bottom and four walls of the cellar. The cellar mud provides the microenvironment for microbial reproduction and habitat.

Cellar mud

Microorganism

Wuduxi yellow mud is the best cellar mud in the world.

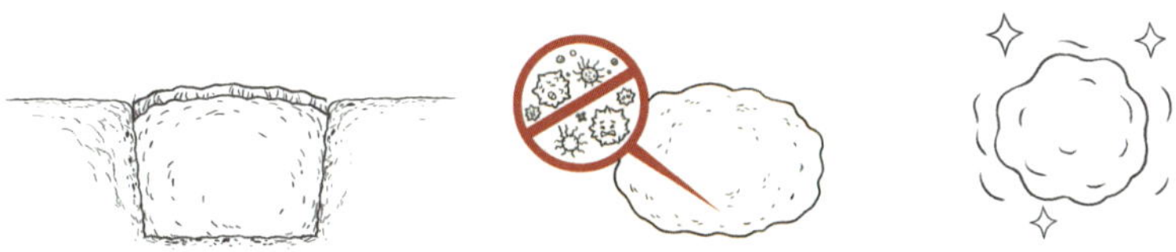

After surveying many times, Shu Chengzong discovered Wuduxi island in many small islands along the Yangtze River in Luzhou.

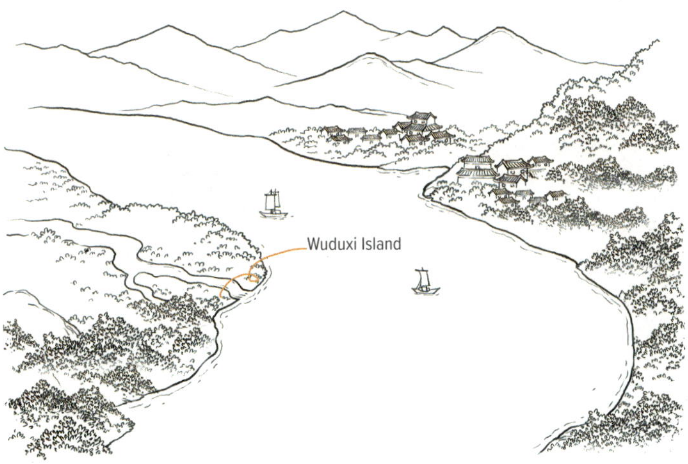

The whole piece of sandstone in the south of the island blocks the lash of the upstream river and the accumulated impurities' sediment, while the mountain spring water in the north plays the role of dredging.

In this way, the water source is in a clean environment for the long growth and development of yellow mud soil.

Hundreds of millions of years ago, the plate motion left a large number of gold grainy minerals that can be rubbed to powder and have strong viscosity. Under the long-term interactive immersion of the Yangtze River water and mountain spring water, the yellow grainy shale mineral, which is not hard and does not contain impurities, has deteriorated and softened and gradually evolved into beautiful golden yellow soil.

Workers immersed pure platinum in molten gold to make a piece of metal. After immersing ten times, they would obtain a deep bronze color.

The formation of yellow mud in Wuduxi is similar to it. However, the former comes from skillful hands, while the latter comes from the hands of nature.

Now, the yellow mud on the island only covers about 1,000 square meters, which is almost the size of three football fields, making the original Wuduxi cellar mud even rarer.

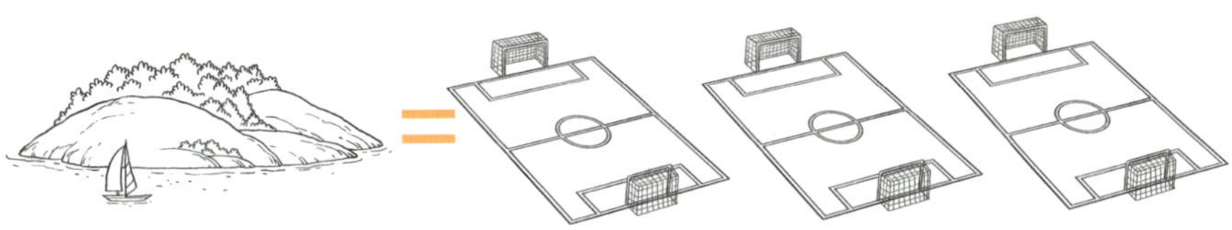

Wuduxi Island

Football field

The quality of liquor relies on the thousand-year cellars, the ten thousand-year fermented grains, and the age of the cellars.

Only with good cellar mud can a good cellar be built; only with a good cellar can we produce high-quality baijiu.

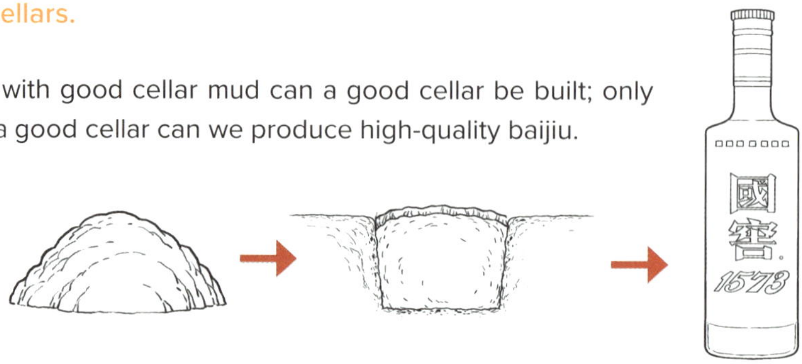

To make a bottle of good liquor, we must go through the steps of saccharification and alcoholization, which must be completed in the cellar.

Distilling liquor in a mud cellar has two characteristics: fragrance produced by mud cellars and the process of adding more materials to fermented grains.

1. Fragrance Produced by Mud Cellars

The beneficial elements and nutrients in vinasse can nourish a large number of microbes during the grain fermentation period. The microorganisms hydrolyze the starch in the grain into sugar, while the yeast uses sugar to ferment into liquor under the conditions of little oxygen or no oxygen.

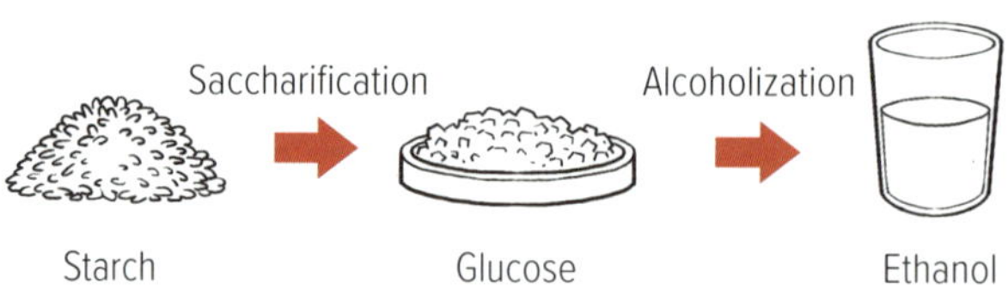

At the same time, during the fermentation process, it produces a series of alcohol, aldehyde, acid, ester and other flavor substances, which enter the liquor with the distillation process and give various typical flavors to baijiu.

As time goes on, after using the cellar for a long time, there are more functional microbial communities. The more microorganisms involved in fermentation to produce the aroma, the more fragrant the baijiu is and the better the liquor is. Just like human evolution:

People are getting smarter and wiser.

Wu Yanyong

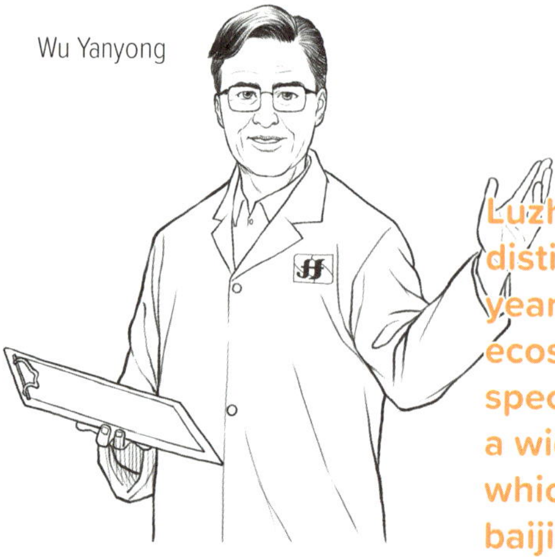

Luzhou Laojiao's cellars have been distilling baijiu for hundreds of years and have created a favorable ecosystem with various microbial species in a high quantity. It has a wide variety of microorganisms, which is a good model for the baijiu-distilling process in China.

Wu Yanyong: the researcher of Chengdu Institute of Biology, Chinese Academy of Sciences

Through the efforts of microbiologists, about 1,700 microorganisms can be detected and recognized in the mud of the 1573 national cellar. Moreover, they are still reproducing every day.

Fang Xinfang

Whoever comprehensively studies the microbes in Luzhou Laojiao can win the Nobel Prize in Physiology or Medicine.

Fang Xinfang: the academician of Chinese Academy of Sciences, Chinese microbiologist, pioneer of Chinese Industrial Microbiology

Later, according to the age of the cellar, the initial cellar can only produce sanqu or erqu. About ten years later, it can produce part of the touqu. The cellar age must be more than 30 years to distill Luzhou Laojiao Tequ Baijiu and Jiaoling Baijiu.

The age of the cellar must be more than 30 years so that it can be called an old cellar.

On September 30, 2018, the sixth session of the Standing Committee of the 13th People's Congress of Sichuan Province approved "The Regulations of Luzhou on the Protection and Development of Baijiu's Historical and Cultural Heritage," which achieved protection for the aging cellars in the Luzhou with a history of more than 30 years by implementing legislative protection.

Luzhou Municipal Government

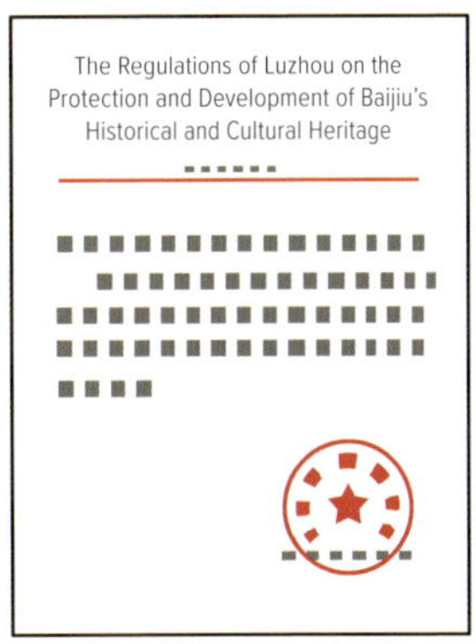

The Regulations of Luzhou on the Protection and Development of Baijiu's Historical and Cultural Heritage

2. Adding More Materials to Fermented Grains

In the baijiu industry, a popular saying is the quality of liquor relies on the "thousand-year cellars and ten thousand-year fermented grains." The problem of "thousand-year cellars" is solved by a "mud cellar producing fragrance." The "ten-thousand-year-old fermented grains" is determined by the process of "adding more materials to fermented grains." After a fermentation period, a quarter of surface fermented grains will be taken out from the cellar cap and replenished with fresh sorghum so that the new grains and old fermented grains can be recycled from generation to generation and repeated year by year.

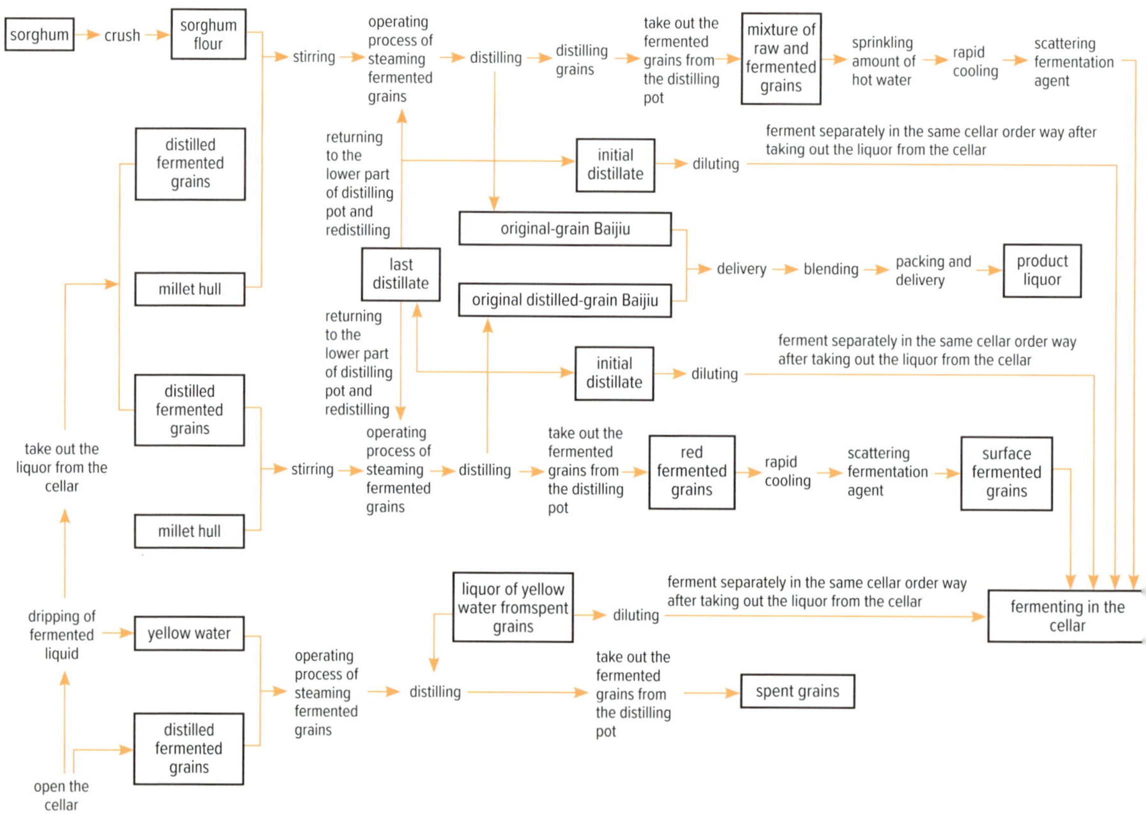

The distilling process flow chart of Luzhou Laojiao

As microorganisms multiply and inoculate from generation to generation, they multiply more complex microbes. Over time, the liquor becomes more and more fragrant.

Without intermission for over four hundred and forty years, it has been creating history every day.

To become a living cultural relic, it must have four characteristics:

"Old," "not," "long," and "special."

1. "Old": It must have thousand-year cellars and ten thousand-year fermented grains. It is impossible to have high-quality strong-aroma flavor baijiu without cellar distilling for more than 100 years. Cellars with a history of more than hundreds of years are the scarcest resource. Therefore, the word "old" determines the scarcity of high-quality strong-aroma flavor baijiu.

The precious 1573 National Cellars are the most ancient, most long-used, and most well-preserved ones up till now in China. It is also acclaimed as the only "living cultural relic" in parallel with Dujiangyan.

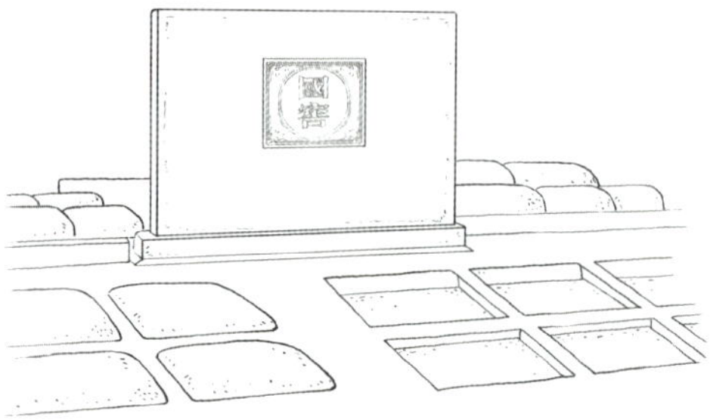

The precious 1573 National Cellars

Dujiangyan

2. "Not": The cellar keeps fermenting, which cannot be duplicated and migrated.

Generally speaking, if the cellar is not used for distilling for half a year, the growth of microorganisms will be inhibited in the cellar, resulting in aging and death. And the cellar will lose its vitality without fermentation. However, the "national cellar" is used all the time.

3. "Long": It is a very important characteristic of strong-aroma flavor baijiu. Strong-aroma flavor baijiu has the longest single-cycle fermentation period in the world.

Types	Strong-aroma flavor	Soya-sauce-aroma flavor	Light-aroma flavor	Rice-aroma flavor	Foreign liquor
Fermentation time	90 days or more	30 days a round	About 28 days	7 to 15 days	7 to 15 days

4. "Special": Liquor is "graded according to quality and priced according to grade. Young and older people all trust it." Therefore, the distillers of all generations stored, packaged, and sold the baijiu according to different grades of baijiu and different distilling seasons. "Tequ" is a superior quality liquor followed by Touqu Liquor and Erqu Liquor. It is the origin of "Tequ Liquor, Touqu Liquor, and Erqu Liquor."

There are no huge ancient buildings, complex and exquisite carvings, or ingenious engineering technology of the precious National Cellars of Luzhou Laojiao, but it has a profound culture. It inherits a long history of distilling techniques and wonderful distilling technology for thousands of years. It covers the contents of three values of cultural relics: history, science, and art. It creates economic benefits for the country, so it has a unique economic value higher than cultural relics and is recognized as a "living cultural relic."
—Luo Zhewen

In short, it means the cellars have not only a long history but also economic and social values.

Luo Zhewen: a Chinese ancient architect and head of the ancient architecture expert group of the National Cultural Heritage Administration

The concept corresponding to “living cultural relics” is “ruins.”

“Ruins” refer to the vestiges of human activities belonging to the archaeological concept. They are mainly shown as incomplete vestiges with a certain regional scope and mostly buried below the surface of the ground.

In November 1996, the State Council announced the precious 1573 National Cellars as one of the “Important Heritage Sites under State Protection,” and it has therefore been called the “Guo Jiao (national cellar).”

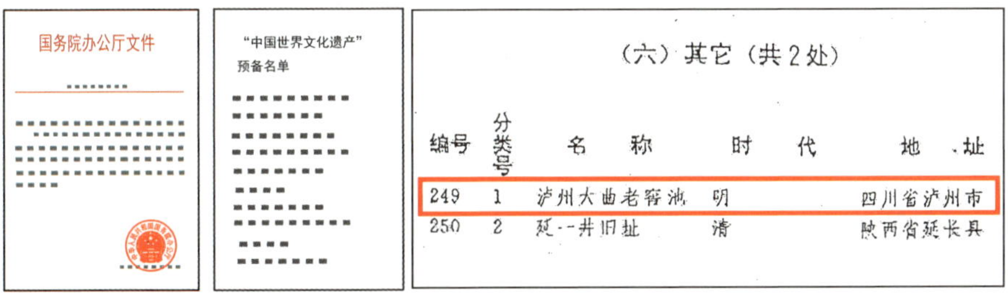

国务院办公厅文件

“中国世界文化遗产”
预备名单

（六）其它（共2处）

编号	分类号	名称	时代	地址
249	1	泸州大曲老窖池	明	四川省泸州市
250	2	延一井旧址	清	陕西省延长县

Luzhou Laojiao has successfully registered the trademark of “Guojiao,” and Guojiao 1573 has become one of the three high-end brands of Chinese baijiu.

Guojiao

Maotai

Wuliangye

"Guojiao" has the authoritative certification of the National Cultural Heritage Administration, the State Administration for Industry and Commerce, and its brand trademark.

In 2006, the Chinese government included "precious 1573 National Cellars" in the tentative list of candidates for World Heritage Sites for their special contribution to human civilization.

In 2013, Luzhou Laojiao's 1619 old cellars used from Ming and Qing Dynasties, the 16 ancient baijiu workshops, and the three major baijiu preservation caves, including Chunyang Cave, Longquan Cave, and Zuiweng Cave, were also announced to be "Important Heritage Sites under State Protection."

Since then, Luzhou Laojiao has become the "previous national" unit with an enormous scale, complete categories, and the highest protection specifications in the industry.

In short, the "cellar" is the "storage" space of western red wine, which is equivalent to the storage hole or storehouse of Chinese baijiu. It only participates in the wine aging process and gives oak barrel flavor.

However, the "cellar" of Chinese baijiu is the container in the process of baijiu fermentation, which participates in the process of fermentation and producing aroma. In English, it can be called the fermentation pit.

In the East: fermentation pit

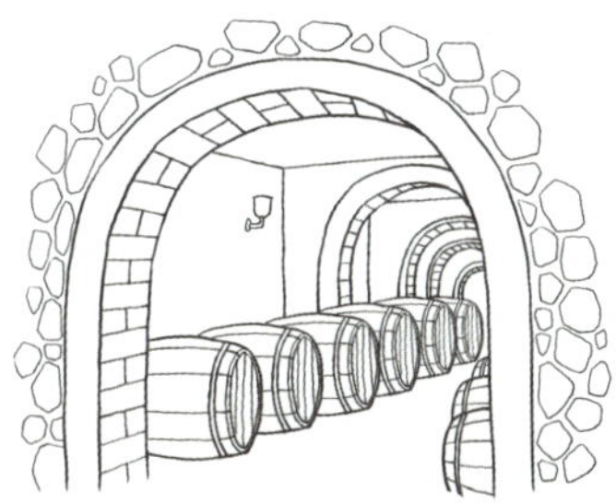

In the West: liquor cellar

Now, everyone should understand why the "Jiao (cellar)" is the central word of the dual brands of Luzhou Laojiao, namely the "Guojiao" and "Luzhou Laojiao" brands. Because "the cellar is the soul of baijiu," "only old cellars can produce high-quality baijiu." According to authoritative statistics, Luzhou Laojiao's cellars, which have a history of more than 100 years, account for more than 91.3% of the industry.

CHAPTER 9

To Carry on Lost Teachings of Ancient Sages—The Secret of Strong Aroma Lies in 516

As the old saying goes, every profession produces its own leading master.

However, why do so many choose to enter the baijiu industry?

Don't underestimate the baijiu-distilling industry, which is a technical job.

How much jiuqu to add?

It is all about sophistication!

Generally speaking, in addition to the owner of each workshop, there is also a key person who is the key to the quality of baijiu-distilling. He is usually called:

A "Da Wa Pian" would take on many apprentices so that the distilling industry was not only crowded, but the skills were also passed down over a long period.

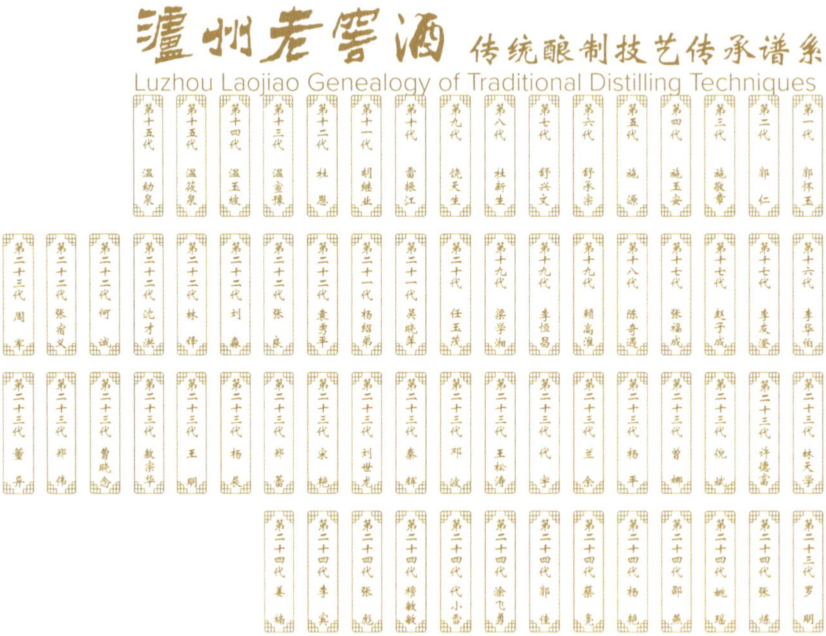

An obvious feature can be found in the genealogy chart.

In the past: father-son lineage

Later: master-apprentice lineage

Why is it so?

Later, the academic qualifications of the distillers got higher and higher.

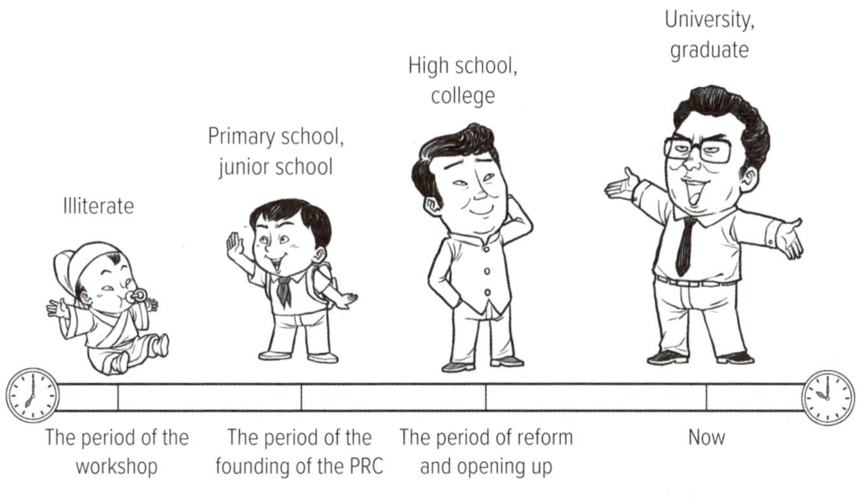

Previously distillers were born to be boss, and now if there is no college degree, distillers are embarrassed to say they are distillers. And now, the universities also set up majors related to distilling, such as bioengineering and food engineering.

As the level of knowledge of distillers has escalated, the distilling techniques have become more sophisticated.

Let's talk about the distilling techniques of Luzhou Laojiao!

The Strong-Aroma Code

The techniques of distilling Luzhou Laojiao liquor are complex, with hundreds of processes in total, but we don't need to remember them all. Come on! Follow the cellar master and read the shorthand.

「516」

National Distilling Techniques

Scatter and hook the fermented grains back into the distilling pot: *tai chi*, which is about the interaction of yin and yang, the unity of heart and hands, and the harmony of rigidity and flexibility.

Baijiu-distilling results from ancient wisdom and brings the ancient concept of "the dome-like heaven embraces the vast earth" into full play.

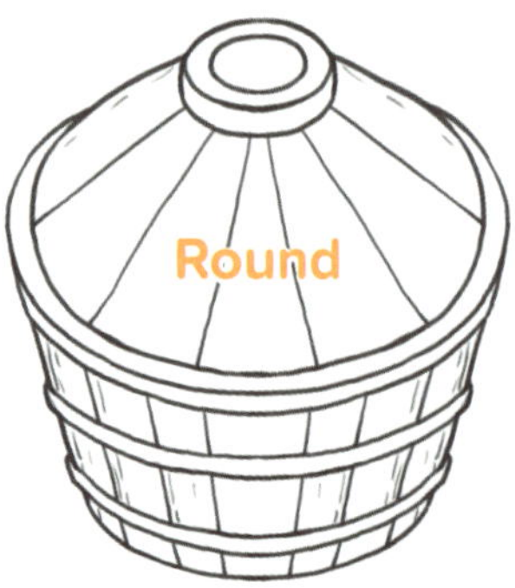

The distilling pot

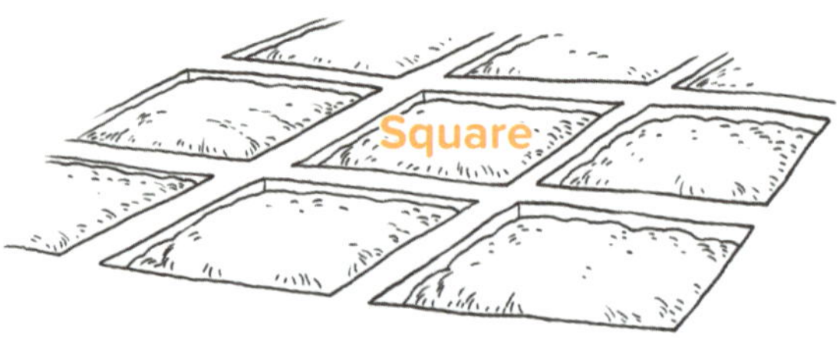

The cellar

The most representative traditional distilling technique of Luzhou Laojiao, "scattering and hooking the fermented grains back into the distilling pot," coincides with the *tai chi* stance.

In fact, the seemingly simple action is not simple, and different work experiences would achieve different results with the same action.

Beginners Skilled workers Veteran technicians

In the operating process of putting fermented grains into the distilling pot, beginners walk around the distilling pot to spread the fermented grains evenly from four directions, called "zhuanzhuanzeng."

Skilled workers usually finish the process from two sides (right and left) and test the rise of the steam with their fingers.

The veteran technician often fixes his position in a standing position, and spreads the fermented grains with both hands in a circular, smooth, one-step manner, spreading about 15 kilograms of fermented grains evenly to the pot surface at one time.

Test the quality of liquor by foam: In the process of distillation to get liquor, the concentration of alcohol will gradually decrease with the flow of time because the boiling point of alcohol and the boiling point of water is different.

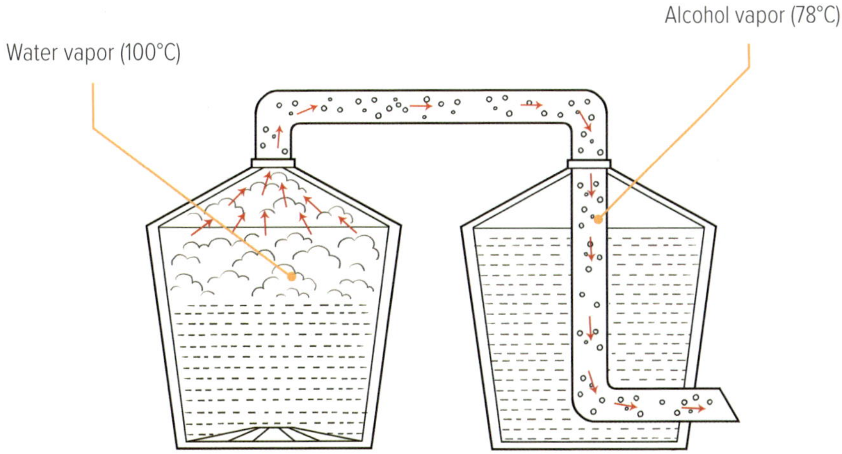

At the time of liquor dispensing, experienced masters drop the liquor onto their fingertips. They twist it gently with their fingers to determine the liquor's degree and state by touching its viscosity.

Look at the foam and pick the liquor: By observing the size of the distillate foam, tasting the liquor, and making other sensory judgments, distillers can determine the degree of the liquor and then pick and store the liquor in sections according to high, medium and low degrees.

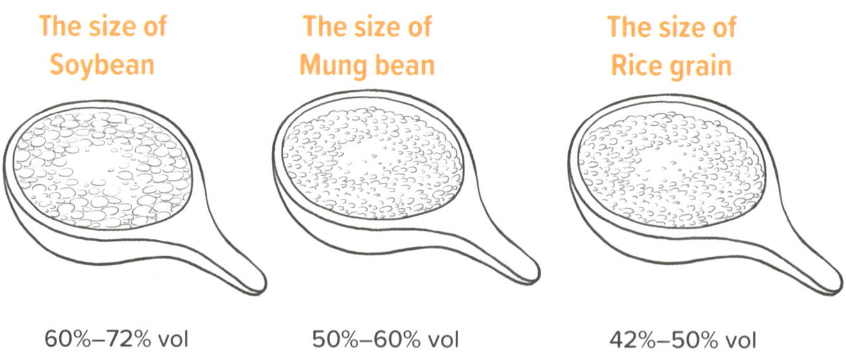

Distinguish the temperature by listening to the sound: After the distillation is over, the mixed grain is not fully cooked, so it continues to steam until the grain is cooked, then the fermented grains is out of the pot, and the distiller needs to make up the right amount of water for the fermented grains; this process is called sprinkling amount of hot water.

The process of sprinkling the amount of hot water is very sophisticated, and the key is to choose the right temperature for the water.

Scatter fermentation agent and rapid cooling: After the process of sprinkling the amount of hot water, take out the fermented grains from the pot for rapid cooling.

After the grain has been dried, the distillers use their hands to sense the most appropriate temperature.

The experienced technician does not rush to scatter the fermentation agent, but it depends on the fermentation of the fermented grains after taking the fermented grains out of the cellar.

Eyes to see the color

Nose to smell the fragrance

Hands to recognize the shape

Tongue to taste the flavor

When the temperature drops to the right level, the jiuqu is added evenly and then returned to the cellar once again for another round of fermentation, waiting for the next opening.

Luzhou Laojiao uses the methods of adding more materials to fermented grains and distilling raw and fermented grains together. Before each distillation, fresh grain and hulls are added to the distilled fermented grains for mixing. After steaming the liquor and steaming the grain, sprinkling the amount of hot water, and spreading the hulls, it is returned to the cellar for fermentation, making the "thousand-year cellars and ten thousand-year fermented grains" today.

And this cycle has been happening for more than 440 years in a row in the Luzhou Laojiao national treasure cellars.

The traditional distilling techniques of Luzhou Laojiao include:

1. Raw grain cultivation techniques

2. Crafting techniques for making jiuqu

3. Cellar maintenance techniques

4. Distillation techniques of crude baijiu

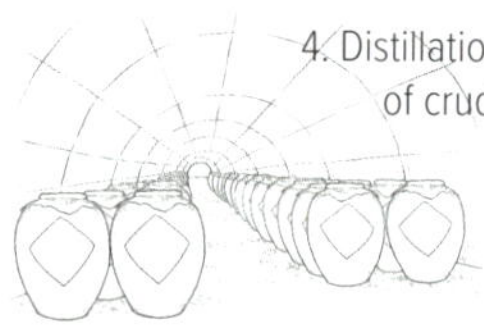

5. Cave storage and aging techniques

6. Tasting and evaluation as well as blending techniques

7. Tasting and appreciation techniques

In 2006, the traditional baijiu-distilling techniques of Luzhou Laojiao were included in the first group of the "State-Level Non-Material Cultural Heritage List," as the only representative of strong-aroma flavor baijiu.

In 2008, Luzhou Laojiao was included in the United Nations "Oral and Intangible Cultural Heritage of Humanity" reserve list for its Chinese baijiu-distilling technique.

CHAPTER 10

Ingenious Yeasts—The Microbes Beyond Your Knowledge

Humans have become the primate of all animals and dominated the world not only because of their intelligence, but also because they like to:

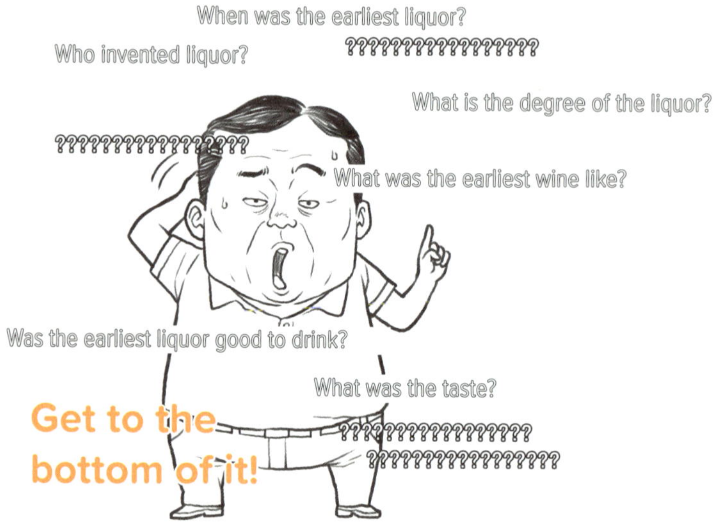

As to who invented liquor, it has remained a mystery.

Whenever in the fruit ripening season, apes hide a large amount of fruit in the stone cellars. Due to the activities of yeasts on the fruit skin or in the air, the sugar in the fruit then ferments into liquor.

So, there was liquor in nature before man learned to make his liquor.

Later, through long-term summary and exploration, people gradually realized that under the action of microorganisms, unexpected changes could occur to foods.

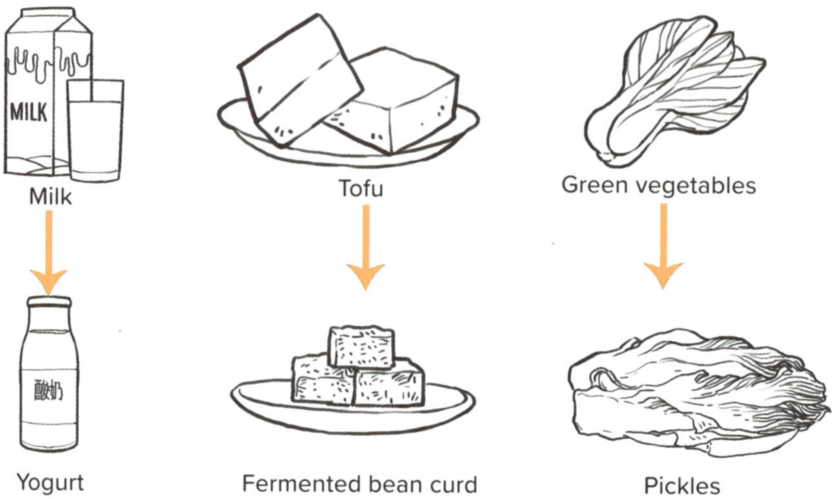

Miyazaki Masakatsu: a history writer, a full-time lecturer in world history at NHK, and a well-known scholar

Scientific practice has shown that once a microorganism enters an environment suitable for reproduction, its population explodes at astronomical levels.

For example, one gram of grape skin, in the beginning, has 100,000 yeasts ...

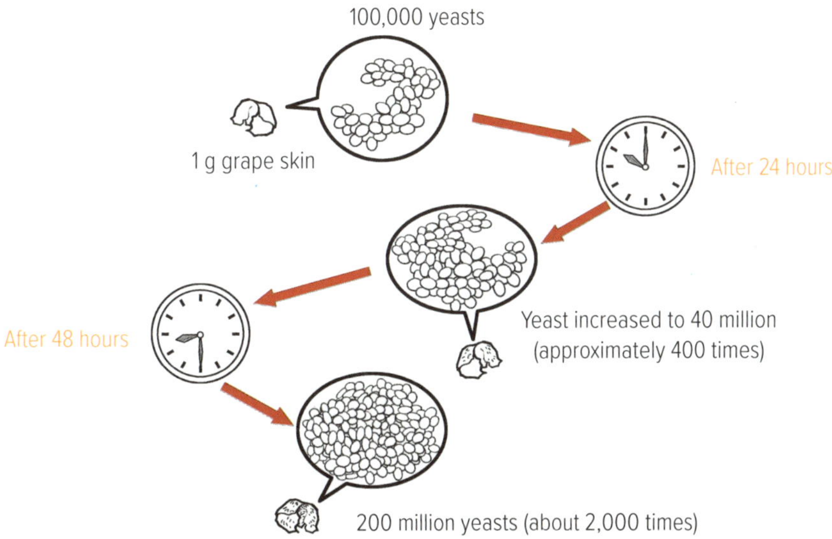

Koizumi Takeo: Professor emeritus, Tokyo University of Agriculture, a representative of Japanese fermentation science

The mysterious microorganisms that transform food into "water of life" are called:

As for what exactly is the jiuqu?

Today we'll talk about it!

A Brief History of Jiuqu

Jiuqu is a saccharifying ferment made from grains containing a large number of microorganisms, which, according to its development history, can be divided into:

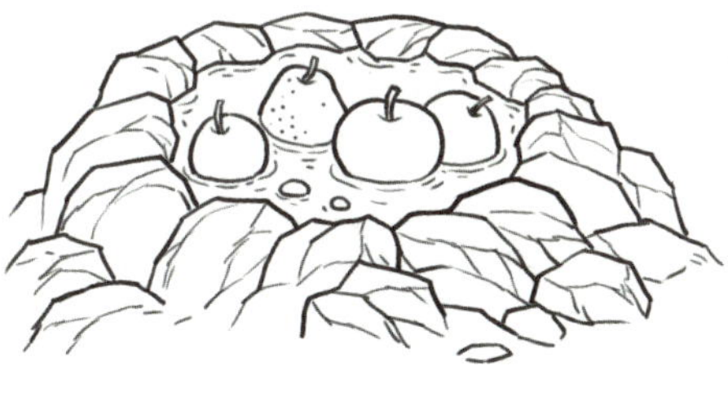

Natural Qu

Artificial Qu

The natural qu, which exists in nature, relies entirely on the natural environment for the distribution and quantity of microorganisms in the wild. So with it, liquor-making is entirely dependent on luck.

Later on, through continuous practice and improvement, people invented artificial jiuqu, so distilling depends entirely on the mood.

The development of artificial jiuqu, which has undergone long changes in China, can be broadly divided into four stages.

1. From Pre-Qin to Jin Dynasties

The ancient name of the jiuqu is Qunie, which was first divided into two kinds of ferments: Qu and Nie.

Sprouted grains

Moldy grains

Nie is a saccharifying ferment made from sprouted grains. The enzyme system comes from the process of grain germination, and the liquor made from the Nie is relatively light (3%–4% vol) and is called Li (that is, ancient Chinese beer).

Legend has it that "Yao Shun can drink a thousand cups, Confucius can drink a hundred goblets." The reason that the ancient sages were good at drinking liquor was the low alcohol content of the liquor!

By the end of the Shang Dynasty, Li was gradually phased out.

Qu is a moldy grain made into fermenting materials, the enzyme system from the growth of mold, the liquor made with qu is relatively strong (10% to 16% vol alcohol), we call it:

The earliest written record of the liquor quotations is in the Zhou Dynasty works *The Book of History · Shuoming*: If you want to make liquor, you must first learn how to make qu.

Our ancestors clearly understood jiuqu early on, not only for distilling but even for medicine.

"Shu Zhan said, 'Is there any wheat qu?' He said: 'No.' 'I am sick in the stomach. What can I do?'"—*Zuozhuan · The Twelfth Year of Duke Xuan* (597 BC)

Later, in the Jin Dynasty, adding herbs to liquor beverages became trendy because the herbs contain vitamins and fragrance components, which are good for the growth of microorganisms and can produce jiuqu with a unique flavor.

2. From Northern Wei Dynasty to Sui and Tang Dynasties

In the Northern Wei Dynasty, China's first agricultural encyclopedia, *Qi Min Yao Shu*, recorded in detail the production process of nine kinds of jiuqu, including Shen Qu, Ben Qu, Bailao Qu, Jiuzhou Baiduo Qu, and Fangbing Qu.

During the Tang Dynasty, the process of making qu was further developed, and distillery estates further emerged. Poets wrote poems and brushed up their presence.

3. Song and Yuan Dynasties

During the Song Dynasty, a large number of documents were published with information on jiuqu and medicinal liquors.

Beishan (North Mountain) Book on Liquor Making by Zhu Yizhong

A Sequel to *Beishan (North Mountain) Book on Liquor Making* by Li Bao

Dong Po Jiu Jing by Su Dongpo

Herbs of Liquor by Tian Xi

Chronology of Liquor by Dou Ping

By the Yuan Dynasty, Guo Huaiyu, a native of Luzhou, had learned the technique of baijiu-distilling from a young age and was not only strong but also smart.

In 1324, Guo Huaiyu developed an innovative new baijiu-distilling jiuqu named "Ganchun" (which means sweet and mellow), which was used to make baijiu with a "strong and sweet aroma and excellent aftertaste." Since then, Guo Huaiyu has become the most famous inventor in the baijiu industry.

Version 3.0 of liquor

The invention of the ganchunqu opened the era of the Chinese Daqu liquor!

In terms of shape, daqu is different from other jiuqu.

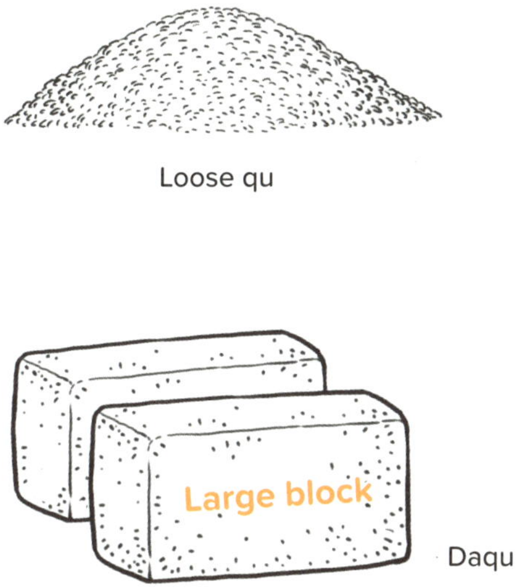

The role of the large block: Because the inside and outside of the qu block are not exposed to the same air, the microbial species inside and outside are different, making the microbial species inside the large block more abundant.

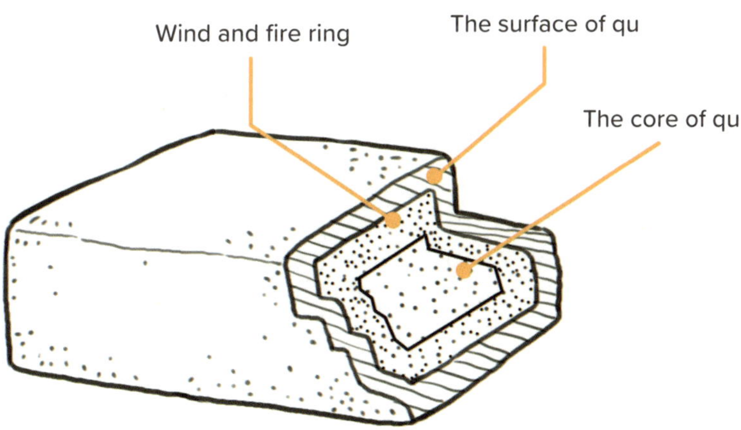

Guo Huaiyu started the history of Chinese Daqu baijiu-distilling and became the first generation to inherit the traditional distilling techniques of Luzhou Laojiao, and as such, is also known as:

...
I think "Yuan drama" may refer to the jiuqu of the Yuan Dynasty.
A little knowledge is a dangerous thing.

4. Since the Foundation of the People's Republic of China to the Present

With the further development of qu-making technology and microbiology, there is a growing variety of jiuqu, and the categories are increasingly subdivided to meet the needs of different functions.

Daqu, in turn, is subdivided into three categories, depending on the fermentation temperature.

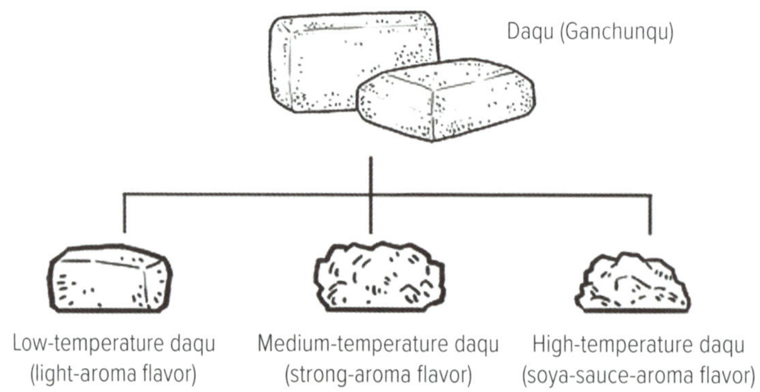

Look at the first places in the world where liquor was made.

Two River Basins in the Middle East: Wine

South Coast of the Mediterranean: Malt beer

Yellow River and Yangtze River Basins: Baijiu

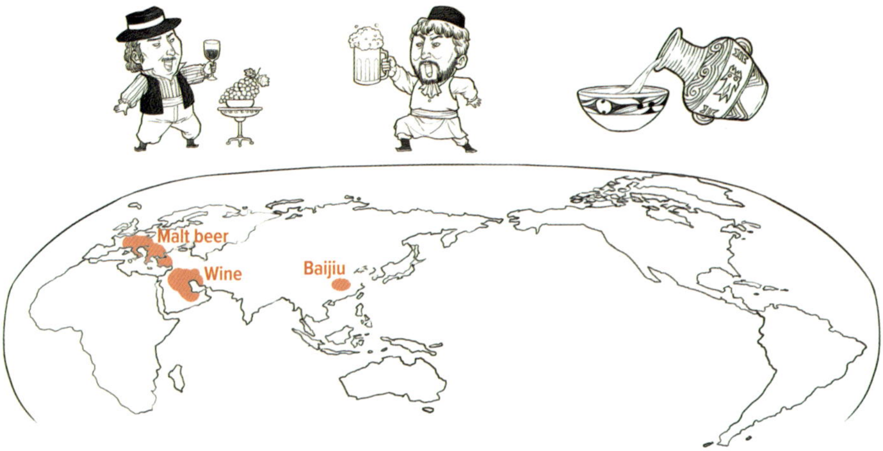

All three places recognize the role of natural microorganisms, except for the difference in ingredients!

However, it was not until the end of the 17th century that the Italian expert Rady proposed the idea of natural microbial fermentation. Only in the late 19th century did Calmette in France create the amylo process of alcohol production.

It can be said that distilling baijiu with qu can be called the fifth invention of ancient China!

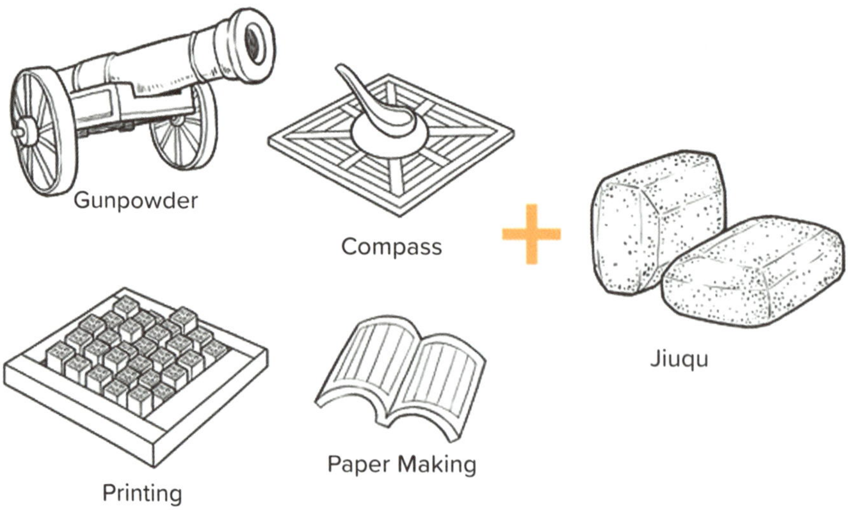

Joseph Needham: a modern British biochemist, and the expert in the history of science and technology

Qu Is the Bone of Baijiu

Many people say that baijiu-distilling is a fermentation process, just like flour fermentation. But this statement is inaccurate and incomplete. To be accurate and comprehensive, the baijiu-distilling process is a complex biochemical reaction process. Simply put, there are two steps:

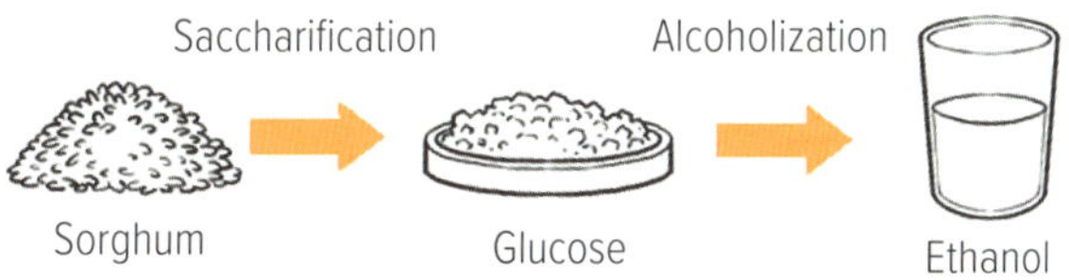

The above two steps, however, cannot be taken out of thin air; they must be done with the help of enzymes. The first step of the saccharification process requires the participation of starch hydrolase; the second step of the alcoholization process requires the addition of alcoholizing enzymes.

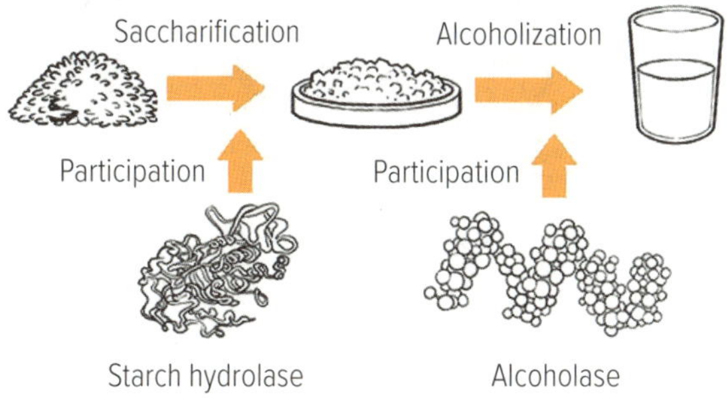

Both of the above enzymes are mainly produced by microorganisms. Starch hydrolase is produced by mycobacteria and bacteria, while live yeast bodies carry alcoholic enzymes.

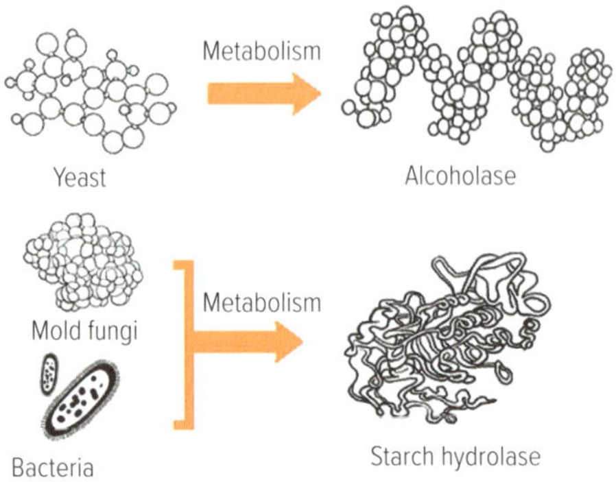

The qu base is a saccharification ferment, a solid medium or "hotbed" for the cultivation of molds, yeasts, bacteria, and actinomycetes, so the basic structure is as follows:

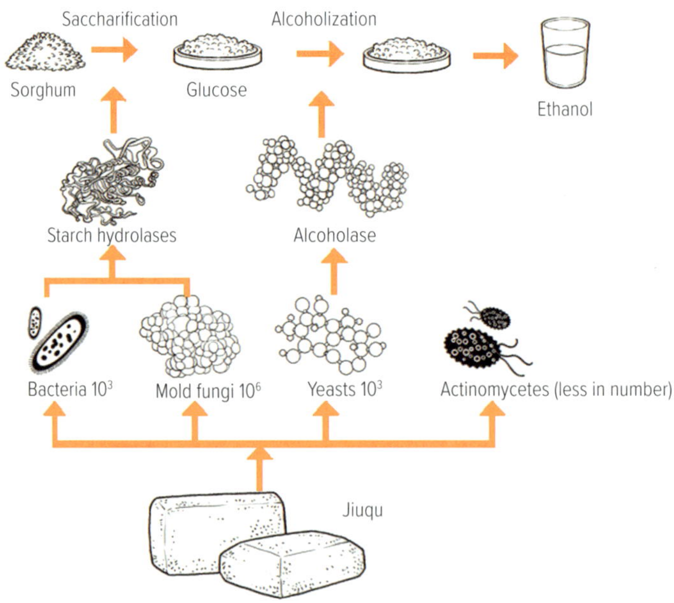

The jiuqu is a carrier of microbial organisms and enzymes

Therefore, to make a good piece of jiuqu, in addition to the theoretical knowledge, you also need the following:

Right time

Favorable location

Right people

There are certain requirements for the selection of time in the making of qu. In summer, where the temperature and humidity is high, the number of microorganisms floating in the air is huge, conducive to the growth of mold on the qu base.

Regarding the raw material, Luzhou Laojiao "Jiuxiang" brand Daqu is made from soft organic wheat, characterized by its high starch and protein content, and is used to make the baijiu more aromatic and richer.

The right time and place are not enough. A set of the scientific production techniques of qu is needed.

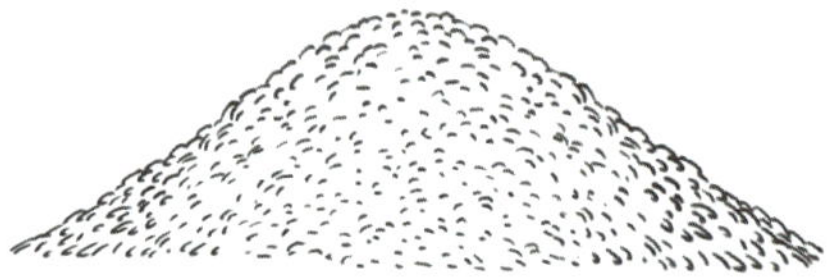

Plum petal crushed grain

Treading qu

Placing raw qu block

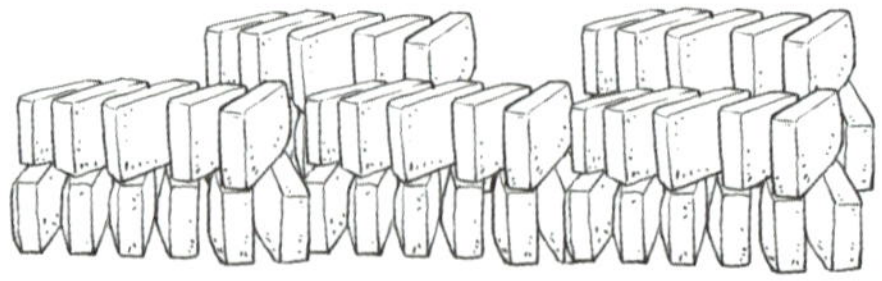

Bacteria culturing and fermenting

All the Subtleties in Distilling

In primitive society, the level of productivity is relatively low, and people will only use the milk of animals, fruit wines made of fruit, and drinking high-degree liquor is impossible.

Later, with the continuous improvement of distilling technology, only then did we start to make qu and distill by ourselves.

It can be said that the artificial production of qu is an important turning point in the history of distilling in China, and the invention of daqu is undoubtedly pushing Chinese liquor to a higher level.

It has been passed down for more than 690 years. Under the care and cultivation of 23 generations of inheritors, jiuqu has undergone evolution and improvement again and again through layers of quality control.

In 1996, Luzhou Laojiao built the qu-making ecological park, which has a strong aroma of qu and has a multi-level, all-round and large-area distribution of high, medium, and low-level microbial flora and microbial spores, enriching, passing down, and domesticating the qu-making microbiota originated from 1324.

Today, the Luzhou Laojiao Qu-making Ecological Park, the largest liquor production base in China, produces the "Jiuxiang" brand of jiuqu, which has won over more than 75% of the liquor market for Daqu Liquor.

It can be said that the "Jiuxiang" jiuqu belongs not only to Luzhou Laojiao, but also to the Chinese baijiu industry.

In 2001, the "Jiuxiang" jiuqu was praised by Mr. Zhou Henggang, a great master in the baijiu industry, as the "number one jiuqu in the world," and became a National Geographical Indication Product.

As the saying goes, the qu is the bone of baijiu, "Jiuxiang" brand jiuqu has mingled in water and fire with the national cellar, together to breed this world's unparalleled liquor.

CHAPTER 11

The Liquor Is Distilled with Spring Water, and Since the Spring Is Sweet, the Liquor Is Superb —The Clean and Unique Ambience Makes Good Liquor

Whenever his girlfriend is sick with a cold, the straight guy will come with a look of concern:

What the hell is water? The panacea?

Today, let's talk about water!

Water Is the Source of Civilization

Earth is the only one of the eight planets in our solar system covered with water. That's why water is also a specialty of Earthlings.

People cannot live without water, and where there are people, there is water. Long ago, the ancient people began studying "water."

Taoism: use water as a metaphor for Tao

Confucianism: use water as a metaphor for virtue

Laozi: The highest good (virtue) is like water. Water benefits everything by giving without taking or contending. It likes the low places others dislike, so it follows the divine law closely. In dwelling, the good thing is the land; in the mind, the good thing is depth; in giving, the good thing is being like Heaven; in speaking, the good thing is sincerity; in governing, the good thing is order; in affairs, the good thing is ability; in activity, the good thing is timeliness. It is only because it does not compete that it is without fault.

Confucius: Water has five virtues. Because it flows constantly, it can benefit all creatures as if it has virtue; whenever it flows, it must be downward, adapting to the shape of the container, either square or long, always follows the order, as if it has righteousness; vast and endless, as if, it has the way; flowing down from the high mountains without fear, as if it has courage; it flows quietly without making any tides, as if it abides the law; it will not conceal what it has and follow others against its will, as if it is upright; it can reach any place, as if it is observant; it always flows from the West to the East, therefore, it is determined; it can wash everything as if it is also good at changes. Water has these virtues, so the gentleman would definitely be inspired by water and reflect on himself when he encounters it.

The West: the Four Elements Theory

The Orient: the Five Elements Theory

Water is the source of civilization, and the origin of human civilization cannot be separated from the water.

Liang Qichao: a famous politician, educator, and historian in modern China

There are four ancient civilizations: China, India, Egypt, and Asia Minor.

In fact, Asia Minor is ancient Babylon!

The selection of human civilizations is a very complex project that depends not only on the presence of human beings, but also on the presence of:

Cities

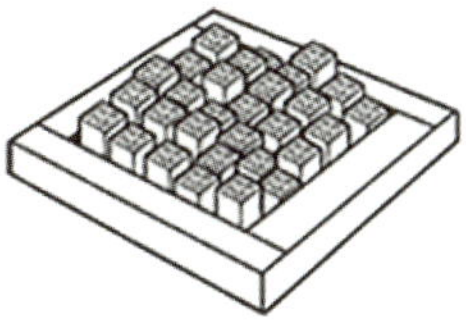

Texts

Complex ceremonial architecture

Synthesizing the four ancient civilizations, we find a common feature: the cities were all built near rivers.

(1) Ancient India is one of the birthplaces of human civilization and represents the civilization of the Ganges and Indus valleys.

The Ganges Valley is one of the birthplaces of Indian civilization, and it is not only the sacred river of Hinduism today, but also the birthplace of Buddhism.

After the fall of the Peacock Dynasty in 187 BC, foreigners invaded and established the Kushan Empire, Mughal Empire, and British India, which led to sharp ethnic and religious conflicts and stagnation of civilization.

(2) Ancient Egypt represents the civilization of the Nile Valley, which is defined as the area from the First Falls of the Nile to the Delta.

Most of Egypt is desert, with only the green belt being washed through by the Nile, and one-thirtieth of the area of Egypt is home to over 90% of the Egyptian population.

Ancient Egypt was a typical water-powered empire, and almost every Egyptian was connected to agriculture in some way. They were either landowners or farmers, and all were familiar with the weather and the rise and fall of the water of the Nile.

Around 30 BC, the Ptolemaic Dynasty was swallowed up by the Roman Empire, and the indigenous Egyptian regime fell.

(3) Ancient Babylon was an important period in the civilization of the two rivers, representing the two-river civilization of the Tigris and Euphrates.

In 539 BC, the Neo-Babylonian Kingdom was destroyed by the Persian Empire.

Thus, three of the four ancient civilizations were dead.

(4) Ancient China, the civilization of the Yellow River and Yangtze River Basins, is also known as the Chinese civilization. It is one of the oldest civilizations in the world and the only one that has lasted the longest without interruption.

To be precise, there are three direct sources of Chinese civilization: the Yellow River civilization, the Yangtze River civilization, and the northern grassland civilization.

Through many dynastic changes, Chinese civilization has flourished and never stopped.

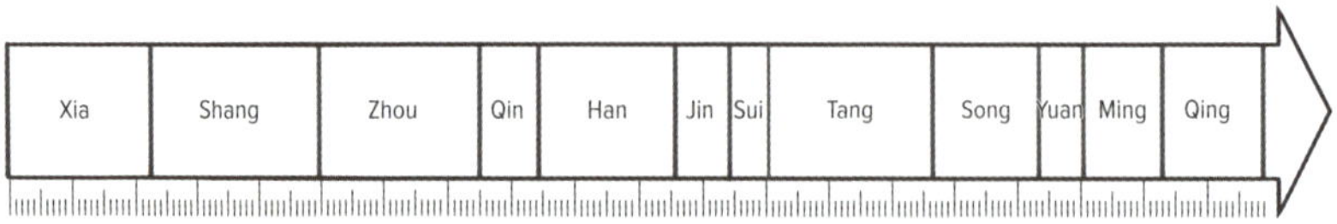

It can be seen from the map that the rivers in China run east-west, while the rivers in other ancient civilizations run north-south.

The north-south rivers have different latitudes, different natural environments, and different agricultural civilizations.

Before the industrial revolution, production was dominated by agriculture. Different eco-agriculture often waged wars over turf.

And after a long time of internal conflict, everyone was tired of fighting, and when a foreign enemy invaded, basically the only way was to surrender.

Therefore, the east-west rivers flow in the same latitudinal zone, and their agricultural civilizations are convergent and stable, which greatly reduces the possibility of agricultural conflicts. This is one of the reasons why Chinese civilization can continue for 5,000 years without interruption.

Water Is the Source of Life

On Earth, 71% of its surface area is covered by water, so it seems the Earth should be more appropriately called "Mercury." It just so happens that 71% of the human body is also made up of water of all kinds.

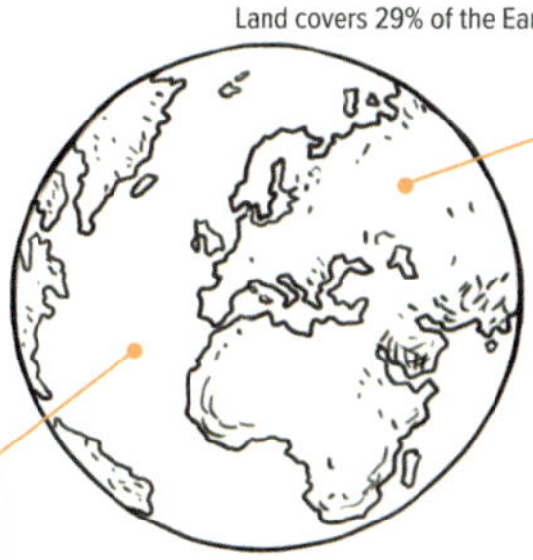

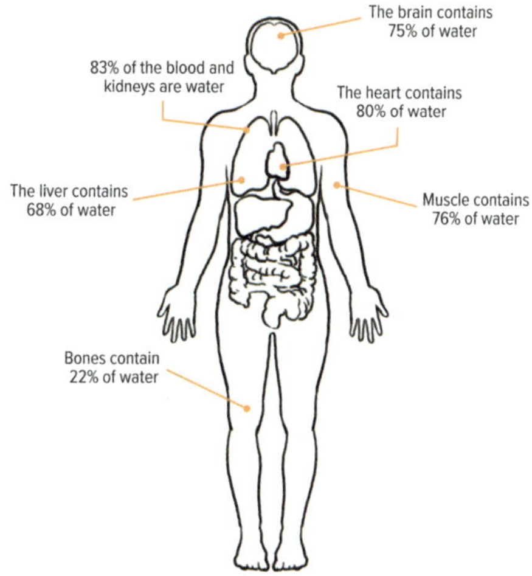

The vast majority of human and animal blood is composed mostly of water. Blood transports oxygen and nutrients to all body parts and participates in the body's macromolecules for metabolism.

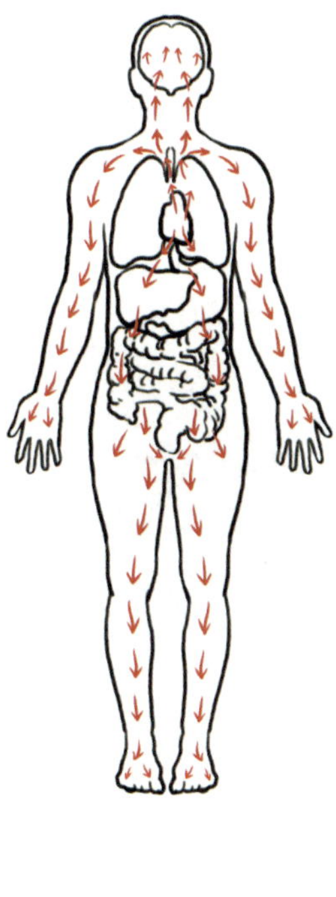

Life is made up of cells, which must be "immersed in water" to survive. Dryness is the main symptom of aging.

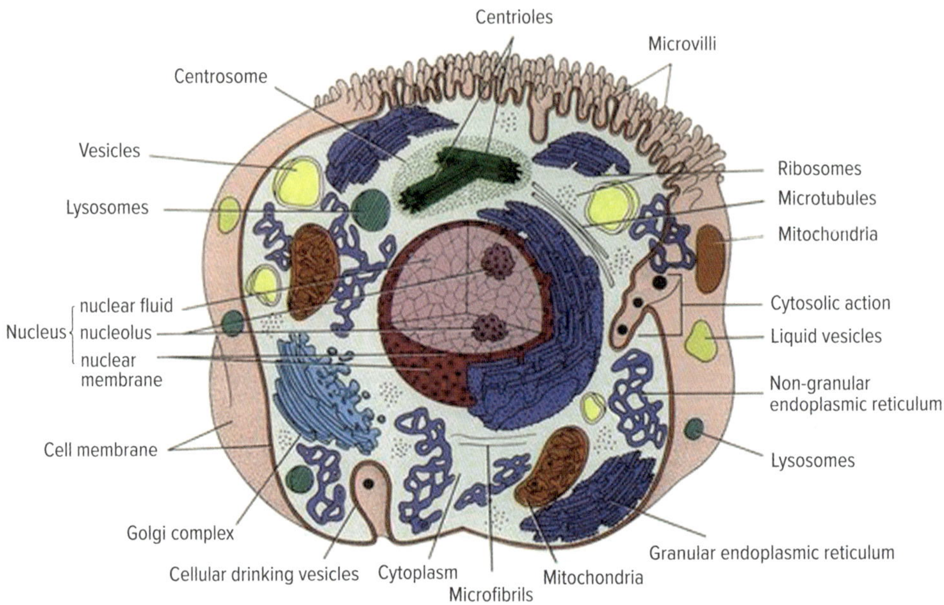

Internal Cell Structure Diagram

Young people have 42% of water in their cells, while older people have only 33%, which results in wrinkles.

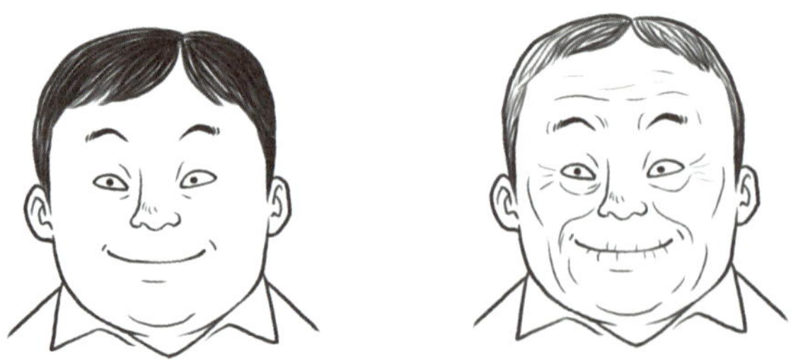

People can go without food for a few days, but not without water for a day. If the human body loses 15% to 20% of its body weight in water, physiological functions will stop and death will follow.

As the saying goes, in the diet, drinking comes first and then eating. Normal people need to drink 1,500 milliliters of water in addition to three meals a day, which is about 6 to 8 cups of water, to meet the needs of human metabolism.

Scientific experiments show that people can live more than seven days without food. Once you leave the water, I'm afraid you cannot live more than three days.

In addition to people and animals, plants cannot live without water, which is the main part of the plant body, and water flows into the roots, stems and leaves of plants to help them transport nutrients.

Some of the water runs out of the small holes in the leaves, which can regulate the temperature of the plant's body and make the air moist.

Water Is the Blood of Distilling

In *The Book of Rites · Proceedings of the Government in the Different Months*, there is "the water is fragrant." Our ancestors knew the important relationship between the quality of water and the quality of baijiu, so the saying that the clean and unique ambience makes good liquor, has become the golden rule for choosing the site of a distillery.

"The liquor is distilled with spring water, and since the spring is sweet, the liquor is superb."
—Northern Song Dynasty, Ouyang Xiu, *The Old Drunkard's Pavilion*

The water in most areas of northern China contains more calcium and magnesium, and the hardness is higher than the alkaline water in the north; the water resources in southwestern China are rich, and the water is clear and sweet, thus creating the Golden Triangle of Chinese baijiu.

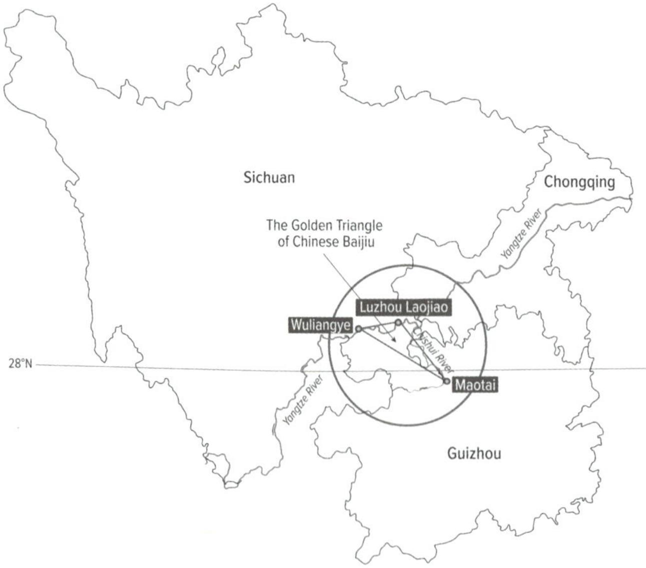

I ask on behalf of the northern "fans," why do you say that the water in the southwest of China is better?

The Yangtze River system, which originates from Mount Geladandong, the main peak of the Tanggula Mountains, and the Tuojiang River system, which originates from the southern foot of the Jiuxiang Mountains, constitute the "main artery" of Luzhou's water supply, which is located in the upper reaches and has an abundant and pure water source.

Luzhou has not only good water quality, but also abundant water resources, with 76 rivers of all sizes, including the Yangtze, Tuojiang, Chishui, and Yongning Rivers, providing a constant flow of clear, living water.

Luzhou is located in the transition zone between the plateau and the mountains, where the water flows rapidly. The quality of the water environment in the Yangtze River Basin has been improved radically, and the water ecosystem has become healthy with the protection and regulation of the ecological environment by government departments at all levels.

Every winter, black-headed gulls migrate to the Yangtze River in Luzhou to stay for the winter.

After talking about the surface water, let's talk about the groundwater!

Due to the geological structure of Luzhou, which is mostly soluble stuff, the water system below the surface is crisscrossed and gushes out of the ground, forming natural springs.

The water from the Longquan Well is pure and sweet, and for generations, it has been used for distilling in the surrounding workshops, with demand exceeding supply. In order to regulate the order, the government began to limit the extraction of water. In the 12th year of the Jiaqing reign in the Qing Dynasty (1807), "a stone monument was erected to set the rule that one person was allowed to carry only one quart of water and take turns to get water ... so that the people would not fight for the water."

As time passed and the Longquan Well fell into disrepair, the surrounding residents took it upon themselves to organize crowdfunding to rebuild the well.

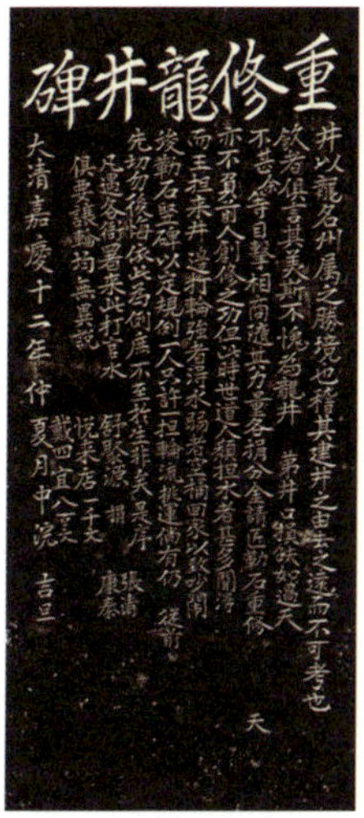

The Restoration of the Longquan Well Inscription

Longquan Well, named after the dragon, is a famous monument in Luzhou. As for why it was built, it is too old to be studied because of its age. People who drank the spring water said the water was good and worthy of the name "dragon well." However, the Longquan Well has been in disrepair for years, and we saw that, after discussing it, each person donated some money according to his ability, hired a craftsman to do the job, and rebuilt the well. Thanks to the work of our predecessors, many people came for the water and drank it, and the strong got water while the weak went home with empty buckets, causing a lot of commotion. So, the monument was erected to set the rules. One person was only allowed a quart, and had to queue up to pick water. When the government offices were here for water, they all had to wait in a queue, no different from the common people. Donated by Shujuyuan, Yue Lai store 1,000 wen, Dai Siyi 800 wen. Zhang Qing, Kangtai.

Zhonghuan in the midsummer of the 12th year of the Jiaqing reign in the Qing Dynasty, one propitious day.

Scientific research shows that Longquan Well water is weakly acidic, which is more suitable for the survival of distilling microorganisms.

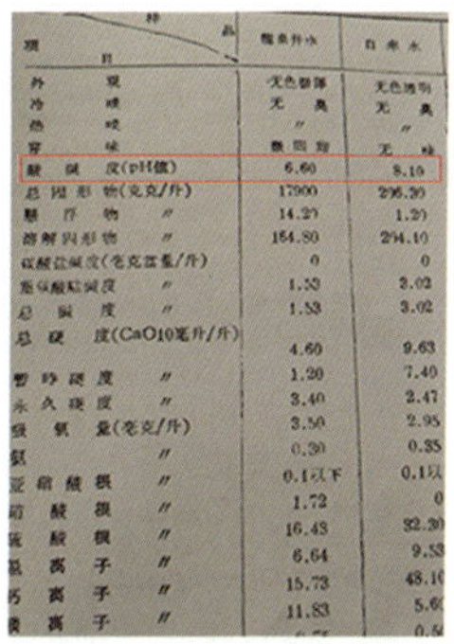

Luzhou Laojiao Daqu Liquor, the first professional textbook on baijiu distilling in New China

Generally speaking, microorganisms grow in an environment with a pH value of 5 to 9, but the most suitable environment for different kinds of microorganisms varies. For example, molds and yeasts are more suitable for growth in acidic conditions.

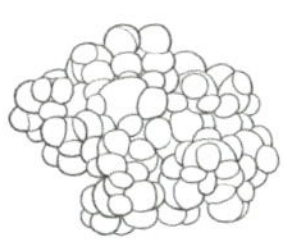

Molds

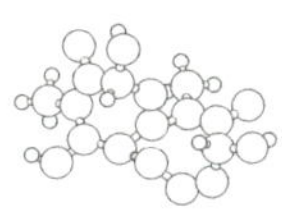

Yeast

Molds produce amylase, which hydrolyzes the starch in the grain into sugar. The enzyme alcoholase uses the sugar and ferments it under anoxic conditions, turning it into baijiu. At the same time, yeasts produce alcohols, aldehydes, acids, esters, and other trace components during fermentation, which are added to the baijiu during distillation.

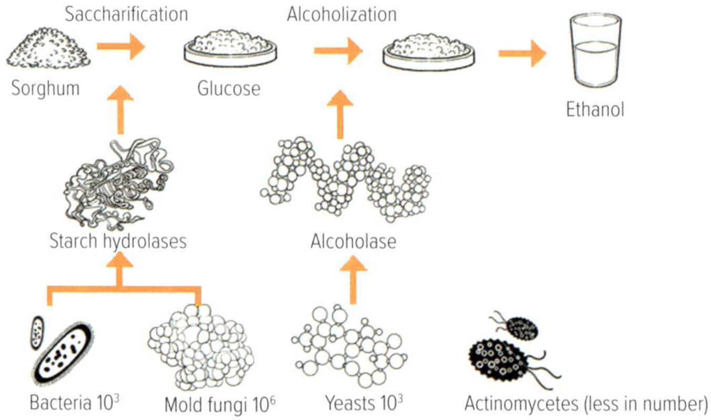

In addition to water for distilling, water is also needed for the design of the baijiu body, i.e., the blending process.

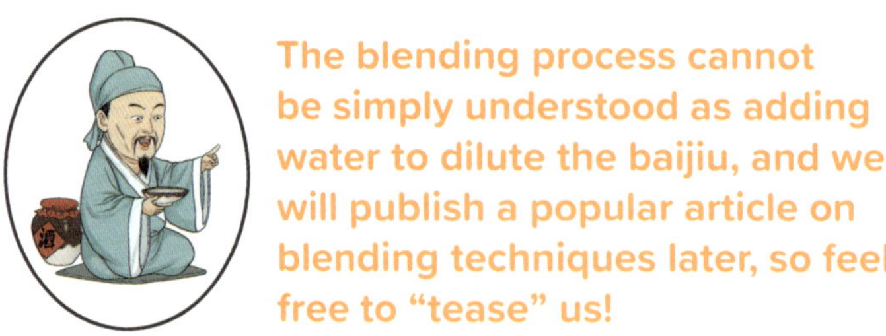

Luzhou Laojiao uses reverse osmosis (RO) water; generally speaking, it takes two tons of distilling water to extract one ton of RO water, and the RO water has the following qualities:

low hardness + clear and impurity-free + low electrical conductivity

Professionals know that the water used for blending and degree reduction must be soft water. The total amount of calcium, magnesium, and other alkali metal salts contained in each liter of water is 10 milligrams, called 1 degree. Hardness below 8 degrees is soft water, and higher than 8 degrees is hard water.

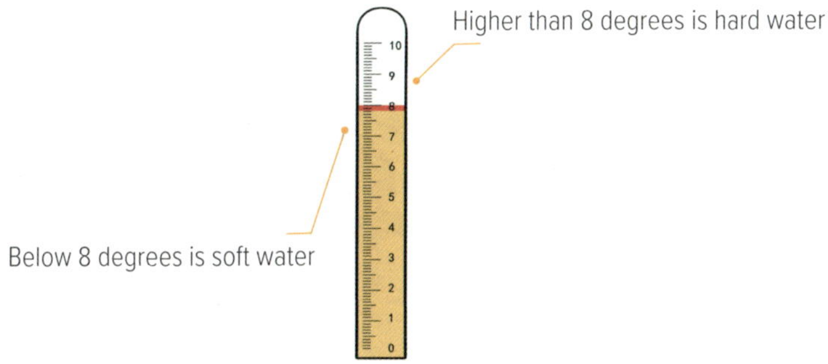

As you can see, the water has witnessed the whole process of distilling a bottle of baijiu, and the baijiu is the water of life. So, the next time when your girlfriend is unhappy:

What is the biggest difference between liquor and water?
酒
Liquor can get people drunk.
酒

Water can be used to describe people. For example, you are so "water," which means you are so fake.

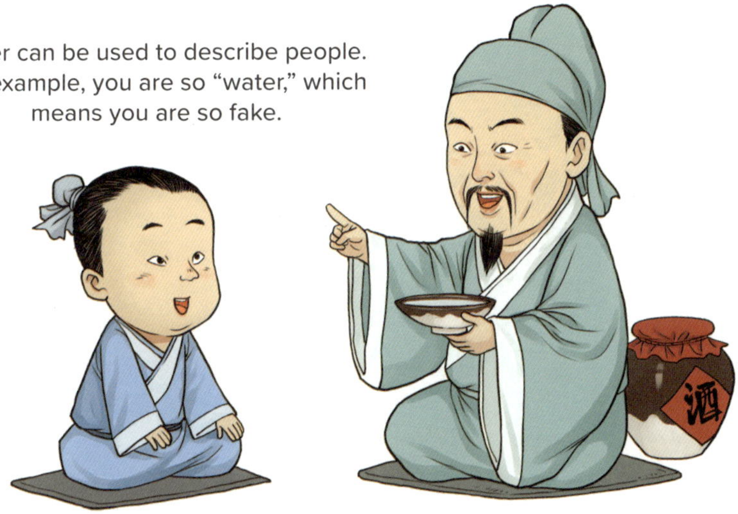

Women are made of water, and men are made of liquor.

CHAPTER 12

Why Sorghum, Being Distilled and Infusing into the Water, Makes the Most Mellow Liquor?

Speaking of sorghum, the first sorghum for human consumption was found in a cave in Mozambique, Africa, and is now 105,000 years old.

Sorghum has spread around the world as humans have migrated. Africa, which has the largest variety, is widely considered to be the birthplace of sorghum.

Sorghum has been cultivated as a food crop for at least 5,000 years in China, where it was formerly known as "corn."

In *The Book of Songs · Xiaoya · Yellow Birds*, there are sentences like: "Yellow birds, listen to me! Don't cluster on my mulberry tree. Or eat up my corn completely."

This is the earliest record of sorghum in our literature. Later, Confucius also wrote about it.

Dr. Wu Qichang, a famous literary historian in China, said that our ancestors grew grain for the purpose of distilling liquor, not for eating. In other words, it was our ancestors' "love of liquor" that brought us to agricultural civilization.

Wu Qichang: a famous literary historian

Dr. Solomon Katz, an anthropologist at the University of Pennsylvania, makes a similar point.

Solomon Katz: an anthropologist at the University of Pennsylvania, USA

In primitive societies 10,000 years ago, humans lived by hunting and gathering, and before they entered the agricultural age, the staple food on which people lived was meat rather than grain.

Later, people discovered that wild grain could be used for distilling, but they could not meet the demand for distilling, so they consciously began to grow grain in order to ensure the supply of raw materials for distilling.

Only later, grain was discovered to be of edible value, and its cultivation was expanded. On the one hand, the "meat-based" lifestyle was transformed into a "grain-based" one; on the other hand, wild prey was domesticated into poultry, and some humans settled down, thus entering agricultural civilization.

In fact, compared with primitive society, people in agricultural society were not happy!

In primitive societies, people only needed to work half a day. The rest of the time could be spent singing and dancing! Mamma mia! In agricultural societies, on the other hand, people had to work at sunrise and rest at sunset, especially during the busy spring and summer farming seasons ...

Why Is Sorghum the Best Raw Material for Distilling Baijiu?

To be the best raw material for baijiu distilling, you have to go through an elimination contest. Because China has a long history of distilling spirits from grain, there are many contestants.

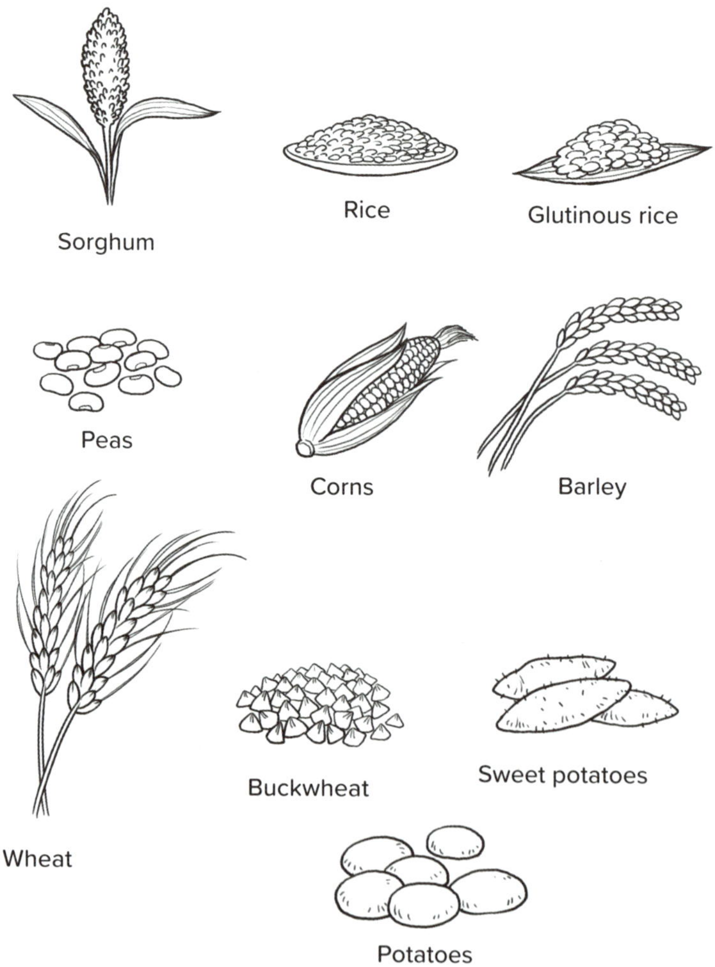

In the beginning, basically, everything that could be eaten was used to make liquor.

In principle, any grain crop that contains starch can be used to make liquor!

However, it does not mean that all of them can make good liquor, which is related to the ratio of the content of the ingredients in the grain.

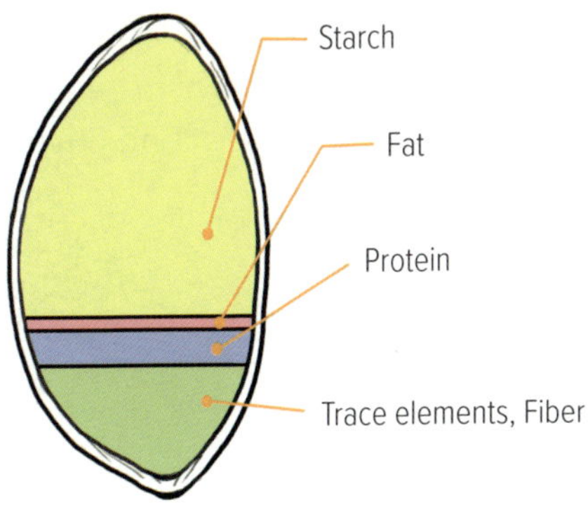

Different grains have different ratios of starch, fat, protein, trace elements, and fiber content, and their liquor varies greatly in flavor.

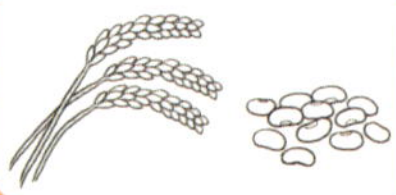

Wheat and peas: The protein content is too high, which produces an unpleasant odor if used as the raw material for distilling alone.

Glutinous rice: It is too viscous, which will make the grains less permeable and fermentation less efficient.

Rice: It has low fat and fiber content, which will produce more odoriferous substances.

Corn: It has high fat content, producing too much evil taste in the baijiu.

Sweet potato, potato: The pectin is too high, and the earthy taste affects the taste of baijiu.

Sorghum stands out with its own distinct advantages. The liquor distilled from sorghum had a rich aroma, so it was elected as the best distilling grain.

First—Fat: Not fat in a real sense, but the high starch content in sorghum, fat and protein content ratio is just right, so that the microbial fermentation produce aroma smoothly and does not lead to the generation of miscellaneous taste substances.

Sorghum composition:

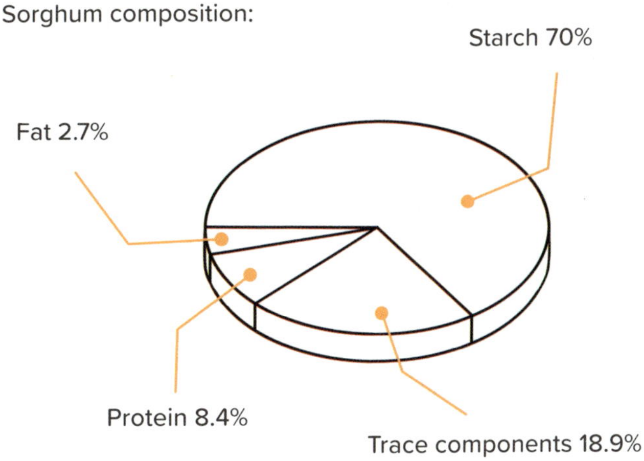

Two—More: Sorghum contains high levels of vitamin B_3, vitamin B_5, and a certain number of tannins.

Modern scientific research has shown that vitamin B_3 and vitamin B_5 increase the aromatic substances of baijiu.

The tannin content in sorghum husks is more than 2%, and 0.2% to 0.3% in the seeds. Trace amounts of tannin anthocyanins are derived into phenolic compounds such as vanillic acid after steaming and fermentation, which can give baijiu its special aroma. This is why it is said that the general nutrition is in the husk!

Three—Easy: Sorghum is easy to ferment, produces aromas easily, and the fermentation process is easy to control.

Why is glutinous red sorghum best for liquor-distilling?

After elimination, sorghum easily outperforms other grains, but there is a wide variety within sorghum, and the competition remains fierce.

By color:

White sorghum Red sorghum Yellow sorghum

By region:

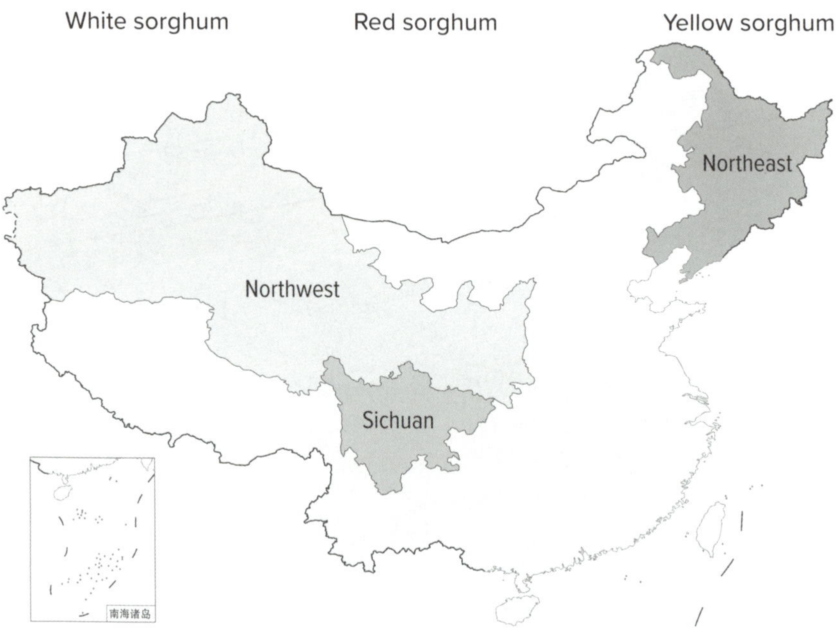
White sorghum
Red sorghum
Yellow sorghum
Northeast
Northwest
Sichuan
南海诸岛

Why is glutinous red sorghum best for liquor-distilling?
There are three reasons.
酒

(1) The amylopectin content of Luzhou's special glutinous red sorghum is higher than that of other regional varieties.

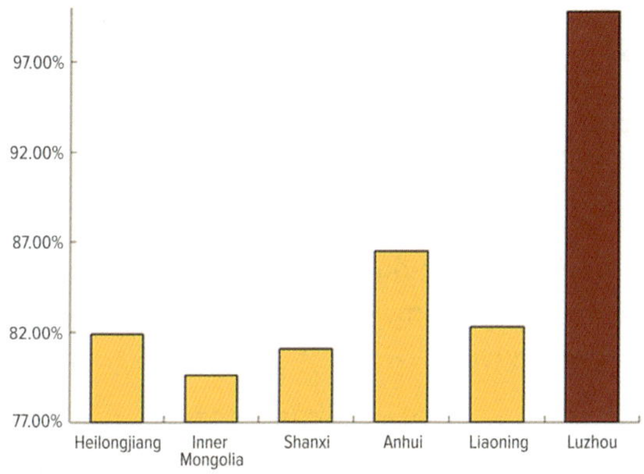

Comparison of the amylopectin content of sorghum varieties in different regions

Here's a quick explanation of what "amylopectin" means.

The starch is divided into amylose and amylopectin, and the latter is easily dextrinized and does not easily gel after cooling. Structurally, it contains thousands of glucose units and has a net-like structure, which can lock water molecules and turn starch into a paste-like sol. It is not easy to age, which is greatly conducive to microbial use in fermentation and liquor production. The former does not easily become paste after boiling, and becomes gel after cooling, and its macromolecular structure contains several hundred glucose units, which are neatly arranged.

Amylopectin   Amylose

Amylopectin helps to lock in nutrients and release them slowly during the fermentation period, making it more suitable for the baijiu distilling process!

Such rich glucose units provide sufficient nutrition for fermentation microorganisms. When the microorganisms eat and drink well, they naturally work well, and the baijiu is produced well.

(2) The fatty acid content of Luzhou's specialty glutinous red sorghum is higher than that of other regional varieties.

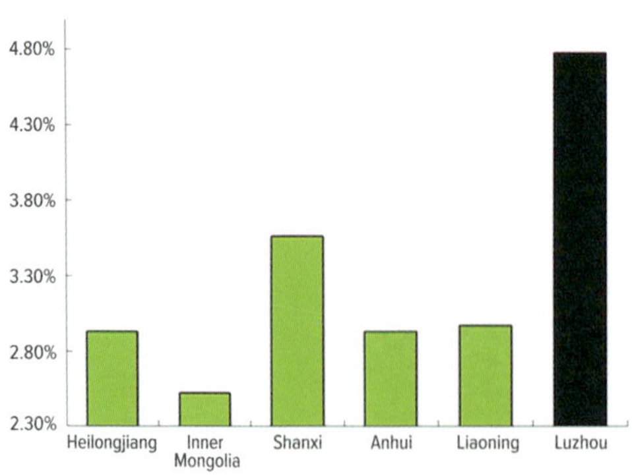

Comparison of the fatty acid content of sorghum varieties in different regions

The fatty acids mentioned here are mainly linoleic acid and alpha-linolenic acid, which are produced by a variety of microorganisms during the fermentation process and brought into the baijiu with the distillation. They play an important role in human health!

(3) The glutinous red sorghum produced in Luzhou is deep purple-red in color and contains anthocyanins, a natural pigment. This type of food is known as "purple food" in nutriology and is currently the most popular health food.

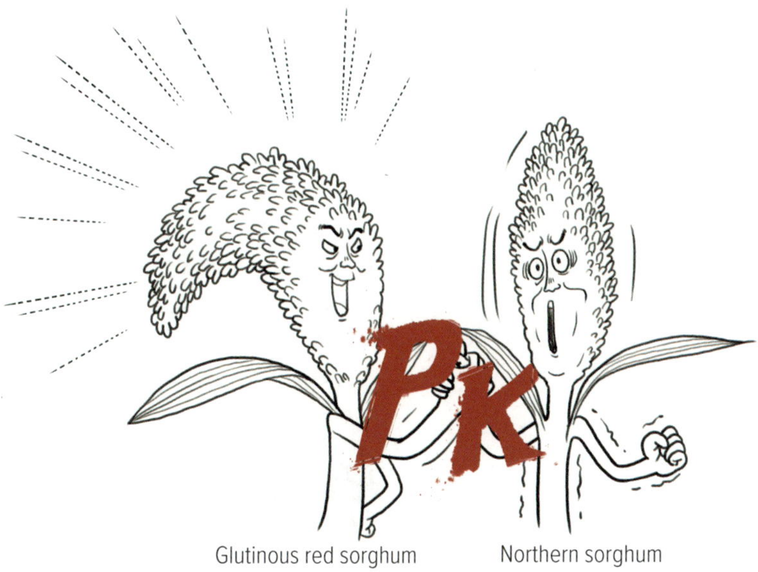

Scientific research has confirmed that anthocyanins are the best and safest free radical scavengers discovered to date. Their ability to scavenge free radicals is 20 times that of vitamin C and 50 times that of vitamin E, making them the world's best-recognized anti-aging health substance!

As for what free radicals are, Baidu it!

After the qualifying round, glutinous red sorghum still leads the pack, becoming a veritable best grain for liquor-distilling and favored by more and more baijiu companies.

Luzhou Laojiao organic glutinous red sorghum base

When it comes to food quality and safety, there are three levels:

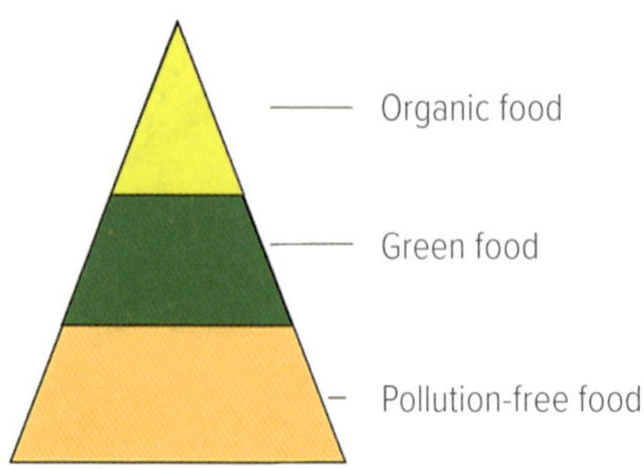

Due to the stringent standards, organic food production is very small. At present, the arable land area of organic crops in the country only accounts for 1% of the national arable land area, that is:

1,349.21 thousand hectares

In 2001, Luzhou Laojiao took the lead in creating "organic glutinous red sorghum farming" to cultivate organic glutinous red sorghum, which is unique to Luzhou.

Currently, Luzhou Laojiao's organic sorghum base in southern Sichuan is the largest organic sorghum growing area in China.

They adopted the "company + research + farmers" model. The government leases the farmers' land, the farmers plant it according to the organic standards set by the research institute, and the company contracts with the farmers to purchase it. In this way, a virtuous circle is formed.

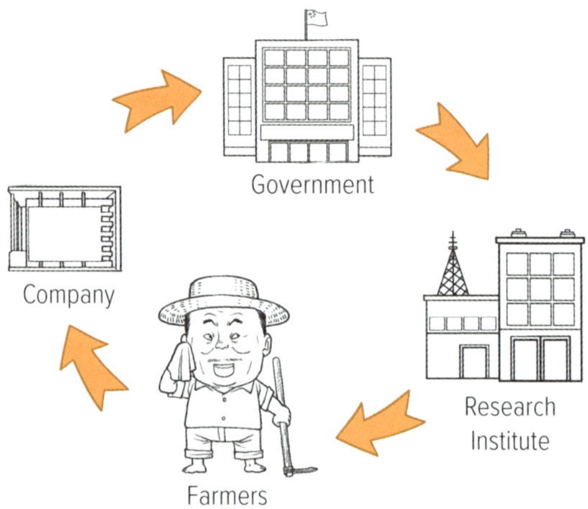

A natural ecological balance method is employed in the whole process, from the growth to the harvesting of organic glutinous red sorghun.

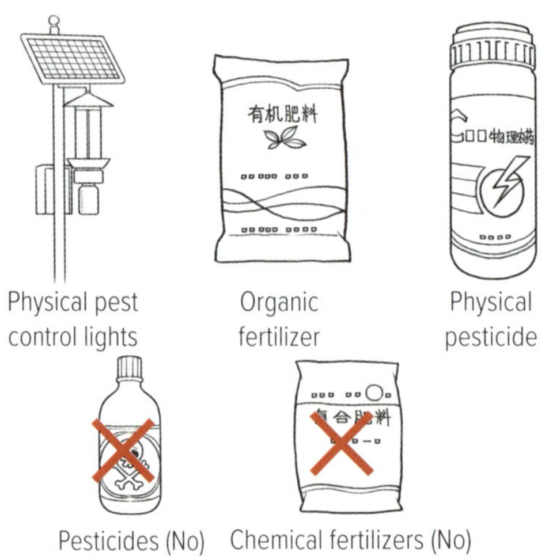

Chinese baijiu is operated in an open environment for natural solid-state fermentation. Organic sorghum ensures that the distilling microorganisms continue to ferment and produce aroma in the most natural and suitable state, thus improving the flavor and quality of baijiu.

In 2008, Guojiao 1573 passed the organic food certification of the China Organic Food Certification Center, and is the only strong-aroma flavor baijiu in China that has passed the authoritative certification.

CHAPTER 13

Aging Liquor by Ages Distills the Aromatic Flavor—Time and Timing Are the Formulae in Making Good Liquor!

One day 2,400 years ago, Lao Kung (the nickname for Confucius) stood at the edge of the Si River, looking at the rushing river, and could not help but sigh:

Time keeps passing like flowing water and never comes back.

And in Zhuangzi's view, life in the world is like a white horse ...

Men's life between heaven and earth, as if the white horse passing a crevice, all of a sudden!

In the *Thousand Character Classic*: "The sky was black and the earth was yellow, the universe was vast and a dark hole."

The character "Yu" refers to space, and "Zhou" refers to the past and present, which refers to time.

In the Buddhist scriptures, there is the concept of "世界," in which the character "世" refers to the past, present, and future, which refers to time; the character "界" refers to the eight directions up and down, which refers to space.

In ancient times, in order to grasp time, people had to rack their brains:

Look at the sun

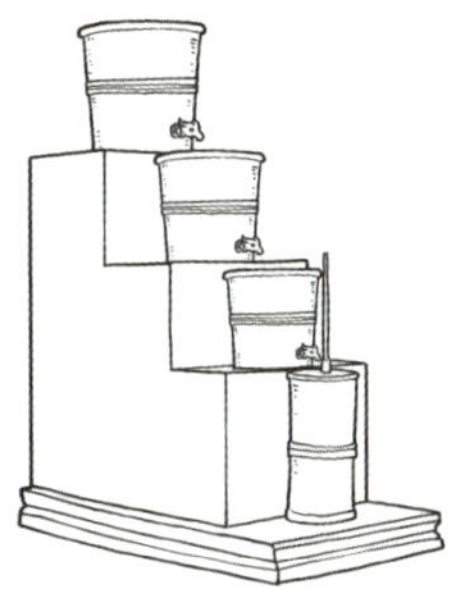

Water droplet timing

Sundial

Hourglass

Stephen William Hawking: a famous physicist at Cambridge University, UK

Since mastering the laws of time, humans have become more regular in their lifestyles.

In two minutes, the cafeteria will be open for dinner.
Is it necessary to be so punctual?

In this chapter, we do not talk about food.
Speaking of food, I'm already a little hungry.
酒

Have you noticed that everything you can eat basically has a shelf life, and time has simply become a cold-faced killer of food?

Sea fish: 1 day

Cabbage: 5 days

Bread: 10 days

Apples: 20 days

However, you may not believe there is something, that has no shelf life.

It is said that nowadays, the most understated show of wealth for tycoons is: drinking "expired" liquor and eating wormy grass.

Why cannot baijiu be sold fresh?

Generally just distilled baijiu, is in its "adolescence," full of masculinity. It's like a newborn Nezha (a Chinese deity in the *Journey to the West*):

"What are you looking at? I'm spitting fire!"

However, with its irascible and spicy temper, many people want to love him but cannot love him.

In fact, new baijiu just distilled contains certain volatile aldehydes, which are irritating.

Therefore, newly distilled baijiu needs several years of aging to be more mellow, and cave storage is an essential process in the distilling process of baijiu.

Today, I will give you a grasp of some things about the cave storage of baijiu!

The Benefits of Natural Caves

As mentioned earlier, the longer the baijiu is distilled, the more mellow it is, but in addition to time, two other issues need to be addressed:

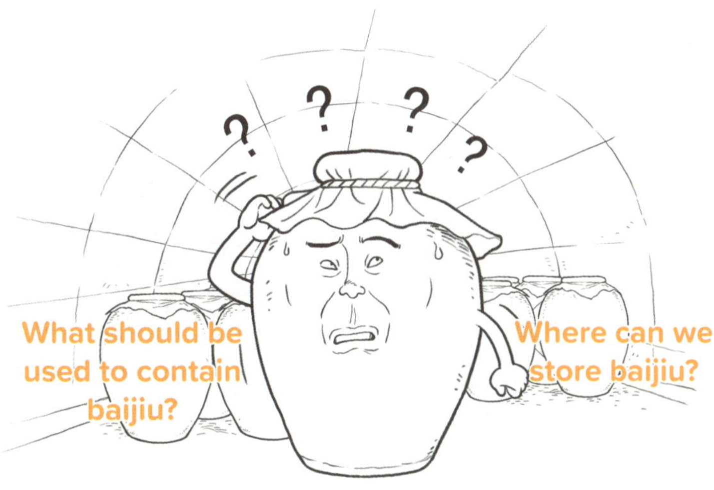

At present, there are many kinds of storage environments in China:

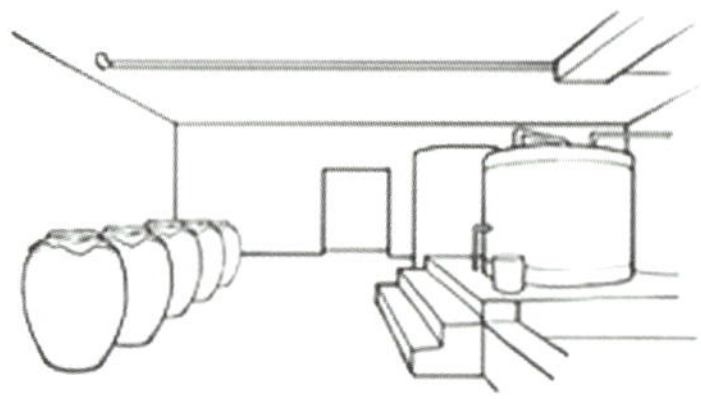

Workshop

Ground

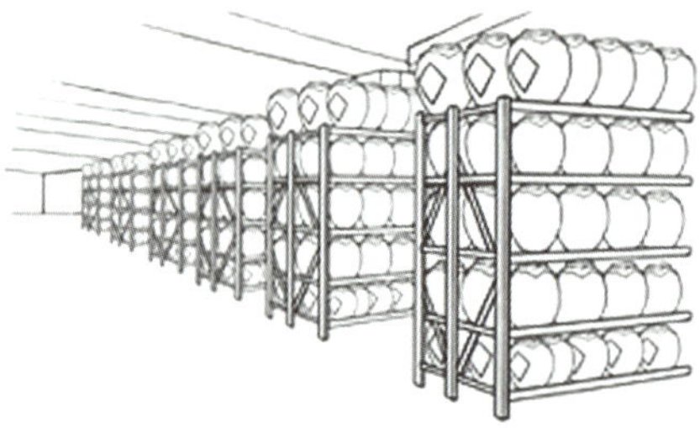

Warehouse

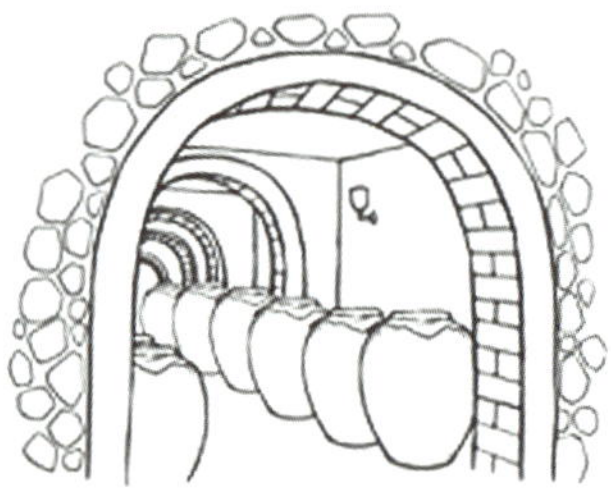

Cellar/Cave

Because the mountain is isolated from the outside world, so the outside climate, air, noise, dust, and sunlight have little effect on the baijiu.

The cave does not see sunlight all day long in all seasons, the airflow is extremely slow, and the temperature and humidity remain stable all year round.

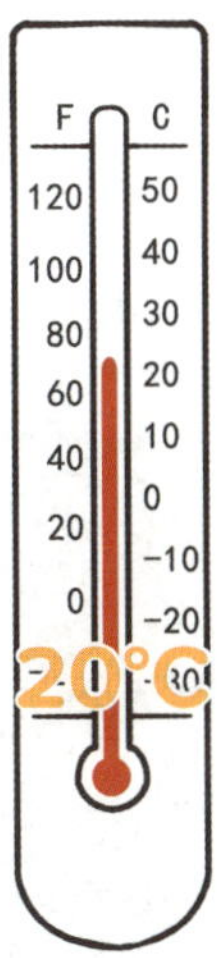

Thermometer

Hygrometer

It is worth mentioning that Luzhou Laojiao has three major natural caves, namely Chunyang Cave, Zuiweng Cave, and Longquan Cave, which has the largest number of natural caves in the industry.

During the War of Resistance Against Japanese Aggression, the caves were expanded into air-raid shelters to prevent bombing by Japanese aircraft.

In the 1950s and 1960s, under the guidance of the idea of "digging deep and accumulating grain," the air-raid shelter was further expanded and extended.

As a result, the cave depot was transformed from a small cave into a large cave, and Chunyang Cave and Zuiweng Cave were connected in the middle of the mountain, forming a 7-kilometer-long Great Wall in the mountain.

Why is it called Chunyang Cave?
Lü Dongbin, called "Chunyangzi," was not only a good poet, but also liked to drink, and it is said that he got drunk here.
酒

Oh, I got drunk that day. I do not remember the things behind ...
I wish the Yangtze River turns into liquor and drinks once in a wave.

The caves are located at the confluence of the Tuojiang River and the Yangtze River. After the two rivers merge, they are strongly blocked by the five peaks of Sanhua Mountain, where they make a "drunken" liquor bend, thus forming the Jiangyang and Xicao peninsulas of Luzhou.

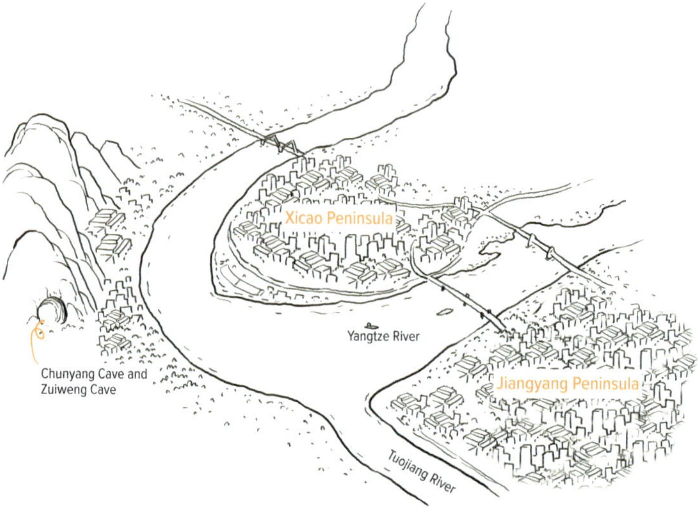

The water of the Yangtze River beats against the mountain and cave walls all day long, creating a continuous resonant wave that has acted on Chunyang Cave and Zuiweng Cave over the years, fully promoting the aging of the baijiu in the pottery jars in the cave.

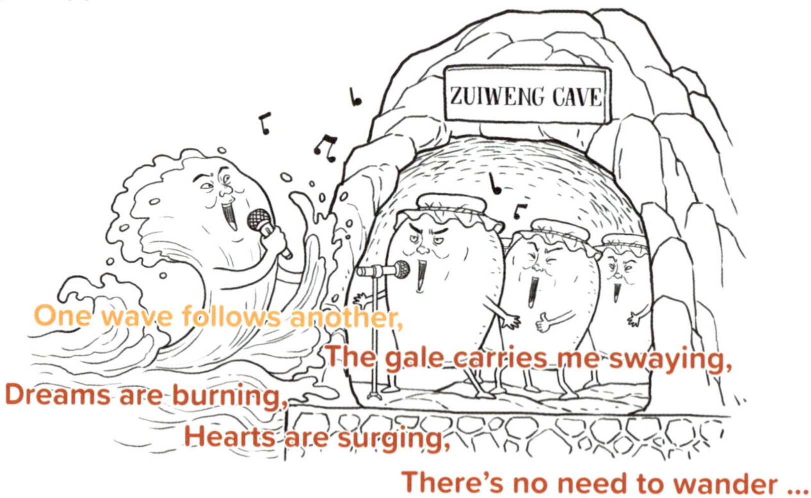

The mountain in which the Chunyang Cave is located is a spotted rock, and the moisture-rich in vegetation seeps down through the rocks into the baijiu cave, making the cave environment, which stretches for several kilometers, extremely shady and humid.

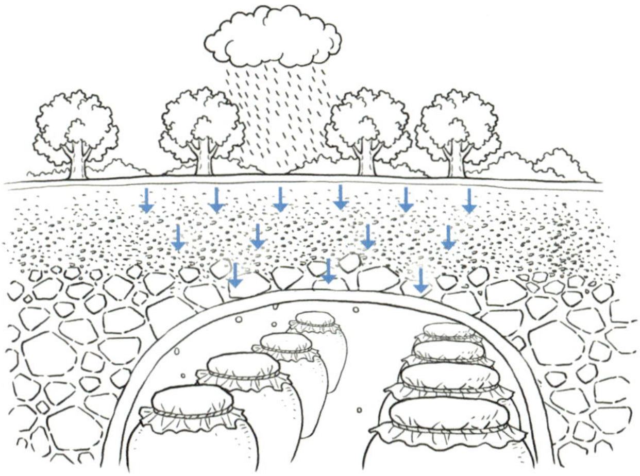

In the cave, the new baijiu undergoes long-term, complex, and slow physico-chemical reactions, and the dry and spicy components in baijiu are gradually evaporated and removed, while alcohol, esters, aldehydes, and other trace components continue to combine and react, making baijiu more delicate, rich, and mellow.

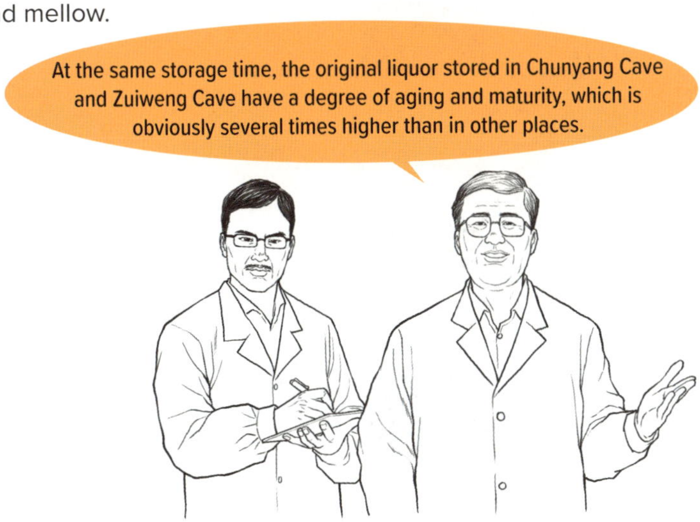

At present, the three major natural caves of Luzhou Laojiao are rated as:

Important Heritage Sites under State Protection

Chunyang Cave

Zuiweng Cave

Longquan Cave

The Benefits of Pottery Jars

With a good cave, you also need a good baijiu container. There is a wide variety of Chinese baijiu storage containers.

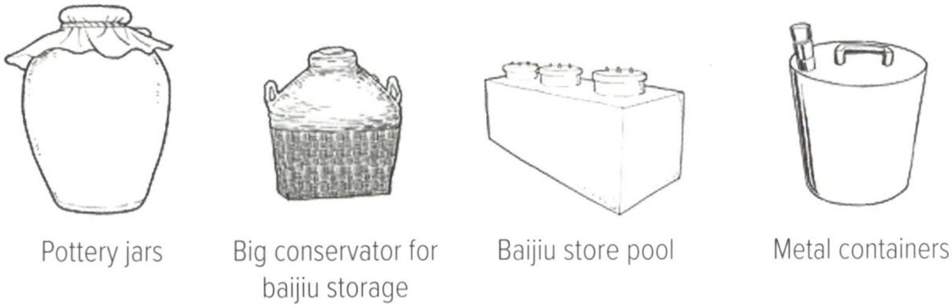

The pottery jar, however, is the best choice for storing baijiu.

The pottery jar of Luzhou Laojiao is made of clay that is unique to the southern Sichuan region and is fired at a high temperature of about 1,000°C. As a result, the organic matter contained in the clay is burned away, and some of the gas components are discharged to form many tiny pores.

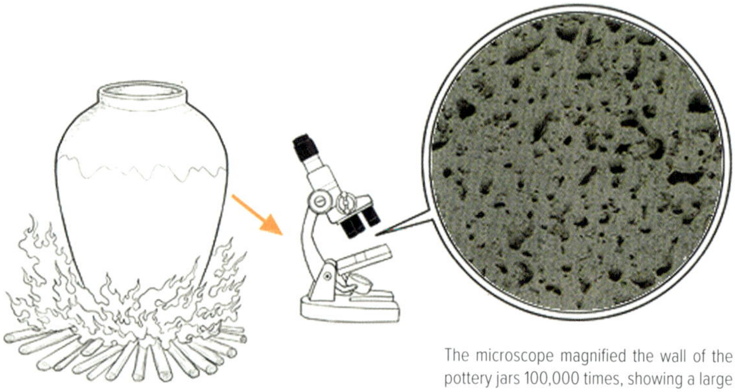

The microscope magnified the wall of the pottery jars 100,000 times, showing a large number of microscopic holes.

The micro-pores are invisible to the naked eye and are the channels through which the liquor body breathes with the outside world. Respiration serves two purposes:

Exhale: Some of the irritating, low-boiling substances in the new baijiu are exhaled through the exchange channels and slowly evaporate.

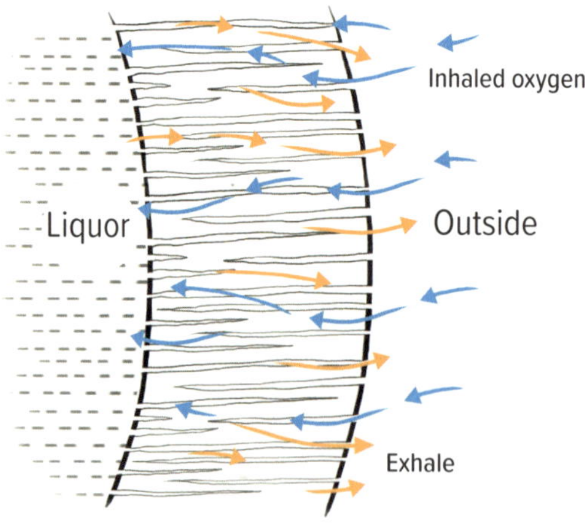

Inhale: Outside air enters the baijiu through the micropores, promoting oxidation and esterification:

Aldehydes are continuously oxidized to carboxylic acids, which then undergo esterification with ethanol to produce esters with an aromatic odor, resulting in a mellowness.

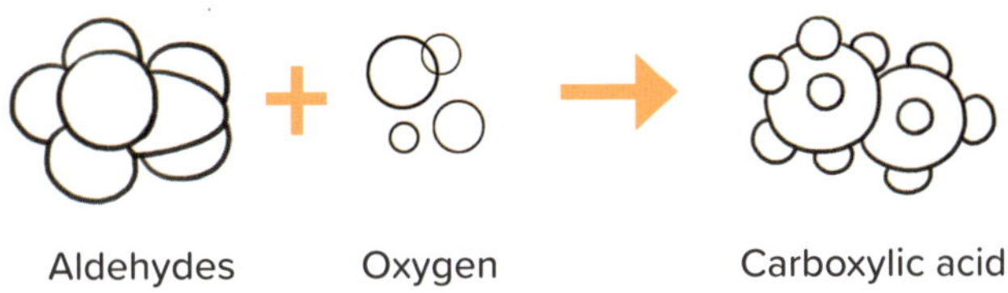

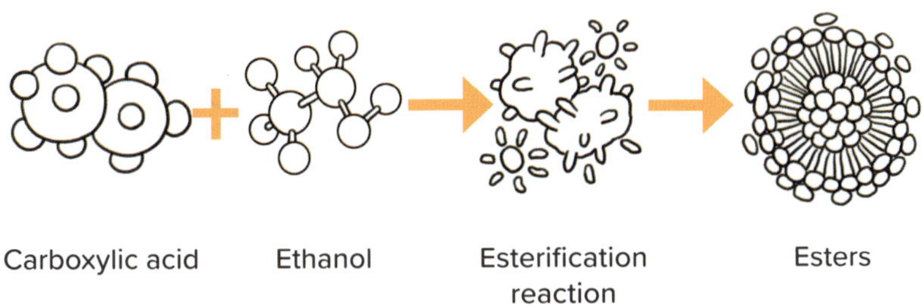

This process of change is how baijiu ages!

During the process of infiltration of the baijiu over time, the active metal ions, calcium, iron, zinc and other trace mineral element ions rich in the pottery jar are partially dissolved into the baijiu, and the original baijiu has a softer aromatic composition and is rich in trace elements that are beneficial to the human body.

Zhuang Mingyang: a renowned expert in Chinese baijiu

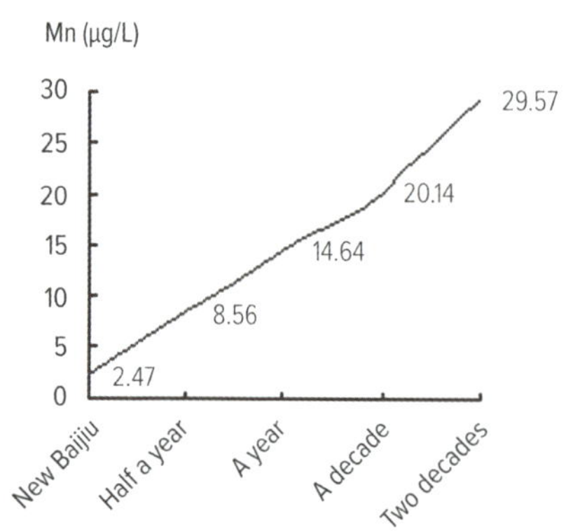

Changes in manganese with storage time in pottery jars

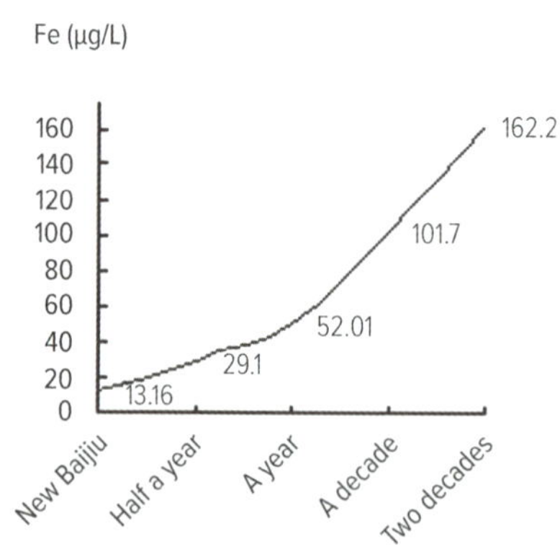

Changes in iron with storage time in pottery jars

The role of zinc in the human body: Zinc is known as the "spark of life" in the human body.

Improves immunity

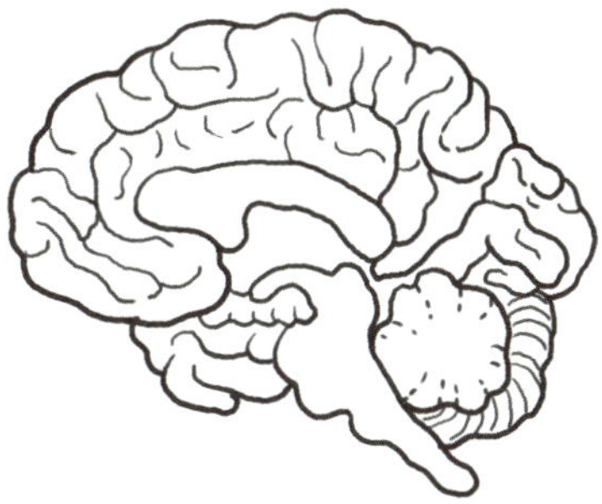

Promotes brain development

Promotes the development of taste buds

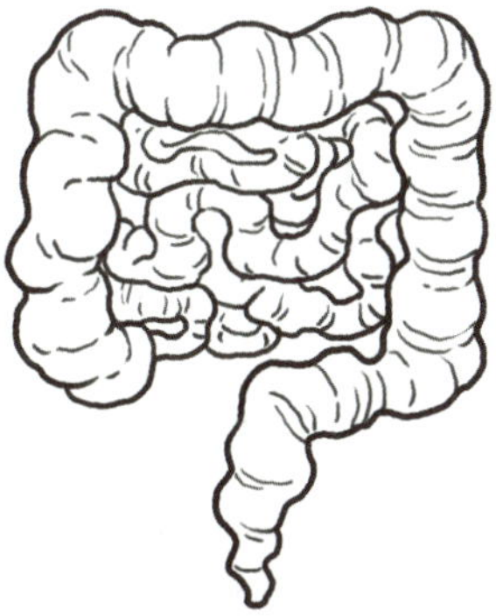

Promotes metabolism

The minerals in the pottery jar gradually dissolve into the baijiu during the storage process, and they react with the aromatic substances in the baijiu, especially the esters, and the baijiu molecules join and rearrange with each other, promoting the formation of a colloidal solution and the aging of the baijiu.

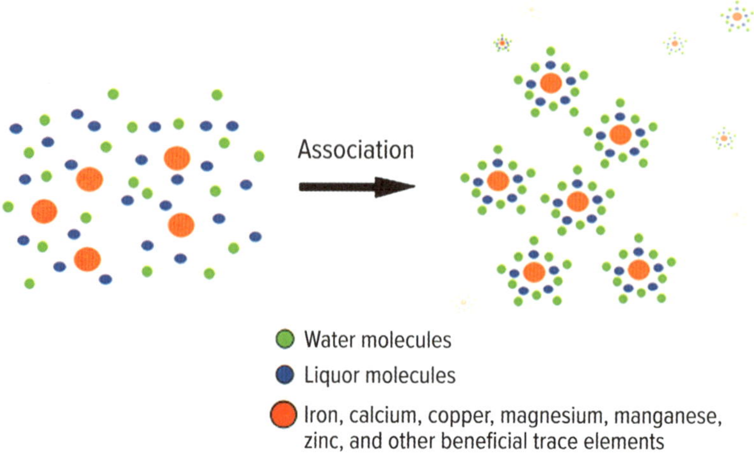

The mechanism of baijiu maturation

Over time, the water molecules, liquor molecules, and macromolecular trace elements form a miniature slow-release capsule.

For hundreds of years, Chunyang Cave, Zuiweng Cave and Longquan Cave have been used for the storage of Luzhou Laojiao's crude baijiu, and they are now not only the hiding place for Luzhou Laojiao's 100 years of accumulated "prominent quality baijiu," but also the place for the cultivation of Guojiao 1573 crude baijiu.

CHAPTER 14

Five Tastes in Liquor, Hundred Tastes in Life —The Art of the Tongue

Many major achievements in history were often discovered by chance, which in turn changed the established rules of the entire world.

Newton Watt Chen Qiyu

Gravity and steam power are learned since childhood, but not many people know the blending technique!

Elementary school language teachers did not teach!

For decades, many uninformed people have labeled the mixing technique as soon as they see it.

In order to eliminate these misunderstandings, today, we are going to blend.

(To show the difference, the word "blending" is used below)

Five Tastes in Baijiu

A really good bottle of liquor must have "five tastes":

Sour

It is mainly from acetic acid, caproic acid, lactic acid and esters.

Sweet

It is mainly from polyols, which is not the sweetness of cane sugar, but more like the taste you get when you slowly chew a white bun.

Bitter

It comes from the taste of tannins, which should not be too much but not too little, either.

Spicy

The pungency and dryness of a new liquor come mainly from the small number of aldehydes that stimulate the senses. For this reason, new liquors should be left for a period of time in order to become more aromatic.

Salty

In high-end baijiu, esters combine with organic acids during the fermentation process to esterify with ethanol, resulting in a salty taste.

This ester is similar to the taste of metal ions, and is the main source of the "salty" taste in baijiu.

Traditionally, we refer to sour, sweet, bitter, spicy, and salty as the "five tastes." However, with the advancement of scientific research, only the four tastes of sour, sweet, bitter, and salty are conveyed by the taste nerves, and "spicy" is not a taste but a sensation produced by stimulation.

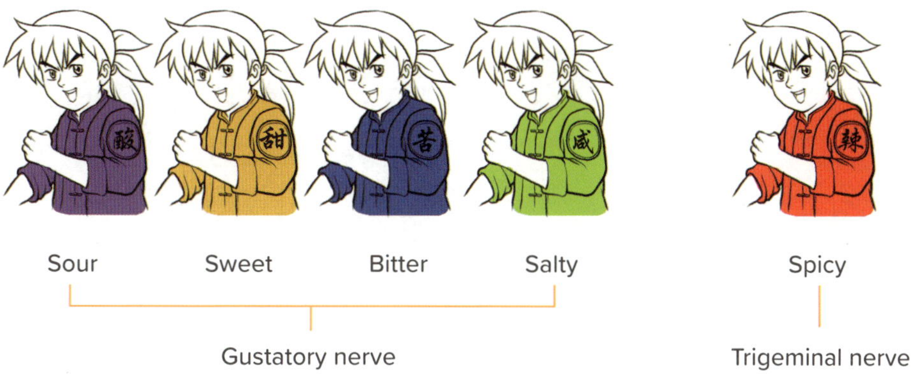

In October 1985, at the Hawaii International Food Symposium, some experts proposed that "freshness" is an independent taste. The main freshness components are monosodium glutamate, guanosine acid, and inosine acid. Since then, "five tastes" has a new connotation.

Everyone's perception of "five tastes" is different. Even if for the same taste, taste perception is not consistent, it is also affected by many factors, such as:

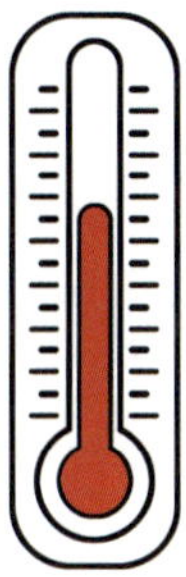

Temperature

Concentration

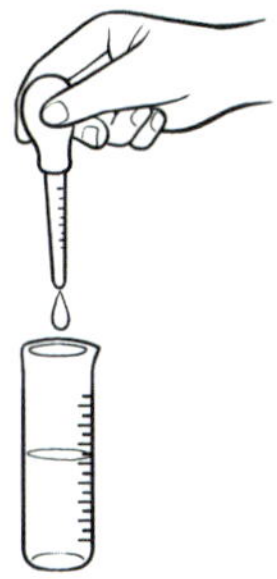

Solvents

Geography and eating habits

For example, the same taste will have a different taste perception at different temperatures. Because of this, so:

Glutinous rice liquor: drink it warm

Beer: drink it cold

In summer, Guojiao 1573 tastes best when drinking at 12°C

People in different regions have different eating habits due to different products and tastes. Some tastes, some people like, while others ...

1. **Multiplication Interaction**

Adding one flavor to another to significantly enhance the original flavor is called the multiplication of flavors.

Research has shown that the water is the sweetest when 0.15% salt is added to 15%–25% sugar water.

2. **Compensation Interaction**

Adding another taste to a taste, so that the taste of the original material is reduced, this effect is called the killing each other effect, also called the offset interaction.

Adding 0.3% vinegar to 10%–20% salt water can greatly weaken the saltiness!

Therefore, experienced chefs will add a spoonful of sugar at the end of the stir-fry.

Chen Qiyu's "Strange Encounter"

Blending is not an ancient product. In the 1950s, Chen Qiyu, the inheritor of the traditional distilling technique of Luzhou Laojiao, discovered the trick of blending by chance.

After repeated tests, he was enlightened. He quickly organized scientific researchers to develop and apply tasting and blending techniques for strong-aroma flavor baijiu.

After more than ten years of exploration and summary, blending was formally introduced as technology and widely used in production practice. It greatly increased the production of high-quality baijiu and strengthened the unique style of Luzhou Laojiao.

Later, under the impetus of Lai Gaohuai, the inheritor of the traditional distilling technique of Luzhou Laojiao, Luzhou Laojiao started distilling technology training courses to deliver technical talents to the national distilling industry. It is no exaggeration to say that many famous baijiu companies have benefited from Luzhou Laojiao's support in their development, thus creating the current world of strong aroma (which means the flourishing of various brands of strong-aroma flavor baijiu).

Blending technology is a very important and essential process in distilling baijiu. Without it, the quality of baijiu cannot be guaranteed, and the taste cannot be stabilized.

Zhou Henggang

Blending is one of the prerequisites for Chinese baijiu to move from "bulk baijiu retailing" to quality, standardization, and brand production.

Dancers on the Tip of the Tongue

After a long accumulation period, Luzhou Laojiao has gradually formed a complete set of blending techniques.

Tasting – Combining – Flavoring – Re-tasting

1. Tasting: At first, each crude baijiu was stored separately, and no one knew each other.

Guest #1 Guest #2 Guest #3 Guest #4 Guest #5

One day, due to some necessity, they are brought together.

Oh! Sorry, it is wrong!

Blending is like falling in love. In order to breed a better next generation, you need a middleman to match up. The tasters then start hosting the job to judge the style and merits of the baijiu.

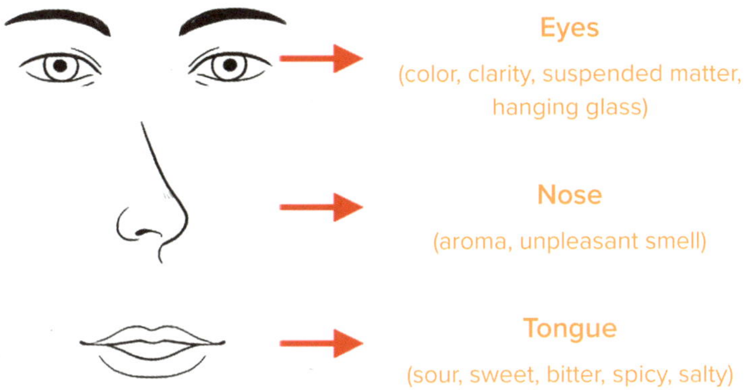

As mentioned earlier, in terms of taste, there are only four taste sensations: sour, sweet, bitter and salty. When tasting baijiu, the taste sensations are different at different tongue locations.

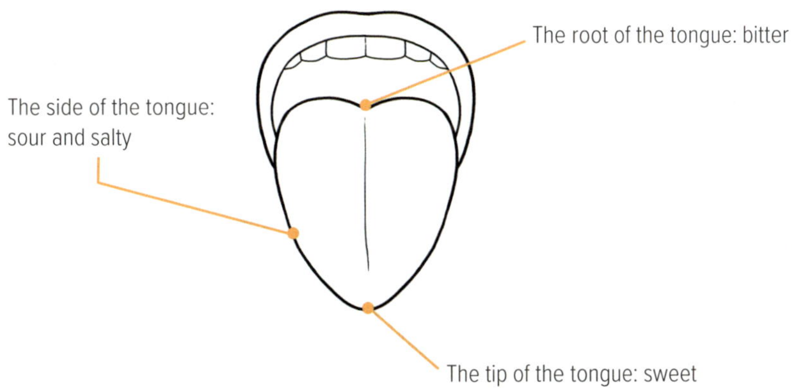

There are 10,000 taste buds in the human mouth, especially on the tongue, but the average person only uses about 60% of them. The master blender can fully utilize these 10,000 taste buds and discover their nuances.

2. Combining: After the tasting, the master blender memorizes the styles of the various baijiu samples and starts to combine them.

After the combination, the quality of the baijiu has improved significantly, but the blender always feels that something is missing ...

Inadequate aging **Inadequate aftertaste**

At this point, it's time for the prominent quality baijiu to come on ...

3. Flavoring: Prominent quality baijiu has the magical effect of adding the finishing touch!

As we said before, 98% of a bottle of liquor is made up of ethanol and water, while prominent quality baijiu affects the other 2% (various aromatic substances).

A few drops of prominent quality baijiu can add the finishing touch.

Additive effects

Balancing effects

Chemical reaction

Molecular rearrangement

Some prominent quality baijiu that is rich in trace aromatic substances will significantly improve the quality of the baijiu at one point or in one aspect.

Rich aroma of aging baijiu

Long aftertaste

Prominent quality baijiu is to achieve a certain degree of coordination and balance in the "color, aroma, taste and character" of baijiu.

It is usually said that the content of prominent quality baijiu is less than one-thousandth of the crude baijiu, but it is this one-thousandth of the "essence" that gives the baijiu its higher quality!

In the natural cave of Luzhou Laojiao, cave-aged vintage baijius range from 50 to 100 years, rare and precious among prominent quality baijiu.

4. Re-tasting: After flavoring, the baijiu is tasted and evaluated, and the best solution is finally arrived at through continuous testing.

After the "small sample" flavoring is determined, the baijiu body may also have some physical and chemical reactions, which may leave the flavor to have some differences from the prominent quality baijiu. Generally, it needs to be stored for a month, checked the quality before organizing the production of large samples, and finally completed the packaging production.

After the finished baijiu comes out, it still needs to go through various tastings and selections.

Tasting Committee　　Baijiu-distilling Technical Expert Committee　　Consumer Tasting Committee

They all have veto power!

CHAPTER 15

High Quality in High Priority Is the Aging Liquor—What Is Good about the Aging Liquor?

The wise Jews are the happiest in the bean-selling world; they never worry about not selling their beans.

If the beans are still not selling, there is another option.

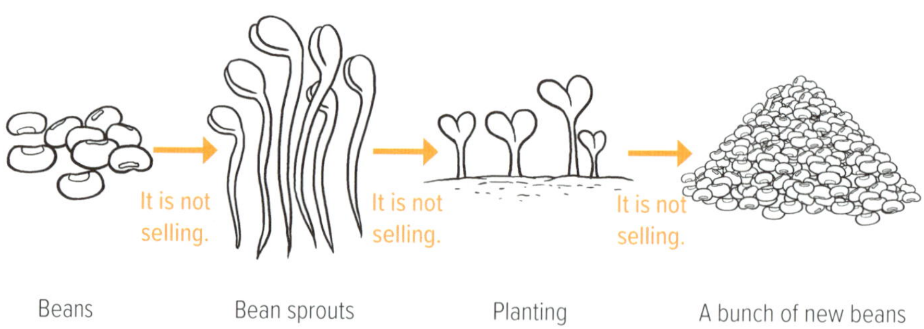

And smart orientalists are the happiest in the liquor-selling world, because if "new liquor" cannot be sold out, it can be sold as "old liquor," and the "bottle storage" vintage liquor has a yearly price!

In October 2021, at the Alibaba Global Old Spirits Festival, a bottle of Luzhou Laojiao Daqu from the 1950s was auctioned for RMB 1.18 million yuan.

This is also true of baijiu storage, as veteran baijiu drinkers know: store new baijiu, drink old baijiu!

New baijiu should not be drunk for a while, and the longer the baijiu is stored, the better it smells!

Therefore, the recent old liquor market is on fire, but besides good-looking, good to drink ... what other tricks can you also find?

But it will be hard for you to survive whenever you are asked a few more in-depth questions. For example ...

How many years do you have to store a bottle of liquor before you call it old?
How do you store old liquor?
Why does old liquor turn yellow?
What is the value of old liquor?

I know you know all the fragmented knowledge, but there are some professional know-hows about liquor!

Today we will systematically talk about: What on earth is good about old liquor?

Part 1: What Is Good about Old Liquor?

First of all, don't think too highly of old liquor. The old liquor, which is stored for a long time, refers to aged liquor. There are old liquors of the following types:

Baijiu | Red wine | Whiskey | Brandy | Yellow rice liquor | Wine | Vodka

Liquor stored for more than five years is usually called old, but generally, there isn't the concept of old beer because of beer's short shelf life.

Although they are both old liquors, the flavor profiles of old liquors in the East and West differ greatly due to the distilling process and storage environment.

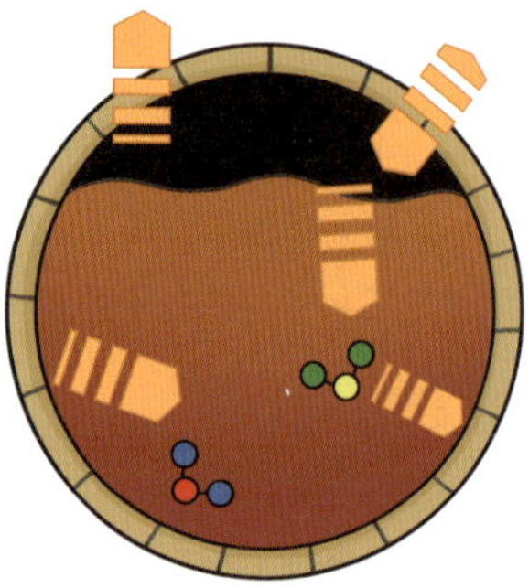

West

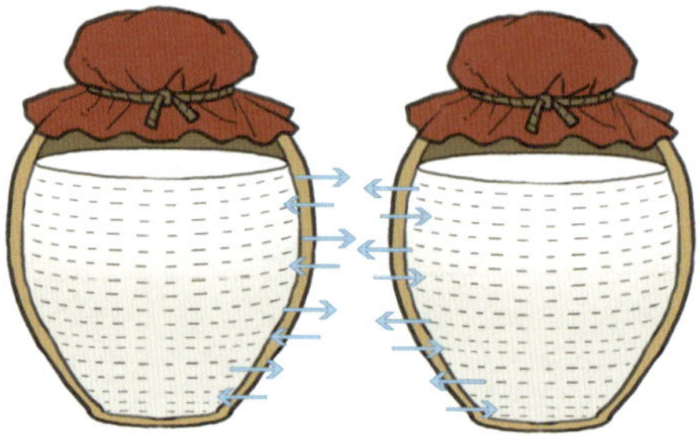

East

About 70% of the flavor of whiskey comes from the interaction between the liquor and the oak barrels.

Baiju-flavor substances come mainly from the metabolism of microorganisms during compound fermentation and transformation during storage.

Over time, the trace components of baijiu undergo slow changes, and the quality of baijiu is sublimated.

Suppose the art of distilling baijiu is the unification of heaven and man. In that case, aging is the further enhancement of its quality and the continuation of the essence of heaven and earth.

Case 1: Good Taste

We mainly like baijiu because of the sensory experience and after-drinking feeling. After some time, old baijiu is significantly less stimulating, more harmonious, smooth and mellow, with a more intense aroma and more prominent aroma, which is pleasant and comfortable to drink.

Sensory Evaluation Chart for Different Aging Times of Strong-Aroma Flavor Baijiu

Level	Sensory characteristics
Ordinary baijiu	The cellar aroma is rich, "sweet, pure, strong."
Three-year-old baijiu	Colorless or slightly yellow and transparent, rich aroma of the cellar, obvious aroma of aging, soft, sweet, net and crisp aftertaste, long aftertaste
Five-year-old baijiu	Colorless or slightly yellow and transparent, rich aroma of the cellar, elegant aroma of aging, the compound aroma of the cellar and aging is beautifully coordinated, mellow and rich, sweet and clean, with a clean mouthfeel and a long aftertaste.
Ten-year-old baijiu	**Colorless or slightly yellow and transparent, rich aroma of cellar, elegant aroma of aging, outstanding aroma of aging, with a beautiful and coordinated complex aroma of aging, elegant and delicate, mellow and soft, sweet and clean, with a long aftertaste.**

Chinese baijiu has different flavors, which have their style and characteristics, and contain different trace components.

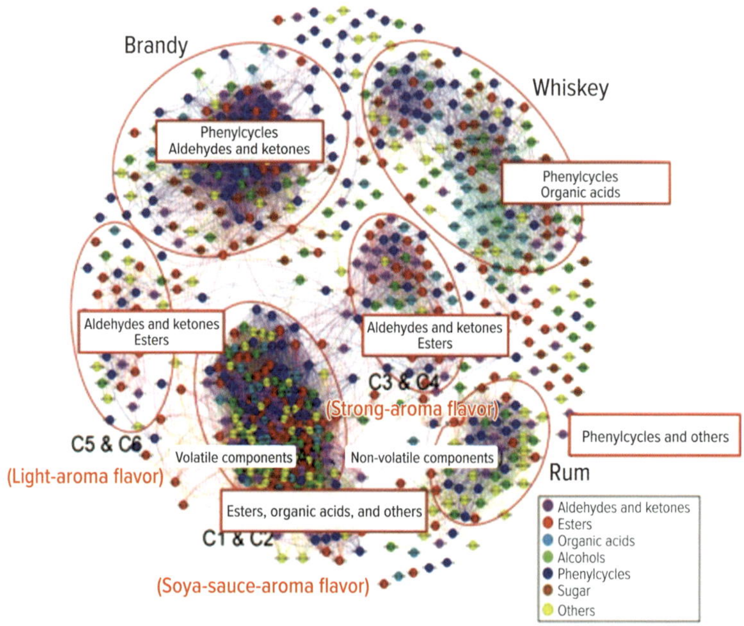

The co-occurrence network characterizes the characteristic components of distilled spirits

The flavor profile of three major flavors of baijiu

For different flavors of old baijiu, taste differences are also found during storage based on different flavor substances.

Flavor	Sensory characteristics
Strong-aroma flavor	**Bright color (or slightly yellow), rich cellar aroma, outstanding aging aroma. Comfortable grain aroma, soft and mellow, mellow and rich, harmonious aroma. Mellow, sweet and clear, long aging flavor (the aging aroma is more prominent)**
Light-aroma flavor	Bright color (or slightly yellow), pure aroma, elegant aging aroma, Soft on the palate, with a long finish (more prominent with aging)
Soya-sauce-aroma flavor	Bright yellow color, the prominent aroma of soy sauce, the obvious aroma of the aging, mellow body; thick and full, long aftertaste, the long-lasting aroma in an empty glass, long-lasting aroma (soya-sauce aroma is more prominent)

Case 2: Healthier

As mentioned earlier, baijiu is composed of 97% to 98% ethanol and water plus 2% to 3% trace ingredients, and the 2% to 3% trace ingredients contain fewer impurities. Through aging, the components of trace ingredients with a healthy flavor will increase, and the impurities will decrease:

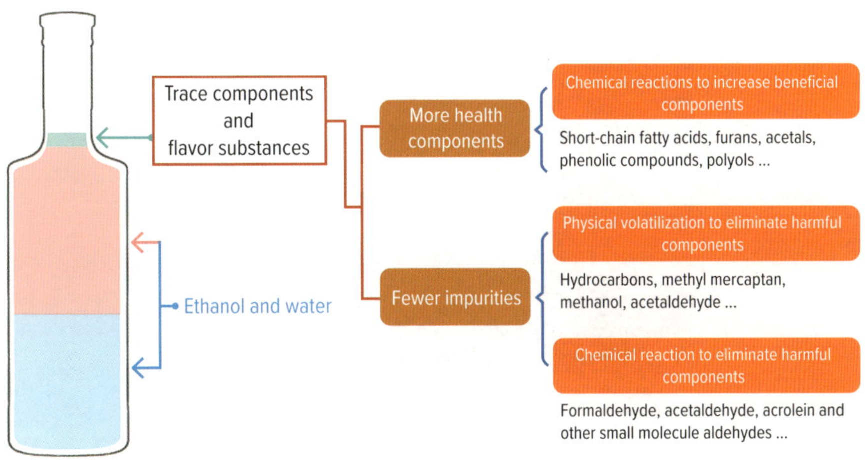

Although the amount of trace components and flavor substances is small, they have a huge effect, and as time goes on, these substances change and become more effective.

Traditional baijiu contains physiologically active substances that give it a healthy connotation that distinguishes it from ethanol. As it is stored for longer, the "temperamental" components are reduced, making it less intoxicating.

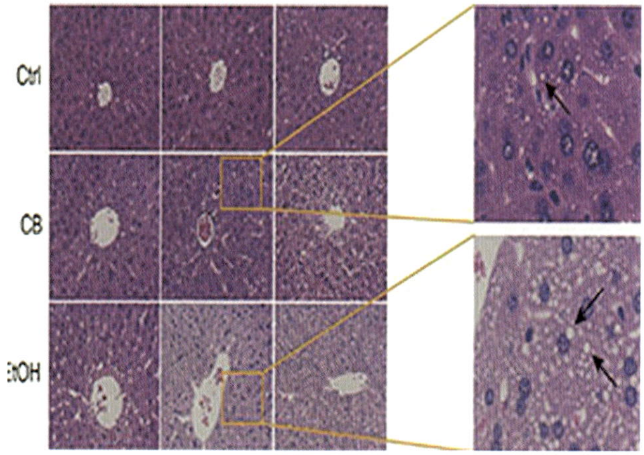

New baijiu

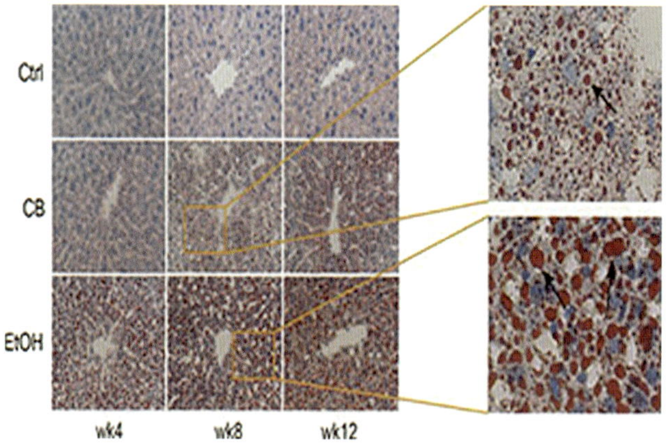

Old baijiu

Case 3: Preserves Honor

The distilling of a bottle of old baijiu is the culmination of many disciplines.

Fermentation and distilling

Microbiology
Chemistry

Distillation

Thermodynamics

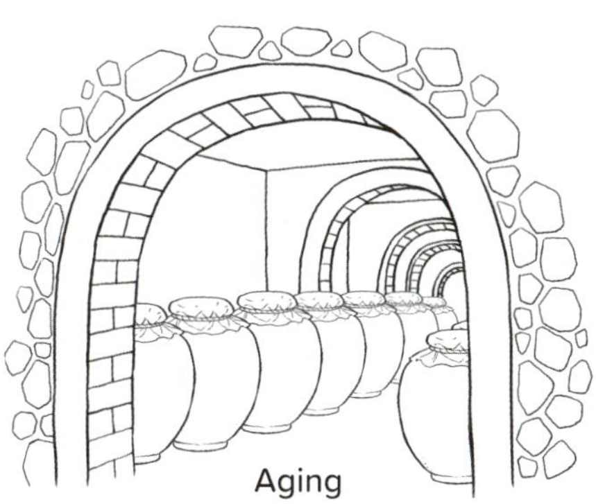

Aging

Physics
Chemistry

And a quality old baijiu is made up of a quality crude baijiu, a storage technique and time; any of these cannot be missing.

Quality crude baijiu (base)

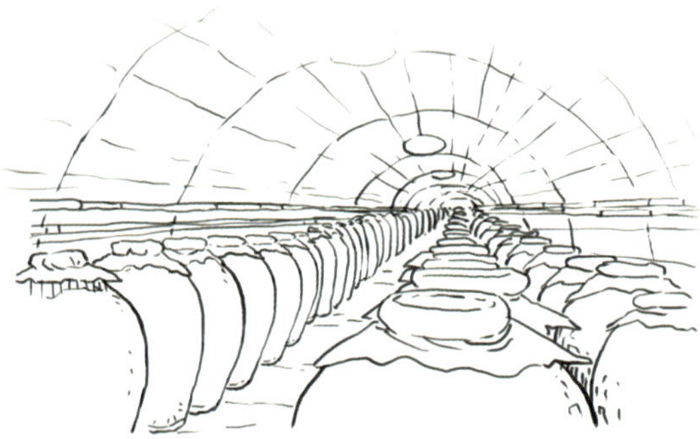

Storage technique (key)

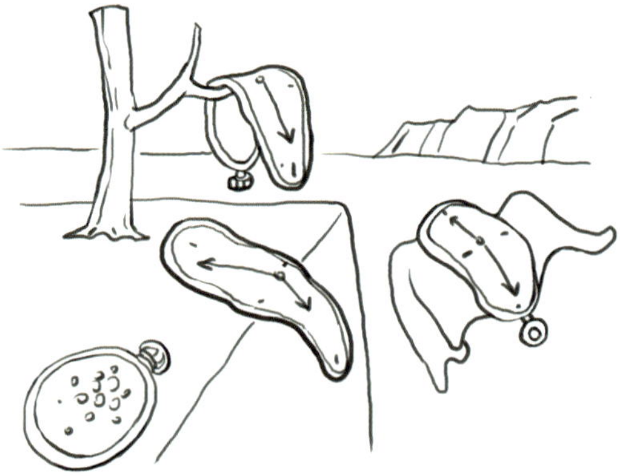

Storage time (guarantee)

In addition, China has a long history of planned economy, so old baijiu stocks are scarce, and as distilled spirits, the cost is high.

That's why things are precious when they are rare, and friends who invite you to drink "expired" baijiu are true friends!

By the way, no microorganisms are involved in baijiu aging, so there are no microorganisms in the baijiu body!

Part 2: What Are the Changes in the Quality of Old Baijiu?

The baijiu industry is the most time-conscious, and during the aging process, the baijiu undergoes complex changes, such as association, volatilization, condensation reactions, Maillard reactions, hydrolysis reactions ...

Each of these sounds very complicated, but it is very simple and broadly divided into two groups:

a: Physical Group

Baijiu undergoes subtle physical changes over time, mainly:

Volatilization

Elimination of harmful components

Association

Stable molecular structure

Arrangement

The regular arrangement of molecules

Combination

The abundance of large and small molecular clusters

Volatilization

Through storage over a period of time, low-boiling substances in the baijiu, such as hydrogen sulfide and methyl mercaptan, are volatilized.

Association

There are two types of association:

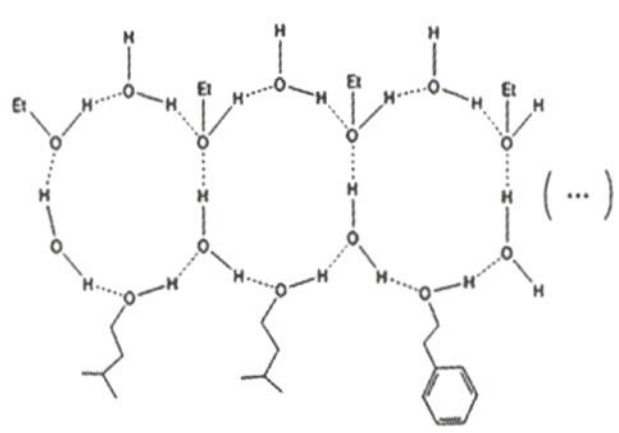

1. Tightly bonded between water and ethanol molecules with the assistance of hydrogen bond donors (acids, alcohols).

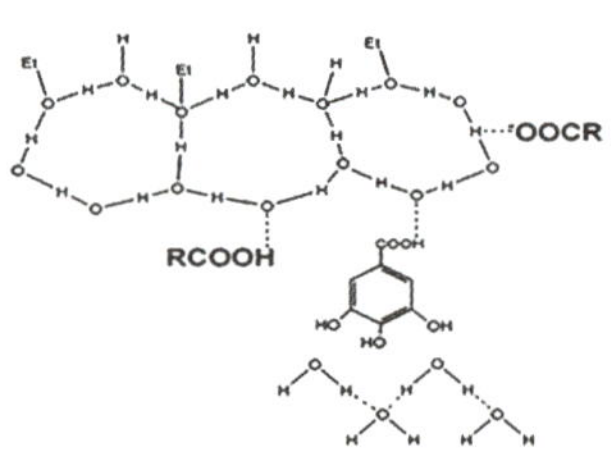

2. Acids, phenols, and other compounds help to strengthen hydrogen bonding.

The strength of the hydrogen bond between ethanol and water molecules in baijiu increases with storage time.

As storage time affects the bonding of ethanol and water molecules, the molecular level conformation also changes.

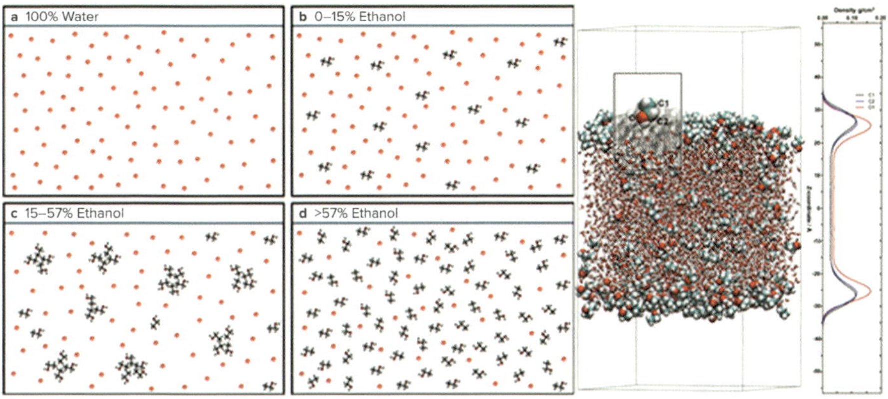

Structure of ethanol and water molecules at the molecular level

Arrangement

Freshly distilled new baijiu particles are disordered and dispersed on the mica surface. As storage time increases, the diameter width and height of particles in old baijiu gradually increase, the number of particles per unit area gradually decreases, and the shape becomes more and more regular.

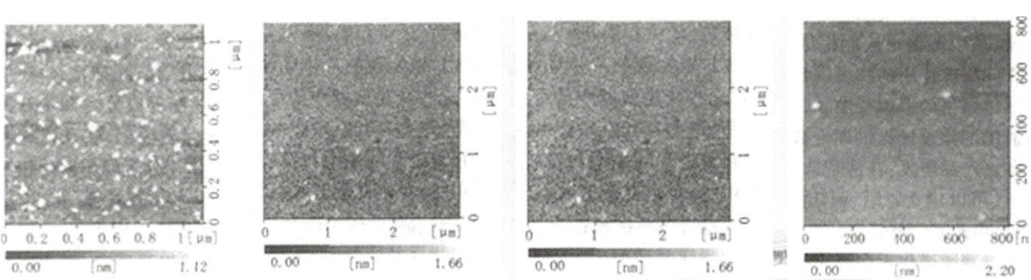

New baijiu 6 months storage 1 year storage 5 years storage

Combination

Studies of stored baijiu using atomic force microscopy have shown that as storage time increases, the small molecular clusters of particles gradually become larger and gradually form relatively stable macromolecular clusters.

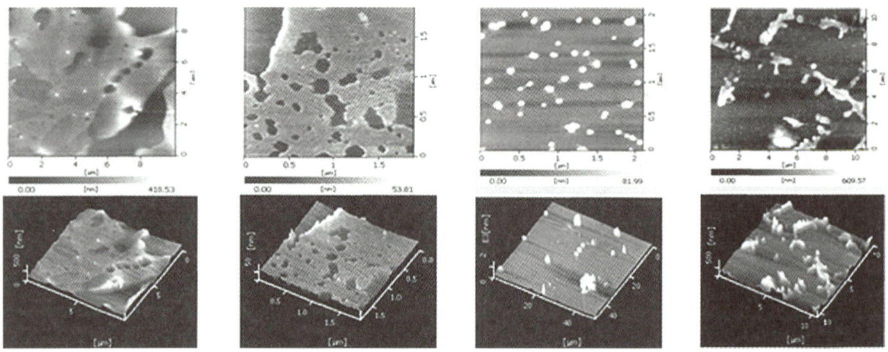

1 year storage | 5 years storage | 10 years storage | 20 years storage

The graph above shows that the formation of macromolecular clusters in baijiu stored from 5 to 20 years causes ethanol molecules to wrap around the surface of the macromolecular clusters, limiting the migration of ethanol molecules and reducing the irritation produced by ethanol.

b: Chemical Group

The aging process of old baijiu undergoes complex chemical changes over the years. Chemical changes are the key to modifying the flavor substances of baijiu, which in turn are the key to its quality.

Condensation Reaction

Alcohols and aldehydes react to form acetals.

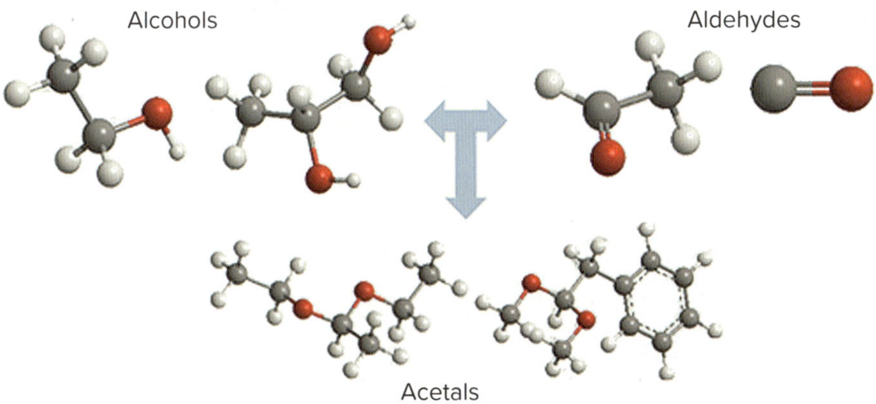

The production of acetal reduces the pungency and harshness of the baijiu!

Maillard Reaction

It is the reaction between carbonyl compounds (reducing sugars) and amino compounds (amino acids and proteins) in the baijiu, which, through a complex process, results in the production of brown macromolecules such as pyrazines, furans, pyridines, and other products that enrich the flavor.

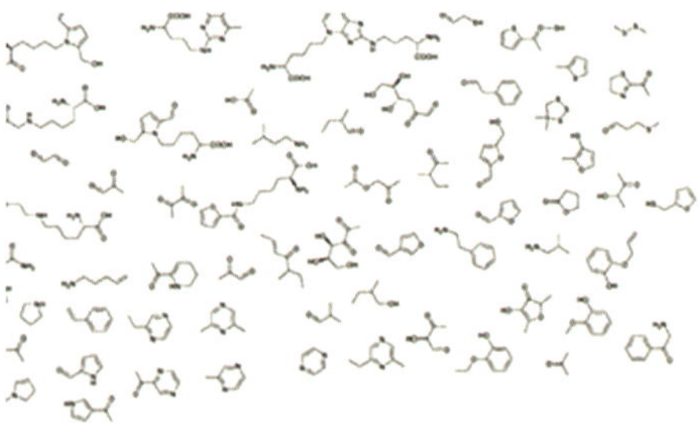

New baijiu   Old baijiu

This is the main reason why baijiu turns yellow! However, it should be noted that the new baijiu becomes yellowish after a long period of storage through the Maillard reaction. That yellowish baijiu is not always old, but maybe "pigmented."

Hydrolysis Reaction

Ester hydrolysis is a reversible reaction: in neutral or acidic solutions, esters, water, acid and alcoholization form a dynamic equilibrium.

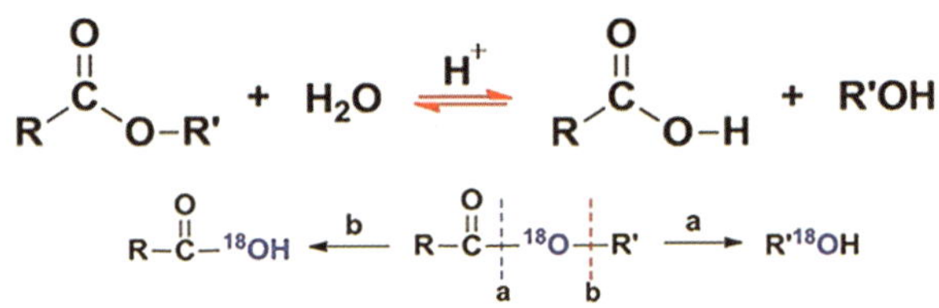

The hydrolysis reaction is the hydrolysis of an ester into an acid and an alcohol. In the hydrolysis reaction, the acid and the ester are interchangeable.

Did you find that if you don't study hard, you cannot even understand the molecular formulae of chemistry?

Oxidation Reaction

Due to the microporous structure of the pottery jar, the fatty acids in the baijiu are subject to oxidation by light, heat and air during storage, and are degraded into ketones and aldehydes, which enrich the flavor of baijiu.

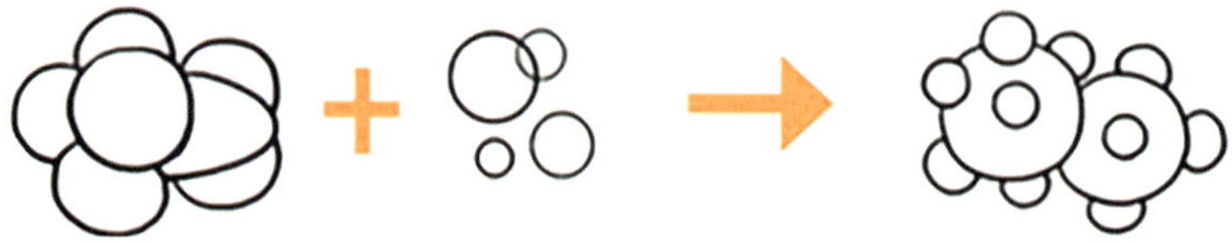

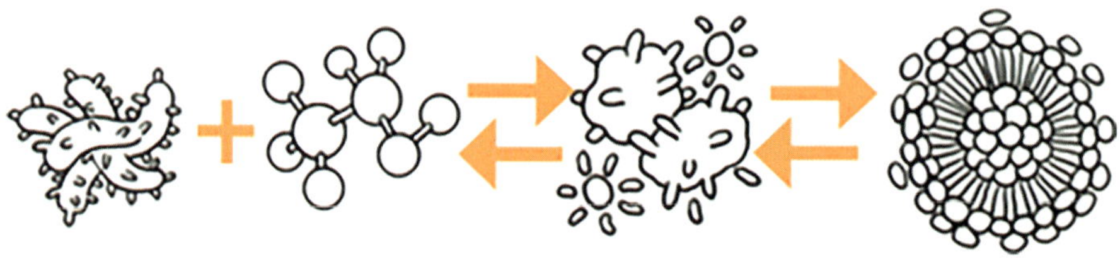

The acid-ester reaction in the baijiu is reversible, resulting in old baijiu with few esters and high acidity.

As a result of a series of physical and chemical changes, there are clear differences in the flavor profiles of new and old baijiu.

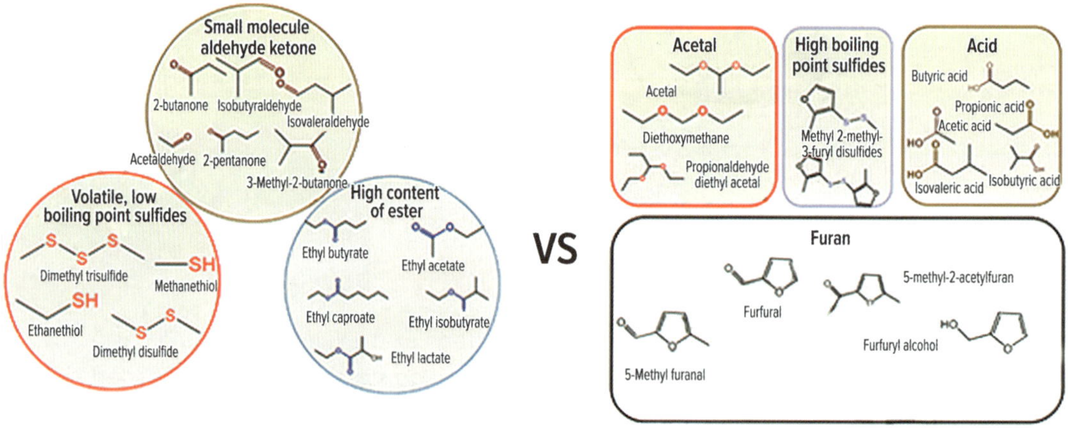

By the way, old baijiu with buried fermented grains, old liquor with buried soil, and old liquor with mold are not good!

Buried fermented grains old ripe

Moldy old liquor

Buried in the earth and ripe

Moldy old liquor

True or false, they are not even qualified in food safety!

There are rules for storing baijiu: avoiding light, keeping a cool, relatively constant temperature and humidity, and drying and preventing mold. For example:

Luzhou Laojiao has three major baijiu storage caves, namely Chunyang Cave, Zuiweng Cave and Longquan Cave, making it the company with the largest number of natural baijiu storage caves in the industry.

Part 3: What Is the Value of Old Liquor?

Having said all that, you may still have a question.

Actually, it's not exactly like that. Generally speaking, the best taste drinking period for a bottle of high-degree baijiu is 5–20 years, meaning its taste declines gradually when stored for more than 20 years.

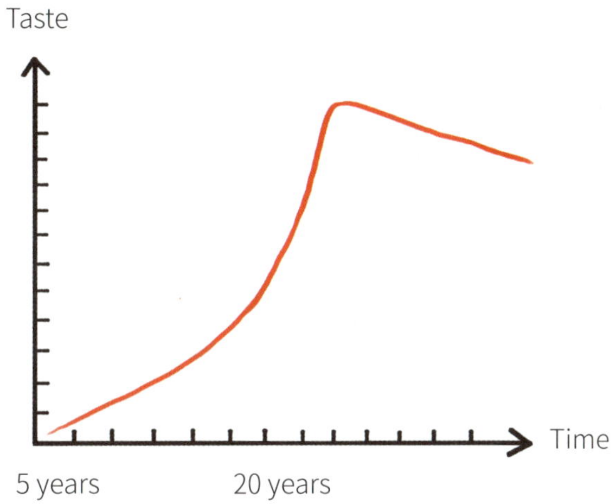

The relationship between the storage time of old liquor and the change of taste curve

Is old baijiu stored for more than 20 years less valuable?

Not really!

Older liquors over 20 years old are indeed declining in taste when consumed directly, but they are the best prominent quality baijiu essences. For example, the caves of Luzhou Laojiao store decades to hundreds of years of old baijiu, which is the gene pool of Luzhou Laojiao's prominent quality liquor.

When the new liquor is aged enough, when will the old friend come?
—Bai Juyi, *Missing Huangfu Shi When the New Liquor Is Ready*

At the same time, since baijiu is largely a cultural carrier, old baijiu stored for more than 20 years also represents the memory of an era and has a very significant cultural value. Even those stored even longer are already considered cultural relics, both in terms of their liquor and containers.

In addition, old friends drink old baijiu. Rather than treasuring old baijiu for years, they treasure friendship for years. The unique emotional value represented by old baijiu is incomparable to any other product.

In summary, old baijiu has a unique drinking value, cultural value, heritage value and unique emotional value.

Line chart of the four major values of old baijiu

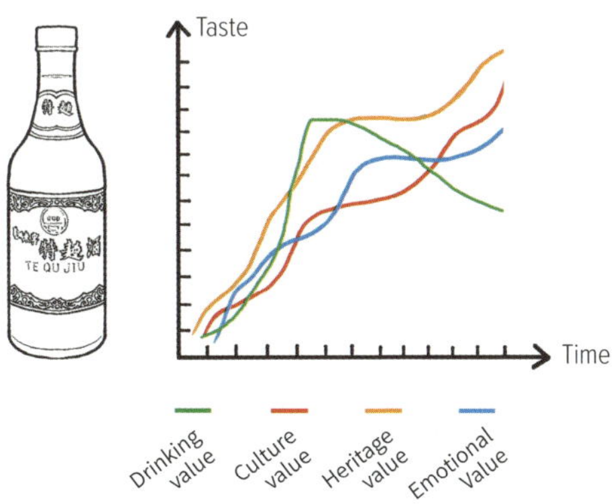

That's why it is said that liquor is fragrant when aged. The more you drink, the healthier you are!

CHAPTER 16

Why Do Those Who Drink Liquor Live Longer in Our History?

Recently, a sudden new coronavirus ravaged the world, causing panic.

With the country's efforts to save the country and numerous medical staff as "heroes in harm's way," the epidemic was controlled in this country, but the various debates over the treatment of the epidemic never stopped ...

What a time to be arguing about this. Is there a need for this?

Yes, there is! Initially, patients of COVID-19 were treated purely with Western medicine, but with poor results.

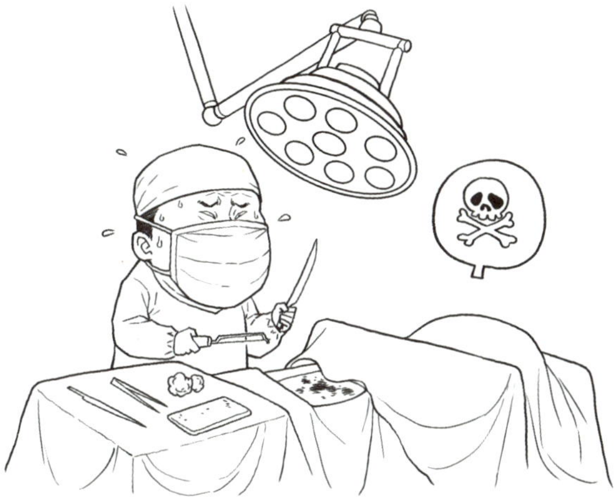

Why? According to the current industry authoritative expert: Modern Western medicine's understanding of the complex human life movement is less than 5%, coupled with a new virus, not encountered before, treatment is like taking a college entrance exam, and the content of the exam ...

All of them are beyond the scope of knowledge!

At this point, you cannot help but ask:

Both are healing and saving lives. Why cannot they sit together?

Chinese medicine has thousands of years of traditional medical experience, while Western medicine has the support of modern scientific theories and technologies, such as physics, chemistry, biology, physiology, and genetic science; although they are both treating diseases and saving lives, there is a key difference between the two, simply put: Chinese medicine is treating sick people, while Western medicine is treating diseases!

Western Medicine   Chinese Medicine

Therefore, no matter what time it is, it is not wise to simply use "only Chinese medicine" or "only Western medicine."

When it matters, we need to combine Chinese and Western medicine!

Okay, 10,000 words are omitted here about the debate between Chinese and Western medicine ...

Today we will talk about another century-old problem: "liquor and health."

The "liquor and health" debate has been going on for a long time, and there are many different opinions in the community. In general, there are two schools of thought.

Pro side　　Anti side

The debate never ends. The International Union of Nutritional Sciences (IUNS) and the Chinese Nutrition Society suggest that:

"Quit smoking and limit alcohol intake," rather than "quit smoking and quit drinking." In other words: drinking in moderation is good for your health! Why? We believe that:

"Medicine and alcohol have the same origin."

Traditional Chinese medicine and liquor are like twin brothers, almost at the same time; since ancient times, "medicine" cannot be separated from "liquor," and "liquor" cannot be separated from "medicine." "Therefore, the traditional Chinese character for "医" (medicine in English) is written as "醫"!

In the Eastern Han Dynasty, Xu Shen explained in *Shuowen Jiezi*: "醫 means to cure diseases." (the traditional character 醫 has three parts: 医, 殳, 酉)

"医" refers to external trauma. (The original meaning is to be wounded by an arrow.)

"殳" refers to massage, hot compresses, acupuncture, and other actions when treating illnesses.

"酉" refers to liquor.

The combination is: After the injury, through massage, acupuncture, and other means, and then internal and external application of liquor, in order to achieve the purpose of treatment, called "醫."

Ancient Chinese medicine believes that "liquor is the essence of water and grain, it tastes sweet and pungent, its nature is hot, its gas is strong, there is nothing it fails to do"; and has the effect of "killing a hundred evil poisonous gasses" as well as "removing the wind-evil and descend qi," "curing diseases with liquor," and other effects.

Liquor comes at the top list of all medicines.
—Ban Gu, *Han Shu · Monograph on Food and Currency*

Sun Simiao

If one person drinks it, there will be no epidemic in a family;
if one family drinks it, there will be no epidemic in a mile!
—Sun Simiao, *Essentially Treasured Prescriptions*

Hu Sihui

Liquor is sweet, pungent, and hot in nature. Liquor is also used as a guiding herb that expels all the pathogenic factors, smooths the circulation of blood, moistures the stomach and intestines, and relieves depression!
—Hu Sihui, *Essentials of Correct Diet and Dietary Cure*

It is also written in the Qing Dynasty works, *Jing Yan Shen Fang*.

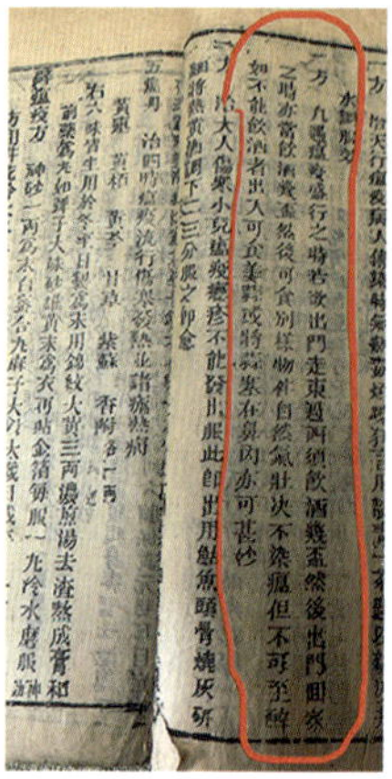

Whenever the plague is prevalent, if you go out, you should drink a few cups of liquor and then go out. When you go home, you should also drink a few cups of liquor, and then you can eat something else, so that your natural strength will not be infected with the plague, but do not drink until you are drunk. If you cannot drink liquor, you can eat ginger and garlic in and out, or put garlic in your nose, which is also very good.
—From the Qing Dynasty, *Jing Yan Shen Fang*

If you eat in a place where hygiene is a concern, you must drink high-degree liquor or eat a little garlic in moderation for antibacterial disinfection!
—Zhou Henggang (a leading liquor expert)

Recently, there is also an internet celebrity who refers to “殳” as “疫” (which means epidemic), which is a “new interpretation of Chinese characters” and is considered the wisdom of the ancient people in creating words, but not the original meaning of the character.

It means that to cure the epidemic, one must always drink liquor! Of course, this is just a saying.

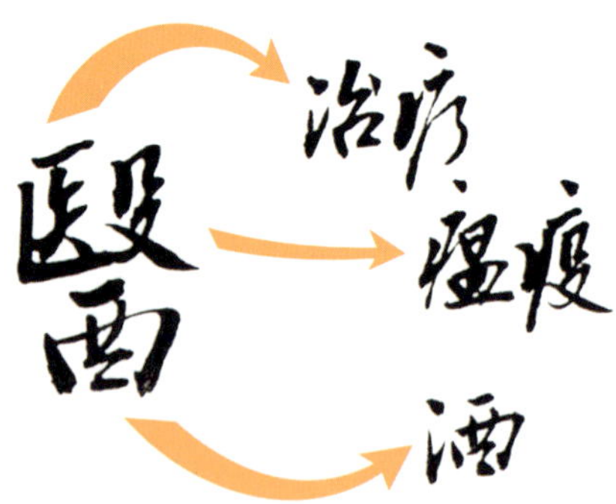

According to Zhang Hua's *Bowuzhi* (*Records of Diverse Matters*), three men, Wang Su, Zhang Heng, and Ma Jun, were walking in the morning in the fog. One drank liquor, one had a full stomach, and the other had an empty stomach.

In the end, the one who had an empty stomach died, the one who had a full stomach was sick, and the one who drank liquor was healthy. As the saying goes, "The power of liquor wards off evil."

Back to the point, often floating in jianghu, how can one just drink liquor, without understanding the "liquor and health" theory in traditional Chinese medicine?

1. Stimulating the Circulation of the Blood and Causing the Muscles and Joints to Relax

Did you find that a few sips of liquor are so refreshing when we work hard all day long? Why? Inspired by my friend Binge's home tap water pipe, this thing can be explained in this way: the human body's blood system is like the tap water network, which has been maintaining the normal circulation of movement.

Once, Binge was on a business trip and was not home for a long time. The scale gathered on the wall of the water pipe. If not solved in time, the water pipe will be clogged, rusted, and perforated.

After middle age, the blood becomes sticky (especially for patients with high cholesterol and high blood lipids), and the cholesterol-like lipids in the blood settle on the originally smooth inner lining of the arteries, forming white plaques of atherosclerosis-like lipids in the inner lining of the arteries, which is called "atherosclerosis lesion."

We all know that when a water pipe is clogged, the caliber of the pipe narrows, and the effect created by pressure is enhanced.

This is how "hypertension" comes about!

And to ensure we pump out the same amount to meet the water demand, the pump will have to run under high pressure for a long time, and over time ...

Sooner or later, problems will arise!

The human body's blood vessels are the same. To ensure the same amount of blood to maintain normal blood circulation, to ensure oxygen and nutrients for every cell, the heart must continue to work under high pressure for a long time, and over time ...

The heart muscle will become hypertrophic!

The "hypertrophy of the heart muscle" requires more oxygen, and once the coronary arteries cannot meet the oxygen demand, resulting in heart ischemia, it will produce "angina."

At the same time, for the local blood vessels, if the plaque further accumulates, it will produce two kinds of conditions: one condition is a complete blockage, and the water pipe cannot flow.

This happens mostly in cardiovascular and cerebrovascular locations, resulting in a "myocardial infarction" and "cerebral embolism"!

The second situation is: As the blockage becomes more and more serious, the lumen of the blood vessel becomes narrower and narrower, and the pressure becomes bigger and bigger, thus middle-aged and older people's blood vessels become more brittle, so they are prone to the phenomenon of blood vessel rupture.

In this case, it mostly happens in the capillary part of the brain, and this is how "cerebral hemorrhage" comes about.

Therefore, the former president of the Fourth Military Medical University and academician of the Chinese Academy of Engineering, Fan Daiming said in a speech that after middle age, it is best to run once or twice a week so that the body can continue for a short period to reach or approach the maximum heart rate.

Personal maximum heart rate = 220 − Age
Aerobic Heart Rate Zone is
Maximum heart rate × 60% to maximum heart rate × 80%

Running speeds up the blood flow, and the high speed of blood flow quickly flushes the blood vessels, like doing a weekly blood vessel cleaning, allowing the substances attached to the walls of the blood vessels to be cleaned out while they are still attached unsteadily.

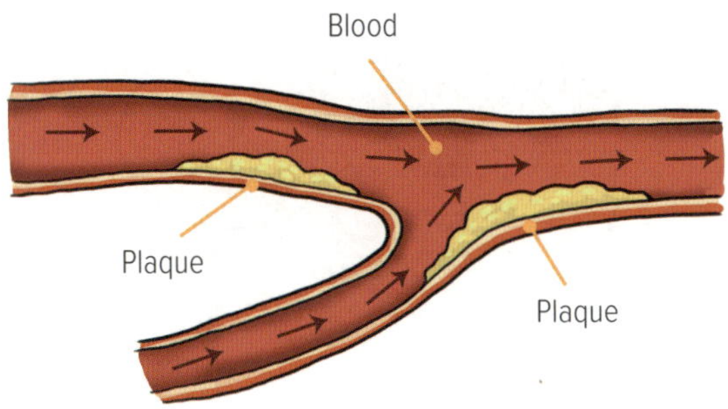

It is said that moderate alcohol consumption can also promote blood circulation, and the principle is the same with running.

Moderate alcohol consumption increases the amount of high density lipoprotein (HDL) in the blood, which transfers cholesterol from the arterial blood vessel walls to the liver, where it is divided and broken down.

I. Transfer

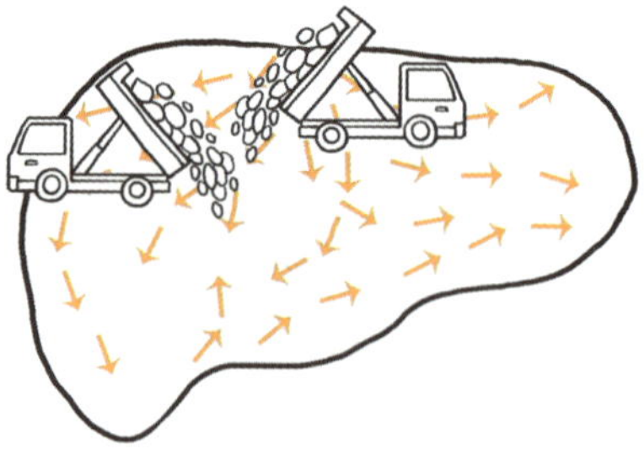

II. Catabolism

HDL can promote fibrinolysis, reduce platelet aggregation and promote smooth blood circulation, significantly reducing the probability of coronary heart disease.

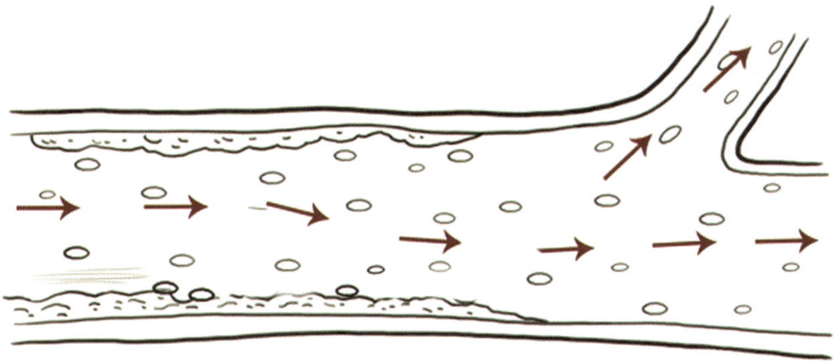

A comprehensive analysis by the National Institutes of Health of 51 clinical studies of prevalent diseases between 2005 and 2010 showed the following results.

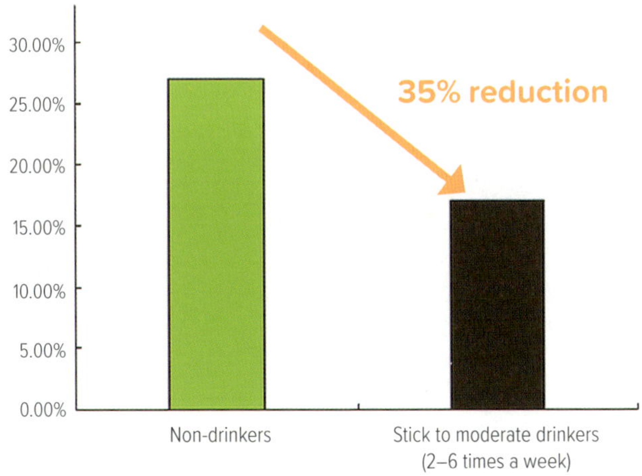

Moderate alcohol consumption and risk of hypertension

A joint research group from the University of Calgary, Canada, the University of Texas, and Harvard Medical School conducted a 30-year study of the relationship between alcohol consumption and heart disease. The survey analysis began in 1980 and, through a comprehensive study of 84 scientific reports and 4,235 samples, showed the following results:

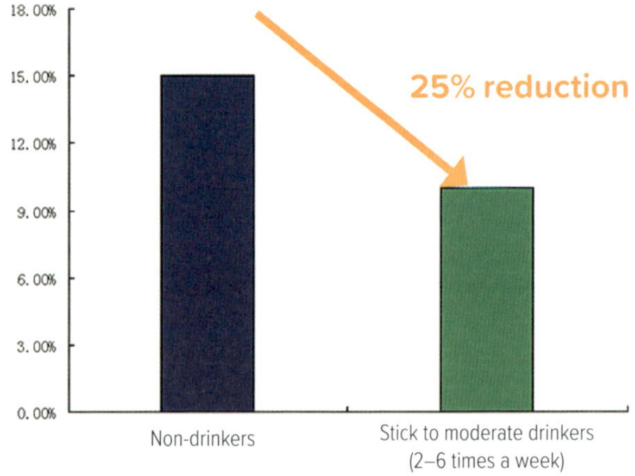

A graph of moderate alcohol consumption and risk of heart disease incidence

2. Chinese Medicine Solvents and Liquors Have a Medicinal Effect

As you know, the extraction of drug ingredients requires a solvent. What is a solvent? It is a medium that can dissolve gases, solids, and liquids into a homogeneous mixture. It is customary to call gases and solids solutes, and liquids solvents.

For a solution composed of two liquids, the component with more content is usually called the solvent, and the one with less is called the solute.

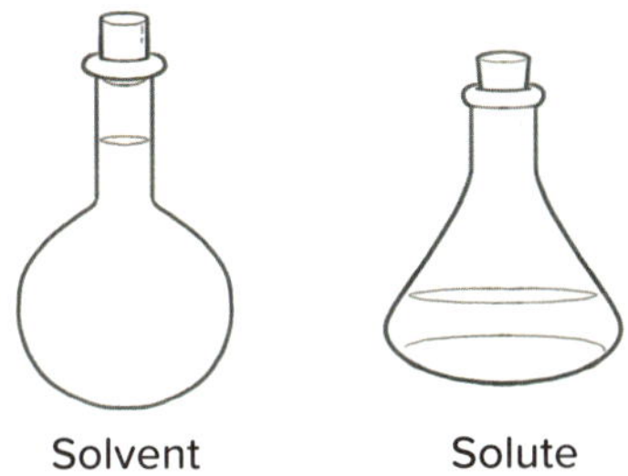

Water is the most widely used inorganic solvent, while liquor, gasoline, chloroform, and acetone are the more commonly used organic solvents.

And for food-grade extraction, the most widely used are:

It is worth mentioning that the vast majority of herbal ingredients are alcohol soluble and insoluble in water, so traditionally the vast majority of herbs are steeped in baijiu.

The expert of the Guangzhou Branch of the Chinese Academy of Sciences

To give a familiar example, in the era of universal anti-malaria, Tu Youyou used ethanol as the solvent to extract the active ingredients of Artemisia annua in the early days. Due to the high boiling point of ethanol, it destroyed the active ingredients of the drug to a certain extent, so it was replaced by its brother, ether, which eventually succeeded in extracting artemisinin.

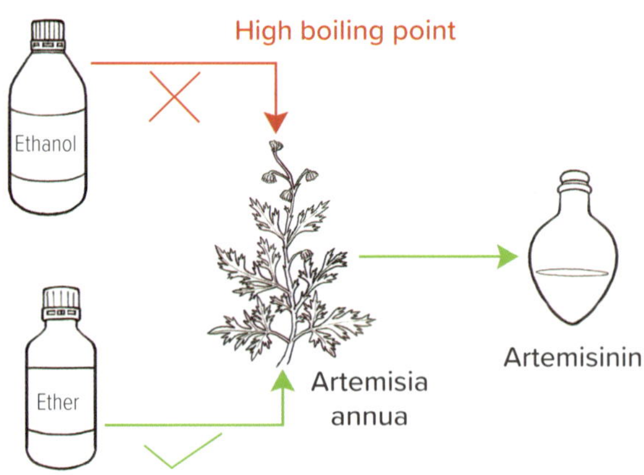

Although this is a less accurate example of ethanol as a solvent, the principle of their extraction is the same. Tu Youyou was awarded the 2015 Nobel Prize in Medicine for this discovery.

Tu Youyou
China's first Nobel laureate in medicine and pharmacologist

Li Shizhen's *Compendium of Materia Medica* details more examples illustrating medicinal liquor's importance for health and healing.

The *Compendium of Materia Medica · Grain Division · Liquor* introduces the therapeutic effects of various kinds of liquor separately and collects 69 liquor recipes, while more than 200 recipes for various kinds of medicinal liquors are also attached to the accompanying recipes in each medicine entry.

Rice liquor
To promote the power of medicine, to open the blood vessels, moisten the skin, disperse dampness, remove poisonous gases, and relieve horses from epidemics and plague.

Yunüejiu
Drink warm frequently and can cure all kinds of malaria.

Tusujiu
This is Hua Tuo's formula. It is drunk on New Year's Day and removes poisonous gases.

Liquor in the ancient medical profession is also known as "soup liquid," more than two thousand years ago, in the book *The Yellow Emperor's Classic of Internal Medicine*, the "Soup Liquid Theory" chapter was dedicated to the discussion.

What about the soup and liquor for the grains and mash?
—From *The Yellow Emperor's Classic of Internal Medicine*

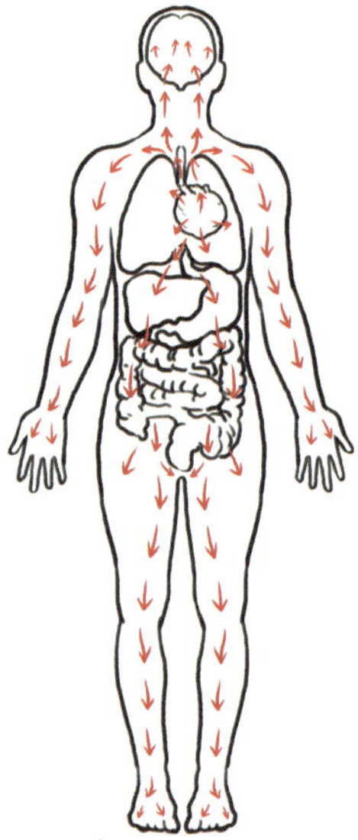

The blood, under the effect of ethanol, acts as a pump to speed up the flow of blood, so that the medicine can easily reach places that it normally cannot. This is true:

Liquor has a medicinal effect!

If you think that baijiu only has the functions of "blood circulation," "medicine potential," and "Chinese medicine solvents," you are wrong!

3. Baijiu Health Function Factor

Baijiu distilling is a science, and baijiu is not equal to ethanol.

Xu Yan, Doctor in fermentation engineering, vice president of Jiangnan University

In addition to ethanol, Chinese baijiu contains 2% to 3% of trace components and flavor substances during its complex process and fermentation.

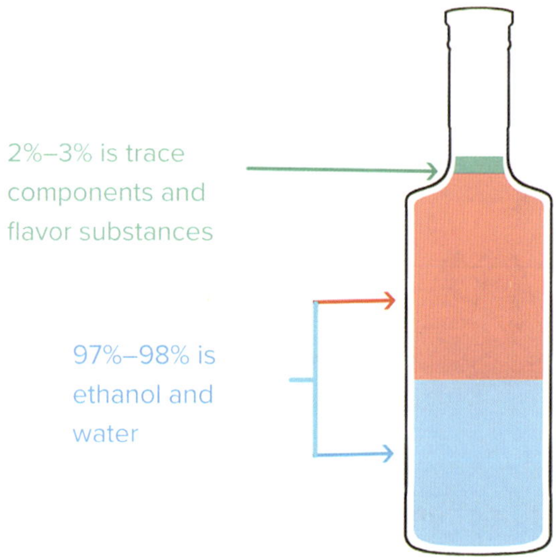

Don't underestimate this 2%–3%, which is the soul of Chinese baijiu.

For the time being, we refer to the trace components and flavor substances that are beneficial to human health as "health function factors," which are mainly the following:

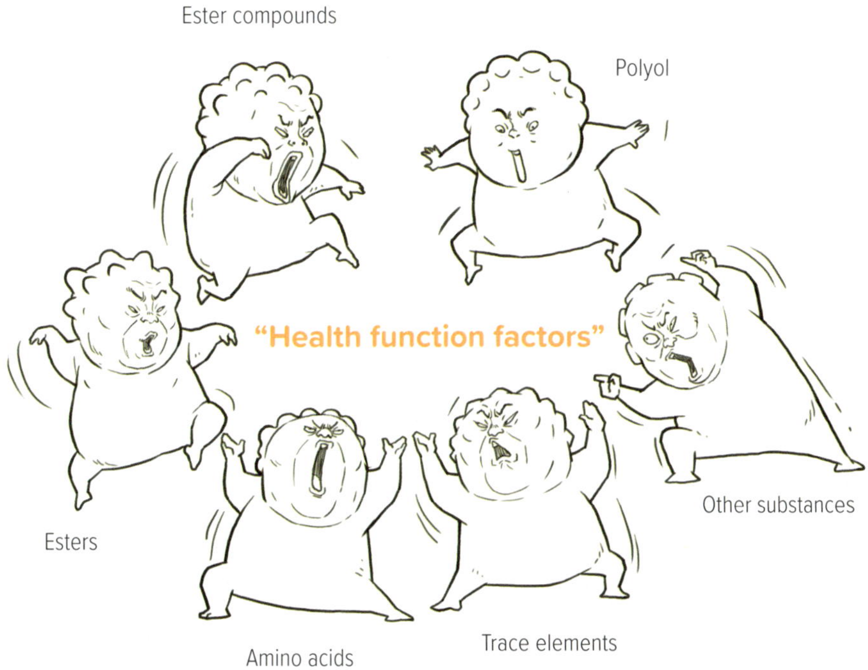

Each name sounds unfamiliar, yet they are all incomparable health-boosting substances.

(1) Organic Acids and Esters

Baijiu contains many organic acids, which are also the main aromatic and flavorful substances of liquor, and are divided into two types according to their volatility:

Strong volatility: acetic acid, propionic acid, butyric acid, caproic acid, octanoic acid, etc.

Weak volatility: lactic acid, malic acid, gluconic acid, tartaric acid, citric acid, succinic acid, etc.

The organic acid is the "big brother of liquor" and plays an important role. That's why there is a popular saying: "Liquor is made into vinegar instead."

They react with ethanol to produce the corresponding esters.

Caproic acid Ethanol Ethyl caproate

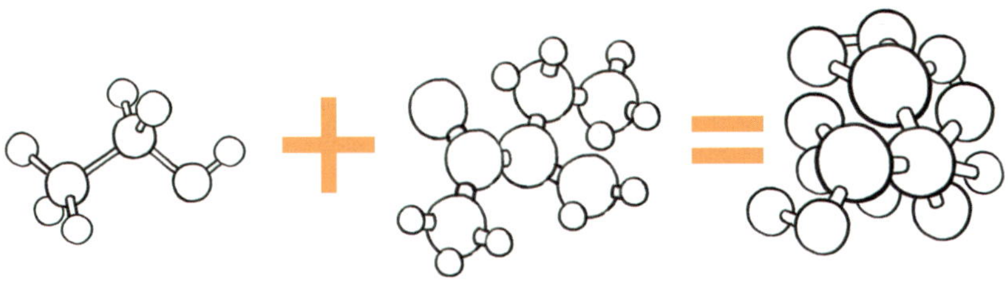

Acetic acid Ethanol Ethyl acetate

The right amount of esters is used to flavor the liquor and bring good taste to the liquor.

Tests show that the content of ethyl caproate in strong-aroma flavor baijiu is more than ten times that of other baijius.

(2) Advanced Fatty Acids and Esters

The strong-aroma flavor and soya-sauce-aroma flavor baijius contain a certain amount of advanced fatty acids and their esters, and advanced fatty acids and their esters also have many "little brothers."

After entering the human body, these advanced fatty acid ethyl esters are hydrolyzed into advanced fatty acids, which can inhibit the synthesis of cholesterol in the body, improve brain cell activity, increase memory and thinking ability, and prevent senile dementia.

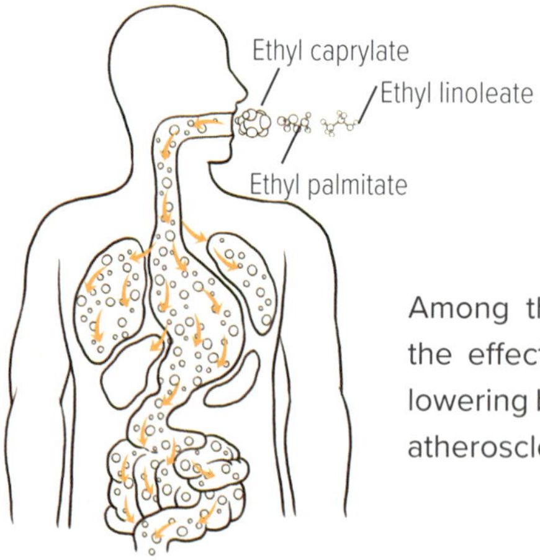

Among them, ethyl linoleate also has the effect of lowering cholesterol and lowering blood lipids, which can prevent atherosclerosis.

(3) Amino Acids

During the fermentation process of baijiu, some microorganisms break down proteins to produce various amino acids that are beneficial to the human body, many of which are essential and semi-essential.

Research results show that strong-aroma flavor baijiu is rich in amino butyric acid, which is an effective component for lowering blood pressure.

(4) Polyols

When we drink baijiu, especially high-quality strong-aroma flavor baijiu, we can obviously feel the "sweetness," which is the role of polyol in it, and polyol also has many "little brothers," and each plays a "tough role."

By the way, according to the national standard, the solid-state fermentation of baijiu is not allowed to add any sugar sweeteners.

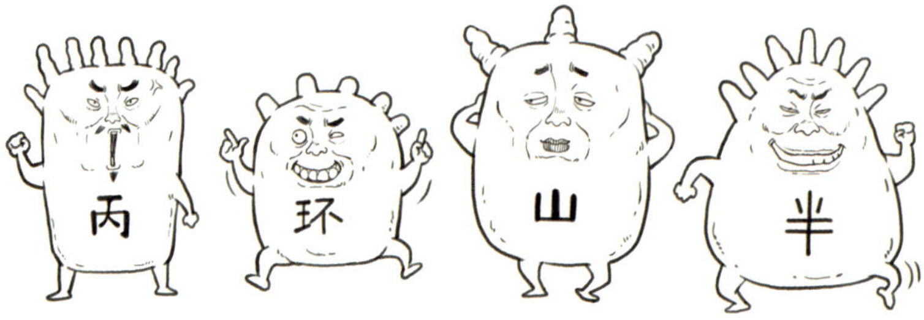

Glycerol Cyclohexanehexol Sorbitol Galactitol

(5) Trace Elements

Traditional Chinese baijiu is produced by solid-state fermentation, solid-state distillation and open production, and during the distilling, distillation and storage processes, various metal elements are incorporated into it. Twenty-nine trace elements, including calcium, iron, manganese, magnesium, strontium, sodium, and zinc, were discovered by inductively coupled plasma emission spectroscopy (ICP-AES).

Because most of these trace elements exist in the form of complex ions, which are bound together stably to form biological enzymes, they can keep the enzymes active and thus participate in chemical reactions in the body. Therefore, Chinese baijiu has excellent health care functions.

Zhuang Mingyang, China's leading expert on baijiu

(6) Other Substances

In 2005, Shen Caihong's team from Luzhou Laojiao discovered that Guojiao 1573 contains superoxide dismutase. Superoxide dismutase, commonly known as "SOD," has the function of scavenging free radicals and preventing aging.

Other-flavor baijius also contain moderate amounts of terpenes and pyrazines, which are beneficial to the human body.

There are currently more than 1,700 health function factors that can be detected. According to the research conducted by Zhang Suyi and Zhao Jinsong of Luzhou Laojiao, these health function factors are not a single component acting alone, but the combined effect of various components acting in synergy with each other.

Of course, how these health factors work together and the mechanism of action is worth further research.

4. The Mood Is Relaxed

If the score of drinking alcohol is good for health is 10, then the first three functions only account for 4 points, while the psychological regulation function of alcohol consumption accounts for 6 points.

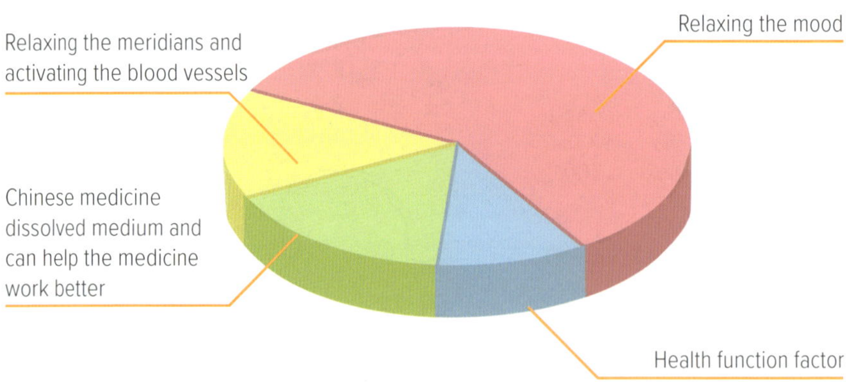

Many human diseases whose causes are still unknown are often caused by psychological depression in the first place, so modern medicine believes that:

Mental health is one of the most important factors in human health!

Robin Dunbar, an anthropologist at Oxford University, England

Traditional Chinese cultural practices:

Make friends, talk business.

The disturbances in the material world, are talked over in two or three cups of liquor; any of the world's hegemony ambitions, would be spent in the pot of tea of the afternoon. After a good drink, you will feel relaxed and refreshed, and your thoughts will flow.

Hi bro, let's get happy!

When I see the clouds in the sky, I cannot help but think of (Lady Yang's) clothes, and when I see the delicate flowers, I cannot help but think of (Lady Yang's) face.

According to modern medical research, people in a state of pleasure can promote the secretion of dopamine in the body. What is dopamine? It is responsible for regulating a variety of physiological functions of the central nervous system, making people excited and free of fear!

This is the proverbial "liquid courage."

5. The Right Time, the Right Amount, Drinking Good Liquor

Although liquor is good for health, everything has a degree. Drinking too little is not enjoyable, too much is not proper, just like leaving the dose to talk about the efficacy of drugs is not scientific! Healthy drinking needs to follow three principles.

At the right time

The right amount

Drink good liquor

First, the Right Time

The ancients have said: "No liquor in the morning, no tea at night."

No liquor in the morning

No tea at night

Second, the Right Amount

Usually, doctors will say no more than two Chinese grams (one Chinese gram = 50 g) at most. But each individual is very different in their drinking capacity, two Chinese grams of high-degree baijiu, perhaps for people with a small capacity, is already too much, but for those who drink by "jin" (one jin = 500 g), obviously not enough. Then the question arises, how much is the right amount?

1. Drinking for health
Drinking 20%–30% of your capacity before bedtime is appropriate!

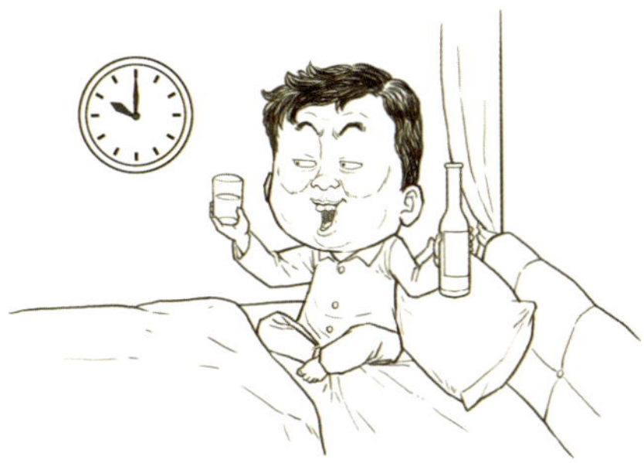

2. Drinking for business
At business parties, drink to 60%–70% of your drinking capacity! "Flowers look beautiful when half open. Liquor should be drunk till you are slightly drunk"!

3. Drinking for friends
A thousand cups would be too little; one should drink as much as he can with friends.

Third, Drink Good Liquor

The old saying still: drink less, drink good liquor! Really good liquor, due to good raw grain, a good distilling process, enough aging years, scientific testing, and other reasons, ensures that there is the richest content of healthy functional substances, and the lowest level of miscellaneous alcohol oils and other substances, so as to ensure the purity of the liquor.

As the saying goes: No liquor is no banquet, but sometimes there can be liquor without a banquet!

Since we cannot do without liquor, it is better to master more knowledge of drinking. Maybe one day you can use it!

If you don't know anything about it, it would be embarrassing ...

Let's drink Chinese baijiu for good health and good taste!

This article has a lot of content, and it is recommended that you recite the entire article ...

CHAPTER 17

Why Is It More Enjoyable to Drink Iced Drinks in Summer?

Whenever it comes to summer, I think the thing we like to do most is to nestle in an air-conditioned room ...

Over old trees wreathed with rotten vines fly crows, under the air-conditioning to eat watermelon with WiFi.

In the summer heat, cooling the heat is the "first priority," regardless of what you just experienced on the hot days outdoors. As soon as you enter the air-conditioned room, you will immediately feel "alive" again.

In general, an iced drink + air conditioning is the standard for summer, and in addition to watermelon and coke, many drinks can be chilled or added to ice, including liquor.

The Chinese traditionally have the habit of warming liquor and drinking it hot, and early on, the ancients used bronze liquor warmers to warm liquor.

Kylin Liquor Warmer: A national cultural relic, now stored in Luzhou Museum

Baijiu, the big brother of the beverage industry, has a very important status in the Chinese mind, and whether it is drunk warm or on ice, it is definitely the "god" of the beverage industry.

In ancient times, the main story of drinking warm liquor took place in winter, when the degree of liquor was low, equivalent to the current rice liquor, and drinking it warm could warm the stomach and taste better.

If the story takes place in the summer, the plot may be as follows.

Oh ...

Here we come to talk seriously about "baijiu on ice"!

When it comes to iced drinks, a little strange, to unfamiliar things, the Chinese are used to asking first:

Part 1: Did the Ancients Really Not Drink Iced Drinks?

In fact, the ancients, like modern people, could not live without ice in summer. When it comes to the use of ice, the ancients were much smarter than we think.

The earliest record of an ice cellar is found in the poem "Binfeng · July" in *The Book of Songs*, which reads, "The ice is chiseled in December of the summer calendar and hidden in the ice cellar in the first month of the year." Lingyin is the name of the ancient ice cellar.

According to *The Chou Rituals*, the Zhou Dynasty, to hide ice and provide ice supply one-stop service, set up a special position—"Ling Ren." (Ling Ren means somebody who is in charge of the ice cellar.)

In the summer, the heat is unbearable; in addition to cooling down, there is another way to relieve the heat—drinking iced liquor!

Ice is used to chill liquor, and ice is used to identify liquor. In fact, from the Zhou Dynasty, there was already a "refrigerator," a high-end tool to avoid heat.

The Chou Rituals · Tian Guan · Ling Ren records: "Sacrifice for ice han." The "ice han" is actually the ancient refrigerator!

Bronze ice han
National cultural relics, now stored in the National Museum of China

The ice han was a large container made of bronze, with two layers, inside and outside, where the food and liquor were placed, and the ice was placed in the space between the two layers. The key is that it is not going to consume electricity!

Utensil containing ice was prevalent in the Zhou Dynasty and was the most primitive refrigerator, chilled fruit and drink, cooling the heat, of course, including chilled liquor.

By the Spring and Autumn and Warring States Period, it became more popular for the vassals in the banquet to drink iced liquor. In Qu Yuan's *Songs of Chu*, there is a record of drinking iced liquor.

In the book, *Songs of Chu · Zhaohun*, it is said that "The liquor is squeezed from the fermented grains and then frozen, and it is delicious and refreshing to drink." Wang Yi notes: "Freezing is also called ice." This means that the liquor is made from the fermented grains and then chilled, which makes it tasty and refreshing.

By the way, in ancient times, those who could drink frozen liquor were not ordinary people.

Part 2: Why Should Baijiu Be Served on Ice?

Well, to solve the ancient mystery of ice drinking, there is still a centuries-old problem—why do you want to promote the iced drinking of baijiu in summer?

In general, each beverage has its own drinkable temperature, and liquors are no exception.

Beer	Sherry	Yellow rice wine
10°C to 12°C	10°C to 13°C	about 38°C

For baijiu, which is a unique Chinese distilled spirit, the ethanol content is usually high, and the aromatic substances are mainly phenols, so a high temperature will destroy the coordination of the aromatic substances, thus highlighting the stimulating dryness and spiciness of ethanol; while the low temperature will inhibit the volatilization of the aromatic substances.

The national standard GB/T33404-2016 "Guidelines for Sensory Evaluation of Baijiu" and "Method of Analysis of Baijiu" state that the room temperature for baijiu tasting is 20°C–25°C. Therefore, when the temperature of baijiu exceeds 30°C, its structure will be broken, and the stable molecular structure of aroma-rich substances will be changed, affecting the taste of liquor.

In the summer heat, the human metabolism is active, and the heart is agitated. Compared to beer and red wine, the alcohol content is higher in baijiu. After being chilled, it is both mellow and cool, and can also eliminate fatigue and tension, dampness, open appetite, and help sleep.

Like human beings, the liquor would be dry and restless in a high-temperature state. It is difficult to understand in heat. But when iced, its low-temperature introverted character is released, the aroma components remain intact and obvious, the layers are rich, and the liquor evaporates more fully and powerfully in the mouth.

Generally good quality 60% vol and 52% vol high alcoholic liquors achieve a perfect blend of liquor and water when blended, giving the liquor a very high quality and a better taste when served chilled. Liquor is hot in nature, so drinking it on ice can correct some of its dryness, making it suitable for most people.

The Song Dynasty's Wu Zimu's notes describing the Southern Song Dynasty's urban scenery *Meng Liang Lu*, "Tea Shops" section wrote:

"Song Dynasty tea shops sold different teas according to the different seasons. Generally, they sold Qibao ring tea, deep-fried noodle cake, scallion tea, or salt and black bean soup in winter. In summer, they sold plum liquor with snow bubbles, and there were many varieties."
—Wu Zimu, *Meng Liang Lu*

Zhu Zhenheng, a medical doctor of the Yuan Dynasty, has repeatedly argued for the benefits of drinking chilled baijiu.

There are three benefits of drinking cold baijiu. The baijiu flows through the lungs and into the stomach. Then it becomes slightly warm. The lungs first get the cold in the warmth, which can replenish the vitality; second, it gets the warmth in the cold, which can nourish the stomach. The cold liquor is slow to travel and is transmitted gradually, so people should not drink it without limit.
—Zhu Zhenheng

Translated, this means that drinking chilled baijiu has two major benefits.

1. It can nourish vitality; 2. It can nourish the stomach.

Speaking of which, by the way, I'd like to mention that in summer, we often put liquor in the trunk, and during transportation, the liquor shakes and becomes unstable due to bumps. In addition to the impact of high temperatures, the aroma evaporates quickly, which increases the acidity of the liquor.

Therefore, the summer liquor needs to be placed in a low-temperature environment or a cool place, and the conditions can be put in a constant temperature box, so that you can enjoy the real taste of the liquor body.

In addition, the car has been exposed to the sun for a long time, the temperature inside the car may often be above 70°C, up to 90°C, and the liquor in the trunk—

Not only is it bad for the liquor, but it's also even worse for the car!

Part 3: What Is the Right Way to Drink on Ice?

As we all know, adding ice to liquor is more common in foreign countries, while in China, it has become popular only in recent years, and is only for champagne, or beer. For baijiu, how do we drink it chilled?

The First Step: How to Choose Liquor

For baijiu, its main composition is ethanol, water, and trace aroma components!

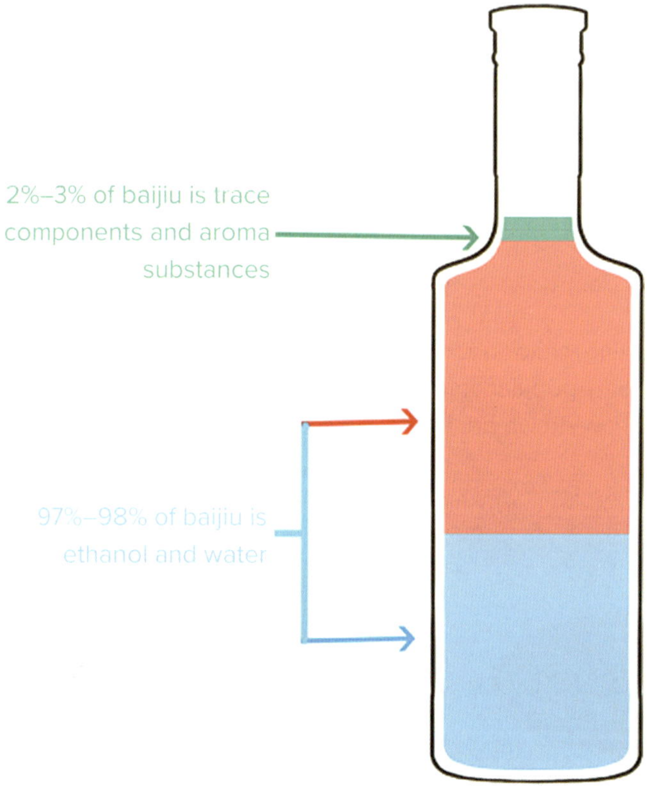

Do not underestimate this 2%–3%, which is the soul of Chinese baijiu.

Usually, after the baijiu is chilled at a low temperature, as the temperature decreases, the aroma substances in the baijiu will condense, and the baijiu body will sometimes turn milky white.

Room temperature
(transparent)

Low temperature
(milky white)

This is a normal physical phenomenon, with no impact on the quality of baijiu.

By the way, two reminders:

1. Chilled baijiu, the temperature cannot be too low!

2. Not all baijiu is suitable for adding ice or chilling!

Researchers have conducted an experiment to compare the effects of chilling seven famous baijius.

Tasting Results of Famous Chinese Liquor Brands on Ice

Sample name	Comment	Clarity
		30%–40% with ice
Guojiao 1573	Elegant and delicate aroma, mellow and sweet, soft and harmonious, comfortable aftertaste	Clear
Luzhou Laojiao Tequ	Soft body, sweet and fragrant, slightly short taste	Clear
A famous strong-aroma flavor baijiu	Sweet aroma, with a prominent raw taste of green vegetables and a bitter mouthfeel	Slightly muddy
A famous strong-aroma flavor baijiu	Elegant aroma, harmonious aroma, short and light taste	Clear
A famous strong-aroma flavor baijiu	A mellow and sweet, soft and short taste	Slight loss of light
A famous soya-sauce-aroma flavor baijiu	The soya-sauce aroma is weakened, the acidity increases, sour and astringent, slightly aldehydic	Loss of light

The chart is from "Guojiao Liquor · 1573—Leading Liquor in the New Times" by Shen Caihong, Wu Xiaoping, and Huang Yanfei, published in 2003 in *Liquor-Making Science and Technology*.

It can be seen that Guojiao 1573 and Luzhou Laojiao Tequ are the most suitable for iced drinking of baijiu among many famous baijius.

No doubt, what you can think of is already thought about by the researchers. They did not only think, but also did this experiment: Although the transparency of the baijiu body meets the standard, but the solid fermentation of grain liquor is still richer in aromatic substances than new baijiu; after adding ice, its disadvantage is even more obvious.

New Baijiu Tasted on Ice

Sample name	Comment	Clarity
A new type of baijiu R	Mellow aroma, light taste. Bitter aftertaste, more astringent ⊠	Clear
A new type of baijiu S	Mellow and clean. Bitterer, shorter, and lighter aftertaste ⊠	Clear
A new type of baijiu Z	The mellow, purer, shorter and lighter aftertaste ⊠	Clear

The chart is from "Guojiao Liquor · 1573—Leading Liquor in the New Times" by Shen Caihong, Wu Xiaoping, and Huang Yanfei, published in 2003 in *Liquor-Making Science and Technology*.

Therefore, solid distilled baijiu is more suitable for drinking with ice than new baijiu. Therefore, it can be said that the ability to drink with ice is a litmus test for the quality of a baijiu, just as only the removal of makeup can reveal the original look of a beautiful woman!

The Second Step: How to Add Ice

How to add ice, there are two ways.

1. Chilled baijiu

2. Baijiu with ice

What specific tricks to master? Here are two examples:

Guojiao 1573

Guojiao 1573 from 10°C–20°C tastes comfortable, especially at 12°C. It has an elegant aroma, rich cellar fragrance, and is mellow, sweet and soft, rich and delicate, with a clean aftertaste.

Usually, when drinking on ice in summer, the amount of ice for 52% vol Guojiao 1573 should not exceed 36%, and the amount of ice for 60% vol Guojiao 1573 should not exceed 60%. The alcohol by volume is 35% vol to 47% vol, achieving the best conditions for drinking Guojiao 1573 on ice.

Add ice to no more than 60%

Guojiao 1573 (60% vol)

Add ice to no more than 36%

Guojiao 1573 (52% vol)

Data from "Optimum Drinking Conditions of Iced Baijiu" by Dai Xiaoxue, Zhang Suyi, Yao Yao, et al., published in *Liquor-Making Science and Technology*, 2019.

Luzhou Laojiao Tequ

Luzhou Laojiao Tequ, combining authentic baijiu with contemporary drinking aesthetics, has created a new way to drink authentic baijiu—

1. The 10th generation of Luzhou Laojiao Tequ is chilled for "10 minutes," which is the best state to drink on ice in summer.

2. When Luzhou Laojiao Tequ 10th generation is chilled to "8°C–12°C," the trace components in the liquor tend to stabilize, and the quality of baijiu becomes calmer, which is the best temperature for serving baijiu on ice in summer.

See what the experts have to say about the process.

In addition to chilling, Luzhou Laojiao Tequ can also be served directly on ice. The baijiu body is crystal clear when ice is added, so that the visual, taste, and smell senses are perfectly combined.

With ice, the baijiu is properly diluted, but the sweetness of it is more evident, so you don't have to worry about it "changing its mind" at all. Oh, no! I mean, don't worry, it would not become "tasteless"!

CHAPTER 18

There Is No Sugar in Strong-Aroma Flavor Baijiu, So How Does It Turn from Slight Bitterness to Sweet Flavor?

Modern people are more and more fond of sweet food, which not only tastes good, but also brings people a special sense of joy!

In order to cater to consumer tastes, not only has milk tea become sweet, but the sweetness of many liquors has also become more pronounced, and to the curious consumers, the liquor sellers will say:

But whenever asked a slightly deeper question, they cannot answer!

Unlike milk tea, where sugar can be added casually, baijiu belongs to distilled spirits, and the state has strict regulations on solids in baijiu, and non-self-fermented sweet substances cannot be added.

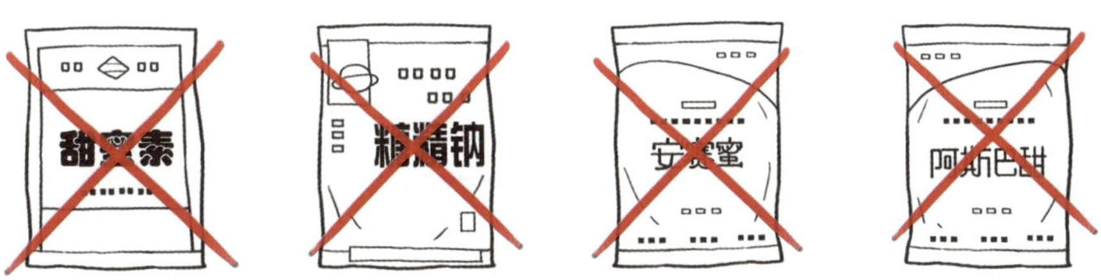

Sweetener (no) | Sodium saccharin (no) | Acesulfame (no) | Aspartame (no)

Tips: According to China's Standards for Food Additives (GB2760-2014), any sweetening additives are not allowed to be added to baijiu.

Therefore, the sweetness in baijiu can only come from itself.

Why is there a sweetness in baijiu when there is no sugar? To figure it out, we must first understand what sweet substances are in baijiu.

Part 1: Baijiu without Sugar, Why the Sweet Taste?

To find out why baijiu has a sweet taste, you have first to figure out how it is made.

During the distillation process, in addition to water and ethanol, various aroma substances go along with the baijiu and water vapor into the spirit.

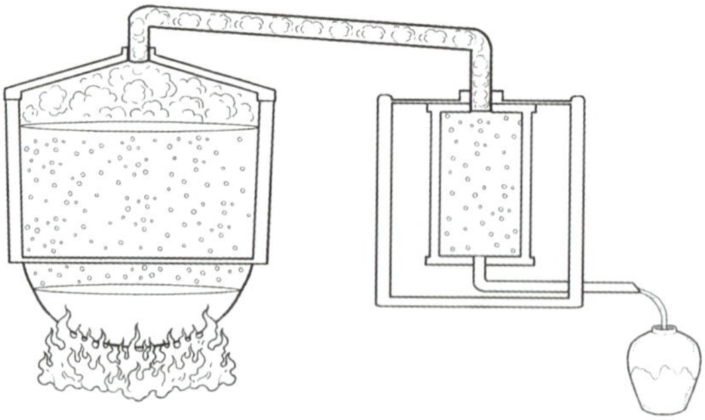

This is roughly how the spirit is distilled!

More than a thousand trace components have been detected from baijiu, mainly including esters, acids, alcohols, aldehydes, carboxyl groups, etc.

Tips: Although the percentage of these trace components is small, they are rich in variety and greatly impact the quality and flavor of baijiu.

Among them, acids, advanced fatty acid esters, and polyols are the main flavor-presenting substances of baijiu.

Different parts of the human tongue have different perceptions of taste.

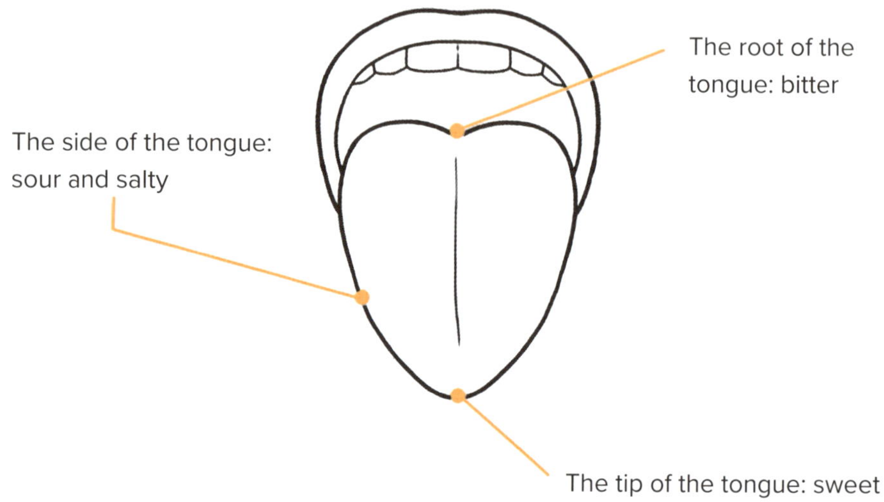

Sweetness, mainly tasted by the tip of the tongue, the following is focused on the sweet substances in baijiu below.

At present, researchers have detected many sweet substances from baijiu.

Sweetening Substances in Baijiu

Name	Molecular formula	Sensory characteristics
Acetic acid	CH_3COOH	Smell estery, crisp, sweet with a sour taste, with stimulation
Butyric acid	$CH_3(CH_2)_2COOH$	Slightly acidic, sweet
n-Pentanoic acid	$CH_3(CH_2)_3COOH$	Slightly acidic, sweet
Caproic acid	$CH_3(CH_2)_4COOH$	Acidic and irritating sensation, more refreshing
Lactic acid	$CH_3CHOHCOOH$	Acidic and stimulating, astringent, thick
Isoamyl acetate	$CH_3COO(CH_2)_2CH(CH_3)_2$	Pear-like, apple-like aroma, slightly sweet with an astringent taste
Ethyl caproate	$CH_3(CH_2)_4COOC_2H_5$	Pineapple-like fruit aroma, like cellar aroma, sweet and crisp
Diethyl succinate	$(CH_2)_2(COO\text{-}C_2H_5)_2$	Slightly fruity, slightly sweet, astringent and bitter
Ethyl isovalerate	$(CH_3)_2CH_2COOC_2H_5$	Apple-like aroma, slightly sweet, astringent
Ethyl caprylate	$CH_3(CH_2)_6COOC_2H_5$	Fruity, slightly sweet
Ethyl nonanoate	$CH_3(CH_2)_7COOC_2H_5$	Aromatic, fatty acid-like, slightly sweet
Ethyl lactate	$CH_3CHOHCOOC_2H_5$	Weak aroma, slightly sweet taste, moderately thick, astringent
Pentyl butyrate	$CH_3(CH_2)_2COO(CH_2)_4CH_3$	Sweet
Ethyl palmitate	$CH_3(CH_2)_{14}COOC_2H_5$	Sweet
Propyl acetate	$CH_3COO(CH_2)_2CH_3$	Fruity, bittersweet when diluted
Ethanol	CH_3CH_2OH	Light narcotic odor, stimulating, slightly sweet
n-Hexanol	$CH_3(CH_2)_5OH$	Aromatic odor, oily, viscous, slightly sweet
Heptanol	$CH_3(CH_2)_6OH$	Fruity, slightly sweet
Phenyl ethanol	$Ar\text{-}CH_2CH_2OH$	Floral-like, sweet aroma, slightly sweet, astringent, bitter
2,3-Butanediol	$CH_3(CHOH)_2CH_3$	Faint odor, viscous, slightly sweet
Glycerol	$(CH_2OH)_2CHOH$	Odorless, viscous, slightly sweet
Acetaldehyde	CH_3CHO	Green leaf and grass odor, pungent, slightly sweet, astringent
Acetal	$CH_3CH(OC_2H_5)_2$	Grassy odor, peculiar odor, slightly sweet, astringent, crisp
Diacetyl	$CH_3COCOCH_3$	Sour and rancid odor, fatty, oily, slightly sweet, crisp
3-Hydroxybutanone	$CH_3COCHOHCH_3$	Sweet-like caramel odor, fruity, slightly sweet, bitter

The content of the chart is from Li Dahe's *Discussion on Sweetness of Chinese Liquors*.

Tips: Due to the large number of trace components in baijiu and the fact that analytical testing is still evolving, there are limitations to current research techniques. Above are the sweet substances that can be found in baijiu, but they are not all sweet substances in it.

At different concentrations, the sweetness of the taste varies greatly.

Flavor Characteristics of Some Sweet Substances in Baijiu at Different Concentrations

Name	Concentration (mg/L)	Flavor characteristics
Acetic acid	1,000	Vinegar odor and pungency, crisp in import, sweet with a sour taste
Acetic acid	100	Slightly vinegar odor and pungency, crisp in import, slightly sour, slightly sweet
Acetic acid	10	Close to the boundary value
Butyric acid	1,000	Aromas of fermented grains and cellar of Daqu liquor, with a sweet and sour taste in the mouth, crisp
Butyric acid	100	It appears to have a slight aroma of fermented grains and cellar mud, slightly sweet and refreshing in the mouth
Butyric acid	10	Close to the boundary value
Valeric acid	1,000	
Valeric acid	100	
Valeric acid	10	
Valeric acid	1	
Lactic acid	1,000	Slightly sour, slightly astringent
Lactic acid	100	Slightly sour, slightly sweet, slightly astringent, with a sense of richness
Lactic acid	10	Slightly sour, slightly sweet, slightly astringent
Lactic acid	1	Close to the boundary value
Caproic acid	1,000	Smells like a big liquor, soft, sweet, and crisp in the mouth
Caproic acid	100	Smells like Daqu liquor, slightly sweet, crisp
Caproic acid	10	Slightly aromatic, slightly sweet
Ethyl lactate	1,000	Weak aroma, slightly sweet, thick, astringent
Ethyl lactate	100	Weakly aromatic, slightly astringent, with some sweetness
Ethyl lactate	10	No odor, close to the boundary value
Ethyl caproate	1,000	Smell like strong aromatic wine, sweet, crisp, with the aroma of fermented grains, thick
Ethyl caproate	100	Smell like strong aromatic wine, short aroma, with bitterness
Ethyl caproate	10	Slightly aromatic, crisp, slightly sweet with sweetness
Ethyl caproate	1	Slightly aromatic, slightly sweet with astringency
Ethyl caproate	1,000	Fruity on the nose, sweet on import
Ethyl caprylate	100	Fruity on the nose, with the astringent aftertaste
Ethyl caprylate	10	No aroma on the nose, slightly fruity and astringent on the palate
Ethyl heptanoate	1,000	Imported with apple aroma, thick taste, crisper, slightly sweet, net end
Ethyl heptanoate	100	Imported with apple flavor, slightly sweet, with astringent
Ethyl heptanoate	10	Slightly fruity, taste with astringency
β-Phenylethanol	1,000	Like rose aroma, slightly sweet, with a stimulating taste
β-Phenylethanol	100	Rose aroma, slightly sweet, crisp
β-Phenylethanol	10	Slightly rosy, slightly sweet, crisp
β-Phenylethanol	0.1	No odor, close to the boundary value

The content of the chart is from Li Dahe's *Discussion on Sweetness of Chinese Liquors*.

There are several theories about the taste mechanism of sweetness, among which Shallenberger's theory is the most complete and popular.

Shallenberger: an American scholar

The AH-B unit on the sweet taste chemistry can interact with the AH-B unit on the taste receptors to form hydrogen bonds, thus producing the sweet taste sensation. Therefore, as long as the AH-B-X system is satisfied, any substance that can bind to a sweet substance can be perceived as sweet.

By the way, there are many sweet substances in baijiu, but the main contributors are the polyols.

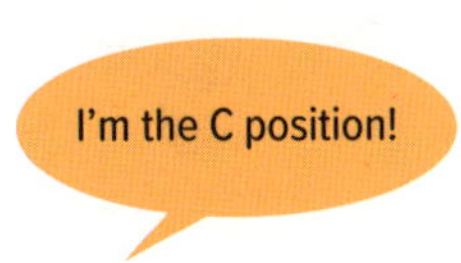

From a distance, a polyol is a person, but when we get closer, we find that it is a bunch of people.

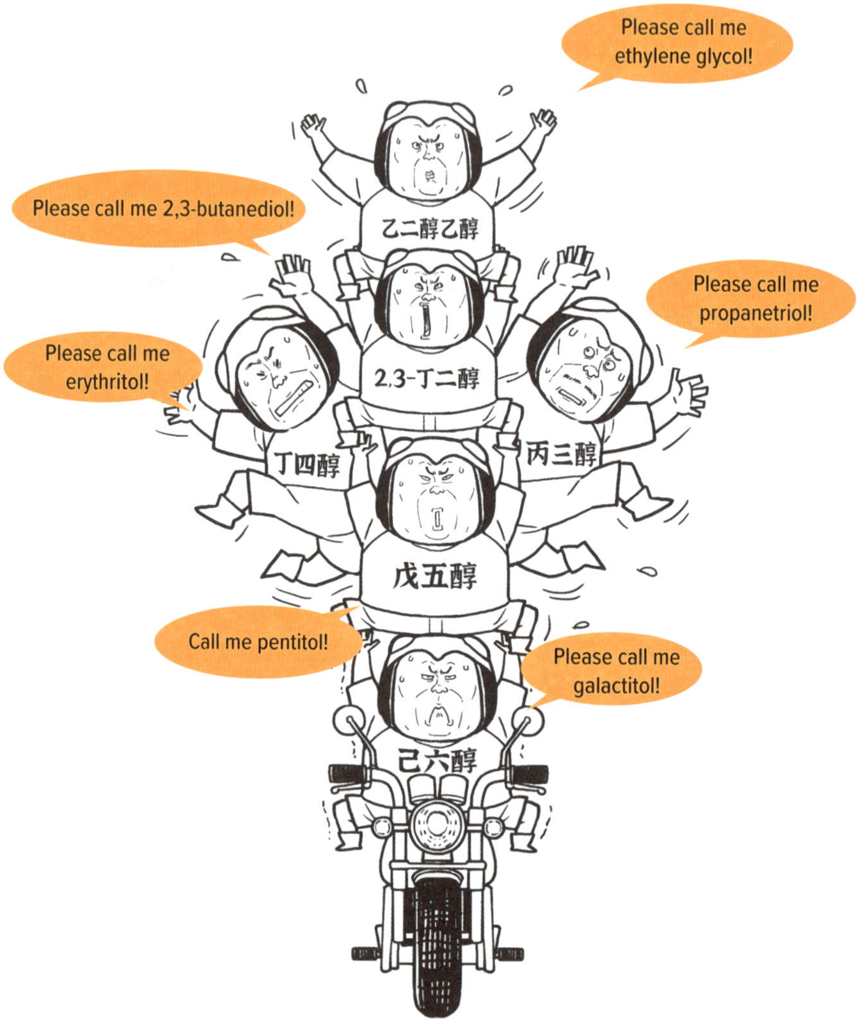

Although they are all born of one mother, their sweetness intensity varies.

Galactitol (Mannitol) > Pentitol (Arabitol) > Erythritol > Propanetriol (Glycerol) > Ethylene Glycol > 2,3-Butanediol

Tips: Polyols are both sweet and viscous, bringing a full-bodied feeling to baijiu and making it taste sweet. Among them, mannitol brings a strong sweetness and is also the main component of fruit sweetness, and erythritol brings twice as much sweetness as sucrose.

In several of China's major basic flavor baijius, there are the sweet substances mentioned above, so strictly speaking, any baijiu distilled with solid pure grains will have a sweet taste!

Pure ethanol will also be mellow and sweet at certain concentrations!

The degree of sweetness varies from one flavor to another because of the different levels of trace components in the baijiu.

Comparison of Some Sweet Substances in Different Flavor Baijius

Components	Strong-aroma flavor		Soya-sauce-aroma flavor	Light-aroma flavor	Rice-aroma flavor
	Single grain	Multi-grain			
Acetic acid	451	465	1442	314.5	215
Butyric acid	129	104	100.6	9.0	/
Valeric acid, n-valeric acid	16.1	15.2	29.1	2.0	/
Caproic acid	361	296	115.2	3.0	/
Lactic acid	332	257	1057	284.5	978
Isoamyl acetate	25	27	6	7.1	/
Ethyl caproate	2232	1984	1407	/	/
Diethyl succinate.	11.8	12.3	5.4	13.1	5.8
Ethyl valerate	73	57	42	8.6	/
Ethyl caprylate	52	52.7	12.0	7.8	2.7
Ethyl nonanoate	12	14	5.7	/	4.1
Ethyl lactate	1616	1354	1378	1090.1	995
Ethyl butyrate	20	30	/	/	/
Ethyl palmitate	65	61.7	27	42.7	50.2
Ethyl heptanoate	42.2	44.3	5	4.4	/
n-Hexanol	66	64	27	7.3	/
Heptanol	0.6	0.9	101	/	/
β-Phenylethanol	3.3	3.5	17.0	20.1	33.2
2.3-Butanediol	22.8	16.3	151	8.0	49
Glycerol	10–40		/	/	/
Acetaldehyde	336	355	550	140	35
Acetal	526	468	1214	244.4	142
Diacetyl	87	118	230	8.0	/
Acetophenol	92	52	405.9	10.8	/
Furfural	14	16	294	4.0	0.9
2-Methylpyrazine	0.021		0.323	/	/
2.6-dimethyl pyrazine	0.376		0.992	/	/
Trimethylpyrazine	0.294		4.965	/	/
Tetramethylpyrazine	0.195		5.302	/	/
2-Ethyl-6-methyl Pyrazine	0.108		0.796	/	/

The content of the chart is from Li Dahe's *Discussion on Sweetness of Chinese Liquors*.

For example, ethyl caproate, which has a sweet taste, is present in strong-aroma flavor baijiu, soya-sauce-aroma flavor baijiu, light-aroma flavor baijiu, and so on, but in strong-aroma flavor baijiu, the content is more than 10 times that of other flavors.

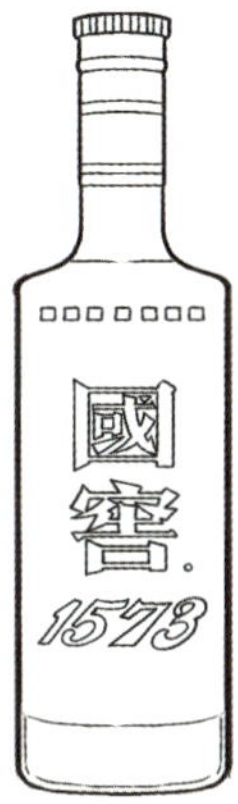

That's why strong-aroma flavor baijiu has the sweetest taste!

Tips: Acids contribute more to the sweetness, such as butyric acid, caproic acid, valeric acid, lactic acid, and heptanoic acid ...

The organic acid content of soya-sauce-aroma flavor baijiu is more than that of strong-aroma flavor baijiu, especially heterocyclic compounds, which are tens to hundreds of times more than strong-aroma flavor baijiu.

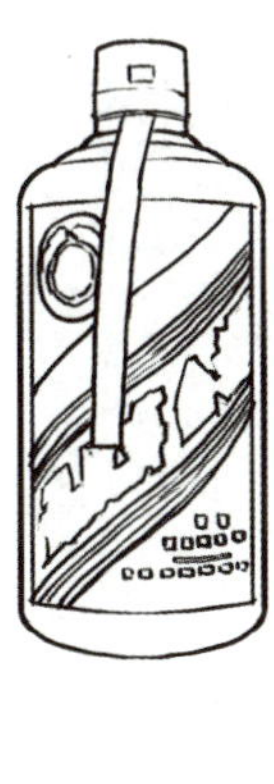

That's why there's relatively little sweetness in soya-sauce-aroma flavor baijiu!

Light-aroma flavor baijiu and rice-aroma flavor baijiu have relatively fewer types and contents of trace components.

Therefore, the sweetness of the two is not obvious!

Tips: Light-aroma flavor baijiu and rice-aroma flavor baijiu have more alcohol, so there is bitterness in them, but the bitterness of good-quality baijiu is not prominent, and is only a momentary sensation.

Therefore, in general, the strong-aroma flavor baijiu has more sweet substances than the soya-sauce-aroma flavor baijiu, and soya-sauce-aroma flavor baijiu has more of those than the light-aroma flavor baijiu and rice-aroma flavor baijiu.

Strong-aroma flavor > Soya-sauce-aroma flavor > Light-aroma flavor > Rice-aroma flavor

Part 2: Why Is the Sweetness of Strong-aroma Flavor Baijiu More Obvious?

As mentioned earlier, polyols are the main contributor to the difference in sweetness, and the polyol content in strong-aroma flavor, light-aroma flavor, and soya-sauce-aroma flavor baijius vary due to different distilling processes.

Chart of Polyol Content in Strong-Aroma Flavor, Light-Aroma Flavor, and Soya-Sauce-Aroma Flavor Baijius

Flavor components	Relative sweetness (equivalent to sucrose)	**Strong-aroma flavor**	**Soya-sauce-aroma flavor**	**Light-aroma flavor**
Glycerol	0.60	3.16	/	0.41
Erythritol	0.81	0.18	/	/
Sorbitol	0.60	0.14	0.28	/
Mannitol	0.50	0.89	/	/
Arabitol	0.70	1.12	1.12	/
Total Sweetness	–	5.49	1.40	0.41

Tips: In general, the polyol content and total sweetness of strong-aroma flavor baijiu are higher than those of soya-sauce-aroma flavor baijiu and light-aroma flavor baijiu, which is an important reason for the sweetness of strong-aroma flavor baijiu.

Therefore, in all the baijiu evaluation sessions, the word "sweet" or "mellow" is inseparable from the comments for strong-aroma flavor baijiu.

Colorless, transparent, richly fragrant, clean and sweet, with a long aftertaste!

The word "sweet and clear" or "clean and sweet" highlights the sweetness of the liquor. So, in the industry, the saying "no sweetness, no 'Lu'" has been widespread.

Here "Lu" is actually a synonym for strong-aroma flavor baijiu!

At the First National Liquor Evaluation Conference, the four most famous spirits were selected and named respectively according to their special distilling processes.

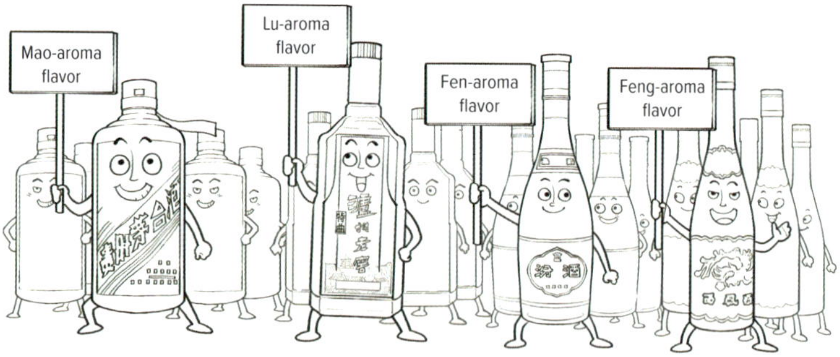

Later, at the Third National Liquor Evaluation Conference, experts formally established the concept of "strong-aroma flavor," "light-aroma flavor," and "soya-sauce-aroma flavor" based on the process and flavor characteristics of several famous baijius, plus the rice-based Guilin Sanhuajiu. The earliest of the "Four Great Flavors" of Chinese liquor was thus established.

Strong-aroma flavor | Soya-sauce-aroma flavor | Light-aroma flavor | Rice-aroma flavor

Polyols are produced when yeast metabolizes glucose. The sweetness of polyol increases with the increase of the hydroxyl group. The amount of its content is related to microorganisms, the number of bacteria and raw material pretreatment, etc., and also closely related to the production process control.

Case 1: Raw Sweetness Depends on Fermentation

1. Thousand-year Cellars

As previously mentioned, the cellar for strong-aroma flavor baijiu is a mud cellar, the cellar for soya-sauce-aroma flavor baijiu is a stone cellar, and the cellar for light-aroma flavor is a underground vat.

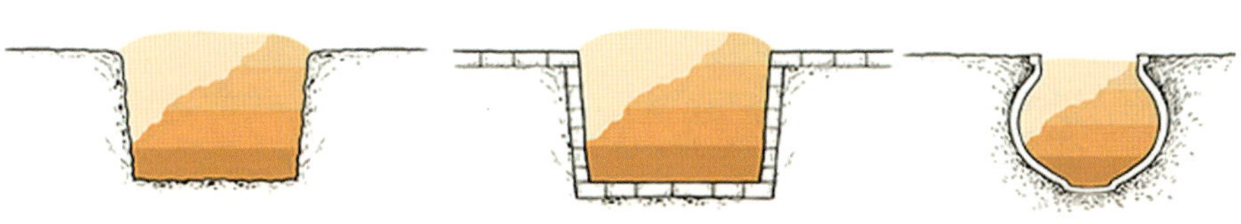

Mud cellar (strong-aroma flavor) | Stone cellar (soya-sauce-aroma flavor) | Underground vat (light-aroma flavor)

The biggest difference between them is that:

The strong-aroma flavor cellar uses a mud cellar!

With cellar mud, microorganisms have a habitat and can metabolize a large number of sweet substances.

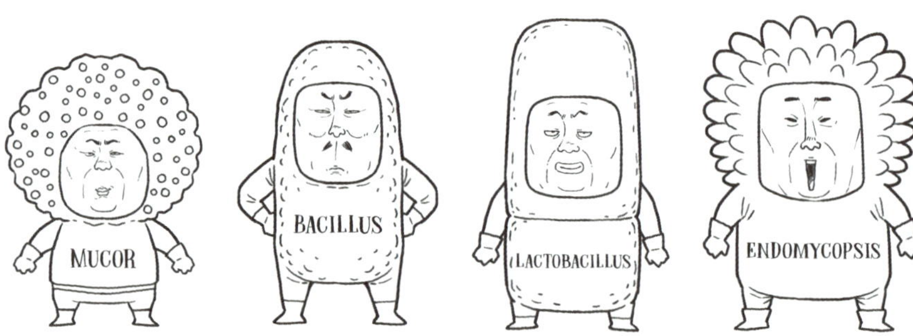

Mucor: It often appears in jiuqu and on the cellar wall, and can produce succinic acid, glycerol, and mannitol.

Bacillus: It can reduce fructose and produce mannitol.

Lactobacillus: Glucose can be used to produce mannitol and 2,3-butanediol, lactic acid, and acetic acid.

Endomycopsis: Glucose can be used to produce mannitol and 2,3-butanediol, lactic acid, and acetic acid.

It has been tested that the mud cellar is the main habitat of anaerobic bacteria, especially bacillus anaerobes, in which bacillus polymyxa undergoes anaerobic fermentation, thus producing 2,3-butanediol.

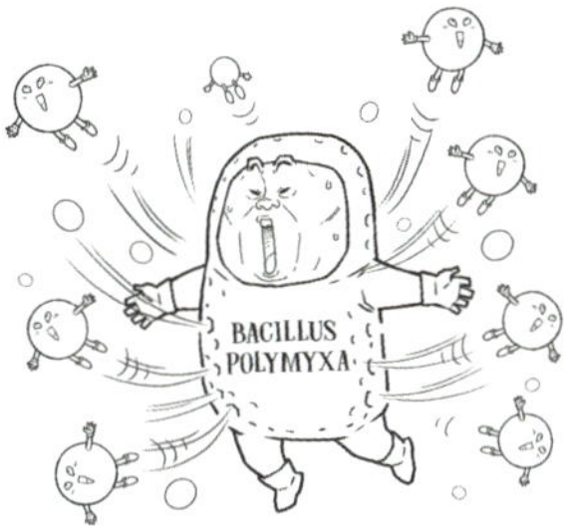

As a result, the fermented grains in contact with the cellar walls and the cellar floor produce a sweeter liquor!

Therefore, in general, strong-aroma flavor baijiu made from mud cellars has more sweet substances than other-flavor baijius.

2. Ten Thousand-year Fermented Grains

Because of the high boiling point of aroma substances, some of them are dragged into the liquor with the distillation of ethanol during distillation, but most of them remain in the fermented grains.

For example, pyruvic acid, which is not easily carried out during distillation (boiling point 165°C), is fermented in the cellar with acetaldehyde to produce acetoin, which is further transformed into diacetyl and 2,3-butanediol, resulting in more α-diketone compounds in the fermented grains.

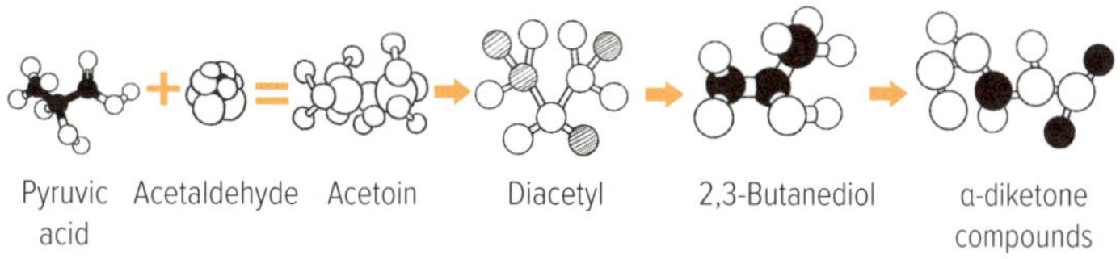

The distilling of strong-aroma flavor baijiu is based on the unique process of "adding more materials to fermented grains," in which 1/4 of the old fermented grains are discarded each time, and 3/4 of the remaining distilled fermented grains are added to 1/4 of the new grain, which is an infinite cycle of new grain and old fermented grains, year after year.

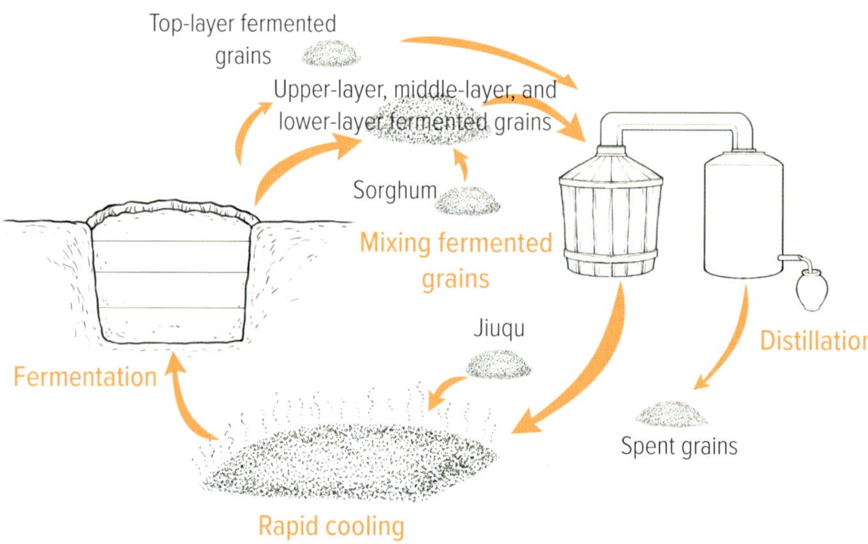

The distilled fermented grains of the previous round are discarded before the next round of fermentation, whether it is light-aroma flavor or soya-sauce-aroma flavor, and there is no such thing as "ten thousand-year fermented grains."

Tips: The sweetness of Luzhou Laojiao is more pronounced than other strong-aroma flavor baijiu because of the use of glutinous red sorghum as the raw grain. More than 95% of glutinous red sorghum is rich in amylopectin, which contains glucose units in a reticulated structure that locks in water molecules and facilitates fermentation by microorganisms to produce liquor.

3. Low-temperature Fermentation

Scientific research has found that the production of sweet substances such as glycerol, propanetriol, and cyclohexane hexanol is closely related to the cellar temperature.

Cellar temperature below 15°C: relatively mellow and sweet, but the aroma is a little lighter

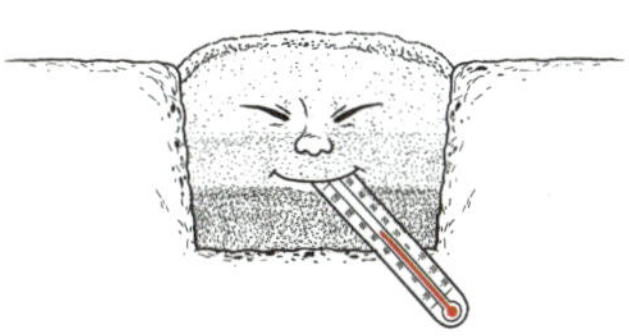

Cellar temperature 15°C–20°C: aroma thickening and mellow sweet still good

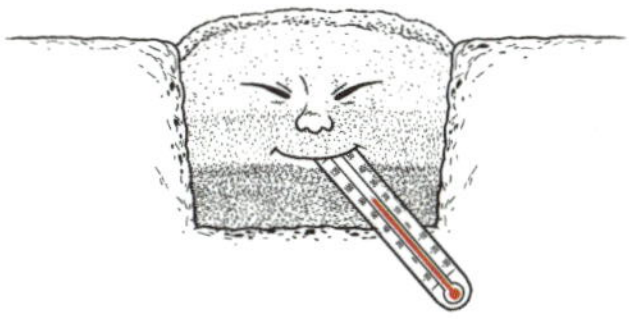

Cellar temperature 20°C–25°C: more aromatic, mellow, and sweet

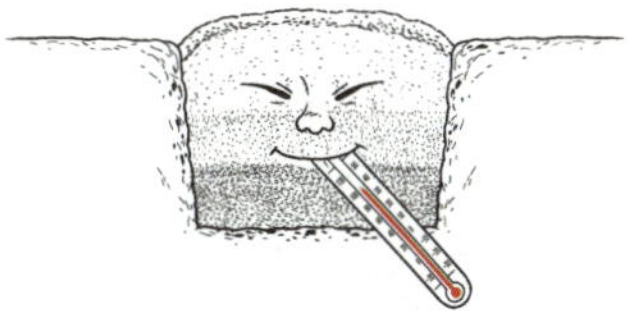

Cellar temperature 25°C or more: the aroma is not very stable, lacks mellowness, sweetness and has some miscellaneous flavors

Different flavors of baijius have different requirements for the cellar temperature.

Strong-aroma flavor Light-aroma flavor Soya-sauce-aroma flavor

Since the cellar temperature is affected by the seasons, strong-aroma flavor baijiu is adjusted according to different seasons.

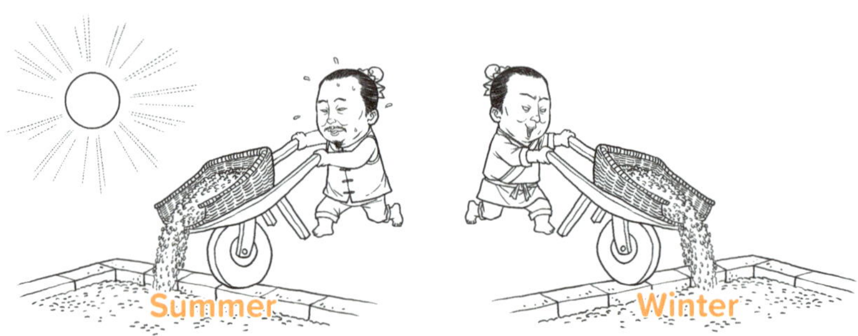

Cellar temperature: flat ground temperature or below ground temperature 1°C–2°C

Cellar temperature: 18°C–20°C

This is why "sweet liquor in winter and fragrant liquor in summer."

4. Long Fermentation Period

The formation of glycerin is slow, mainly in the fermentation period of 60–90 days.

Strong-aroma flavor	Soya-sauce-aroma flavor	Light-aroma flavor	Rice-aroma flavor
≥ 90 days	30 days per round (7 times a year)	28 days or so	7–15 days

The fermentation period for light-aroma flavor, soya-sauce-aroma flavor, and rice-aroma flavor baijius is so short that distillation begins before the sweet substances are produced in large quantities!

It is worth noting that it is not the case that the longer the fermentation period, the sweeter it is. Glycerin is not produced indefinitely during the fermentation process; it accumulates to a certain level and then does not continue to increase.

Case 2: Sweetening by Distillation

Staged Collecting of Liquor

Since sweet substances have a high boiling point, liquor with a strong sweetness is generally concentrated on distillation, so only slow distillation is more conducive to collecting sweet substances into the liquor.

Unlike other-flavor baijius, strong-aroma flavor baijius are distilled slowly, and the quality of the baijiu is picked. After distillation, the crude baijiu is stored separately according to different styles and in separate jars.

Case 3: Sweetening by Blending

1. Pottery Jar Storage

Chinese liquors are stored in pottery jars.

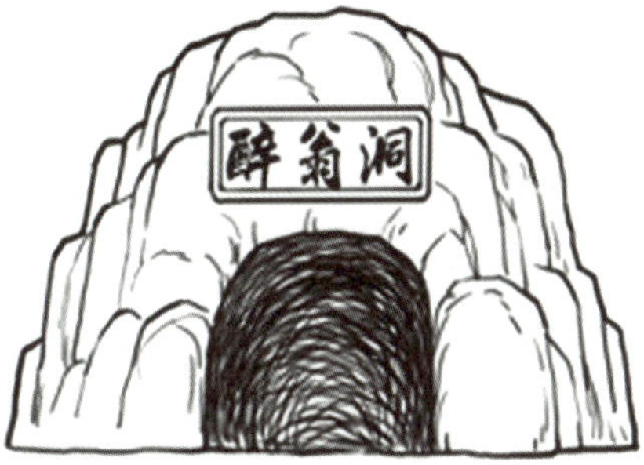

Natural liquor cave

Pottery jar

When a pottery jar is fired at a high temperature, the organic matter contained in the clay is burned off, and the gas is removed to form tiny pores.

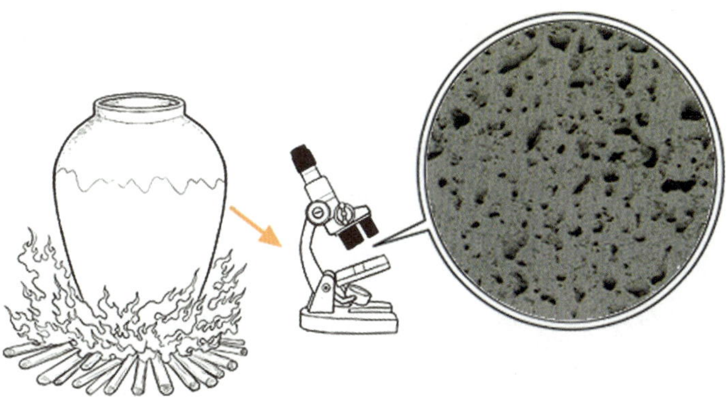

A microscope magnified 100,000 times reveals a large number of tiny pores in the wall of the pottery jar!

The micro-pores are invisible to the naked eye and are the channels through which the liquor body breathes with the outside world. Respiration serves two purposes:

Exhale: Some of the low boiling point components (aldehydes) and sulfides in new liquor are exhaled through the channels of exchange, slowly evaporating and reducing the unpleasant odor in the liquor, which can highlight the sweetness.

Inhale: Outside air enters the liquor body through micro-pores, prompting oxidation and esterification, such as the action of acetaldehyde and acetic acid phases, which produce diacetyl through condensation, increasing the relative sweetness and making the liquor taste more rounded.

As the storage time increases, the organic acid content increases to promote the sweetness of the liquor.

2. Baijiu Blending

Baijiu blending pays attention to the five flavors of sweet, sour, bitter, spicy, and salty. It doesn't work without sweetness, but it is also not all about sweetness. Normal taste, in addition to good coordination, also pays attention to the following:

Strong-aroma flavor baijiu with the preceding fixed quality picking, sub-jar storage of the base, in the blending process, usually divides the prominent quality baijiu used for blending according to the level of sweetness into a number of levels:

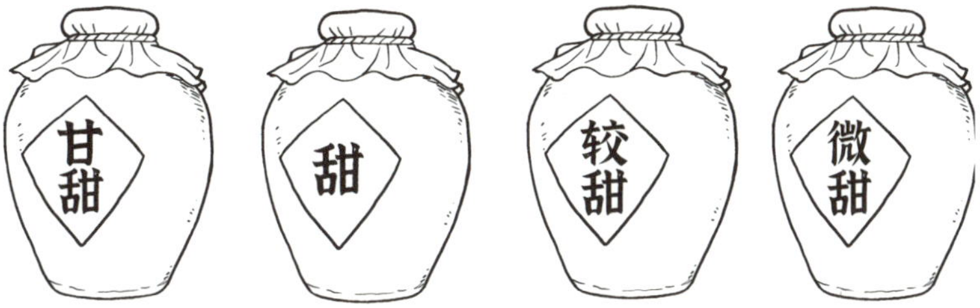

Very sweet　　Sweet　　Relatively sweet　　Slightly sweet

Tips: In the blending process, such as the occurrence of first sweet and then bitter (i.e., in mouth sweet aftertaste bitter), first bitter and then sweet, sweet in the middle of the tongue, sweet to cloying and sweetness for a long time, sweetness is too heavy, etc., are not very good.

From the blending of the body of baijiu, the sweetness of liquor is affected by the interplay of a variety of factors, which have a multiplier effect on the aroma, so after completing the blending, it needs to be stored for a month to check the quality before the enlarged sample production.

By the way, the "sweetness" of Luzhou Laojiao was analyzed more systematically, mainly by analyzing the sensory and flavor components of Luzhou Laojiao, in order to find the characteristic components of its sweetness.

The sweetness of Luzhou Laojiao liquor is mainly reflected in its soft, mellow, and refreshing sensation of baijiu, in the mouthfeel of the liquor, which leaves a long aftertaste and sweetness in the mouth, refreshing the heart and soul, with a crisp or clean feeling. This feeling is called "sweet and cool."

The polyol content and total sweetness of Luzhou Laojiao are higher than that of its competitors, which is an important reason for the sweetness of the liquor.

In short, the sweetness in liquor is not only the presence of its own substance, but also the result of the coordination of all the flavors. As long as the formula is right, the proportion of coordination is to be called good liquor!

What is good about strong-aroma flavor baijiu besides its sweetness?
More likeable!
國窖
1573

CHAPTER 19

Why Do Some Foreign Liquors Go to the Head More Easily Than Baijius?

Many people have had this experience: drinking and drinking, you cannot stop.

In fact, blackout drunk is not terrible. The terrible thing is to wake up the next day. There are a bunch of people to help you remember ...

"Blackout drunk" has always been a hot word in liquor circles.

Drunkenness is actually a common occurrence, but many people get drunk and have a splitting headache.

Especially in American dramas, you can see the handsome hero shaking his glass of liquor one second, emitting a cold charm in the night.

The next second ...

Don't think it's okay if you are handsome; the special lady never favors the handsome guy.

In life, there are indeed cases of drinking that go to the head, but many people reflect that drinking foreign liquor more easily goes to the head than baijiu.

In the following, we will talk about why foreign liquor is more likely to "go to the head." But to clarify this issue, we must first understand ...

Part 1. What Is "Go to the Head"?

First of all, let's look at what's in foreign liquor.

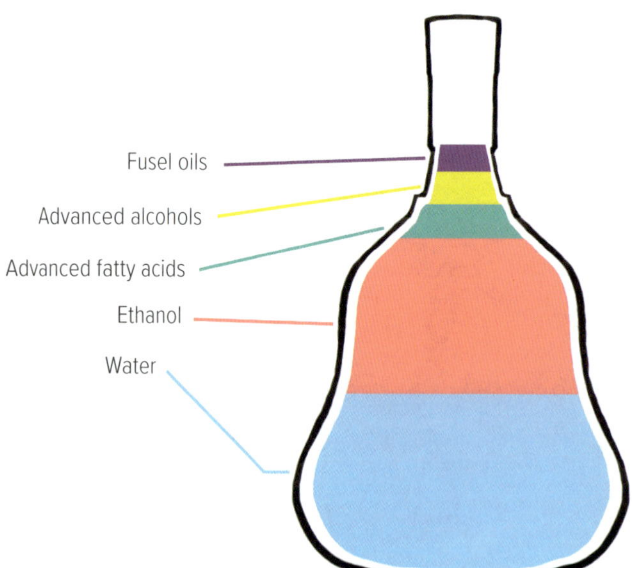

In short, many things cause drunkenness, and fusel oils contribute the most to the drunkenness caused by foreign liquor.

Tips: Fusel oils are advanced alcohols other than methanol and ethanol, which are inevitable byproducts of the fermentation process.

But, then again, fusel oil is not all bad. It has two sides: On the one hand, it can give the liquor a special flavor, and set off the ester aroma, making the aroma more perfect; on the other hand, it is also the culprit of "going to the head."

When a glass of liquor enters the body, it first enters the stomach through the mouth.

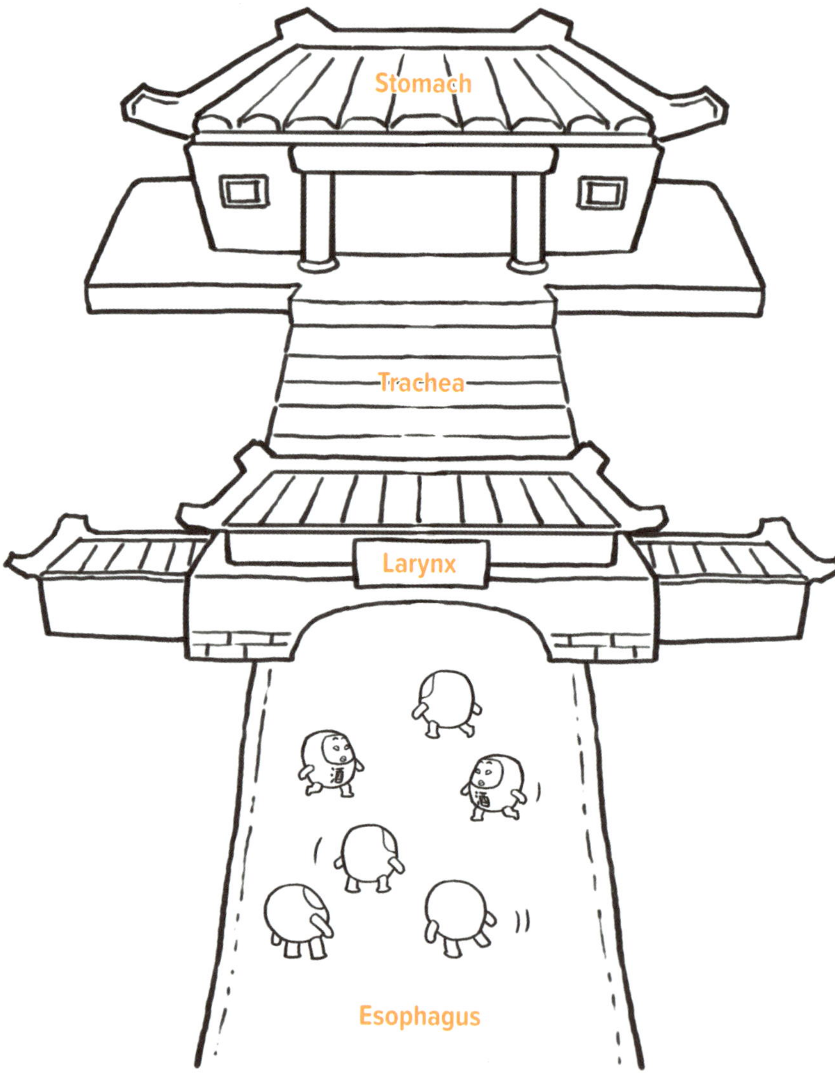

Then it penetrates the blood vessels.

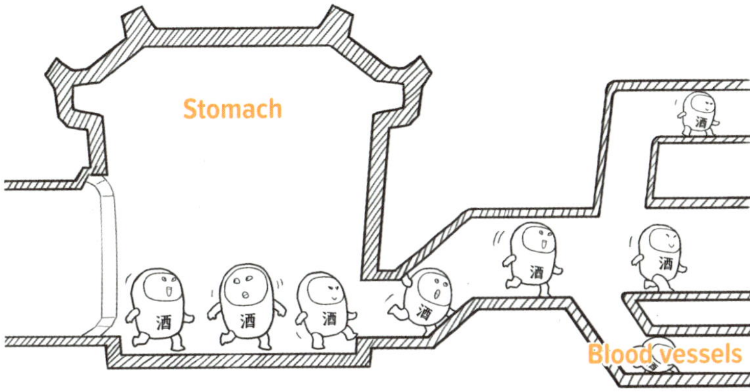

The next door "neighbor" (liver) starts to break down the ethanol and acetaldehyde in the blood vessels through the enzymes it constantly provides.

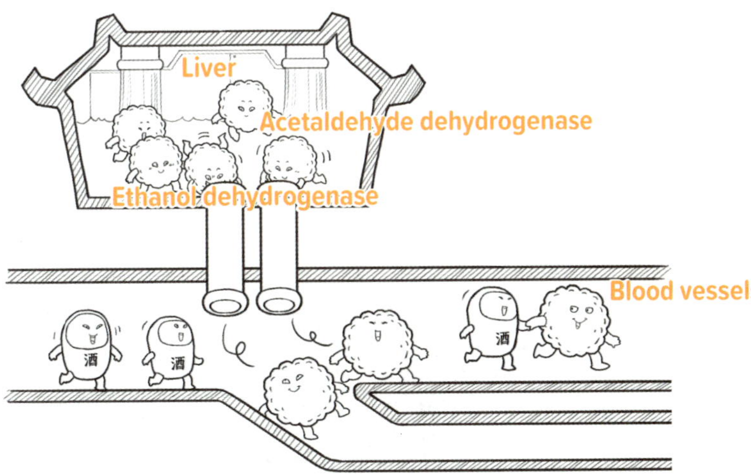

In this way, ethanol is transformed into acetaldehyde, acetic acid, and eventually water and carbon dioxide, and is happily excreted.

The body's permeable tissues refuse to allow the passage of these substances.

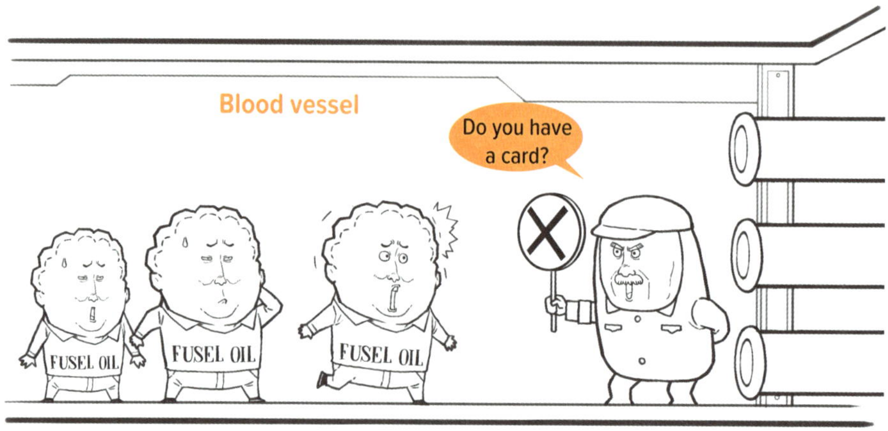

They can only return to the digestive organs by the same route, and then go to the head.

On the one hand, fusel oil has a vasoconstrictive effect, which causes insufficient blood supply and oxygen supply to the brain.

On the other hand, fusel oil stimulates the sympathetic nervous system of the body.

Moreover, the decomposition and metabolism of the fusel oil in the body is extremely slow, so many people will have a headache until the next day.

Part 2: Why Is Foreign Liquor More Likely to Go to the Head?

1. Ingredients

Fusel oil is a byproduct of fermentation distilling, and is made from proteins such as leucine and isoleucine that have been degraded.

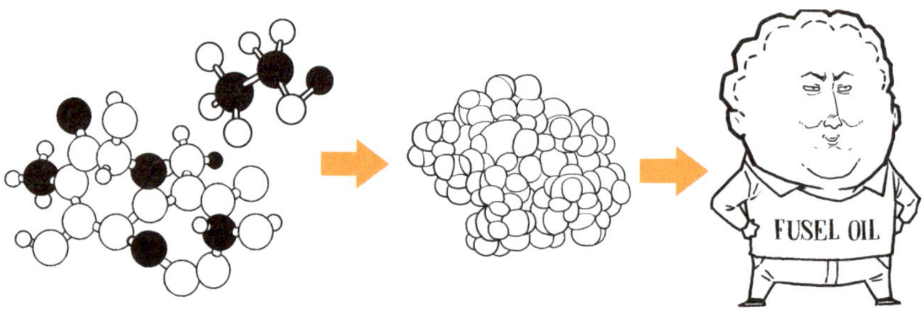

Protein Yeast Fusel oil

Compared to baijiu, the raw materials used in distilling foreign liquor are more random.

Tips: Whiskey is distilled from fermented barley; rum is fermented with sugar cane molasses; brandy is distilled from wine ...

Vodka is more accessible and can be made as long as it can be fermented.

Tips: Some foreign liquors are made from high-purity alcohol diluted and later stored in oak barrels, or with other flavors added ...

Therefore, when there is a lot of protein in the raw material, the amount of fusel oil in the liquor is also high.

2. Process

Unlike baijiu distilling, foreign liquor relies on a single strain of microbial culture, and the process is basically as follows.

Grapes or barley are crushed, and a large amount of water is added.

The liquor is placed in a closed fermenter in liquid form, and pure yeast is added for rapid fermentation.

Tips: Closed liquid fermentation is used in the brandy, whiskey, and other foreign liquor distilling processes, which take the form of liquid into a closed fermented jar, and then pure yeast is added for rapid fermentation.

The key point is that foreign liquor would not be fragrant without fusel oil, and foreign liquor also goes easily to the head because of the high proportion of fusel oil.

Because the single yeast fermentation speed and temperature of foreign liquor rise quickly, starch glycation into ethanol is also fast, but other fats, proteins, and other components cannot keep up with the pace, which will lead to incomplete transformation, resulting in a large amount of fusel oil.

Tips: The time for the liquid fermentation of foreign liquor is only 2–3 days, while the solid-state fermentation time of baijiu is generally 30–90 days, which shows a significant gap that is unmatched by most foreign liquors. Except for whiskey and brandy, gin, vodka, tequila and rum, which do not need to be aged, it takes a few months at most from production to finished liquor for foreign liquors.

Although there are several distillations and purification processes for foreign liquors, the distillation technology alone finds it difficult to remove the fusel oil completely, and its content still far exceeds the "1981 version of the distilled spirits health standards" based on the pure grain solid fermentation distilling process in China.

Tips: Foreign countries do not have a separate test for fusel oil, nor do they have a limit on the amount of fusel oil required; more often than not, the fusel oil is treated as an aromatic component of liquor.

By the way, the liquor is stored in oak barrels, in a closed barrel environment, so it is difficult for the liquor to exchange with the outside world, and it is also difficult to volatilize the fusel oil.

During the WTO (World Trade Organization) negotiations, China's request for a limit on fusel oil was opposed by many liquor producers, who saw it as a trade protection policy.

Your liquor is over the limit of fusel oil!
That's the flavor component!
Your liquor is over the limit of fusel oil!
It is trade protection!
Your liquor is over the limit of fusel oil!
You have no scientific basis!

In the end, the assessment report submitted by China did not provide sufficient scientific justification for a strict limit on the amount of fusel oil in distilled spirits. As a result, the indicator was later removed from the Hygienic Standard for Distilled Liquor and Formulated Liquor (GB2757-1981) released in November, 2006.

In addition to the high content of fusel oil, the use of additional flavors in foreign liquors is also an important reason for its going to the head, which will be briefly mentioned here due to limited space.

Case 1 Edible Alcohol

Among the six distilled spirits, vodka, rum, and gin are typical liquid fermented spirits. They are usually made from sugar or starchy raw materials, and are distilled after fermentation with yeast.

Compared with pure grain alcohol, edible alcohols have more impurities such as aldehydes and alcohols, and are more likely to cause headaches.

Case 2 Flavors and Fragrances

Many people are fascinated by the noble color and rich aroma of foreign liquors.

In fact, fragrances and colors are added to many of them and often after drinking, drinkers will have a headache and dry mouth.

Tips: Especially in bars and nightclubs, a lot of high-priced poor-quality liquors are mixed in. The poor-quality foreign liquor additive is too much, with an imbalanced ratio, often causing an after-drinking headache and a dry mouth.

Part 3 Where Does the Charm of Baijiu Come From?

In contrast, Chinese baijiu is produced in a pure grain solid state, with sorghum and wheat as raw materials, and is fermented in an open environment with the input of solid forms of grains.

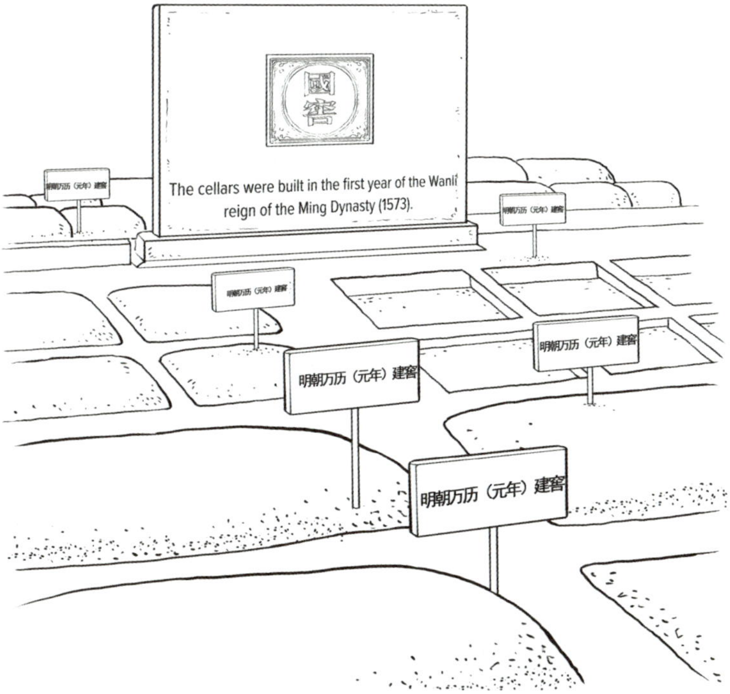

Tips: Scientists have experimented and found that sorghum liquor has the lowest content of fusel oil, followed by grain liquor and corn liquor.

This process makes full use of the underground to keep the temperature constant during fermentation, so that fermentation can proceed slowly at relatively low temperatures, thereby inhibiting the production of fusel oil.

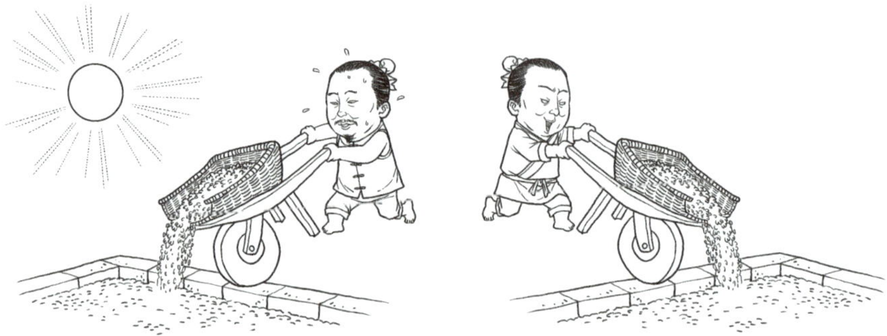

Summer

Cellar temperature: flat ground temperature or below ground temperature 1°C–2°C

Winter

Cellar temperature: 18°C–20°C

At the same time, a large number of different kinds of microorganisms in the cellar mud of the daqu environment will participate in the fermentation process, making the fermentation microorganisms very rich, coordinated, and balanced with each other to control the fermentation rate, thus further inhibiting the production of fusel oil.

In addition, Chinese baijiu storage containers are usually pottery jars.

Natural cave

Pottery jar

When a pottery jar is fired at a high temperature, the organic matter contained in the mud is burned off, and the gases are expelled to form many tiny pores.

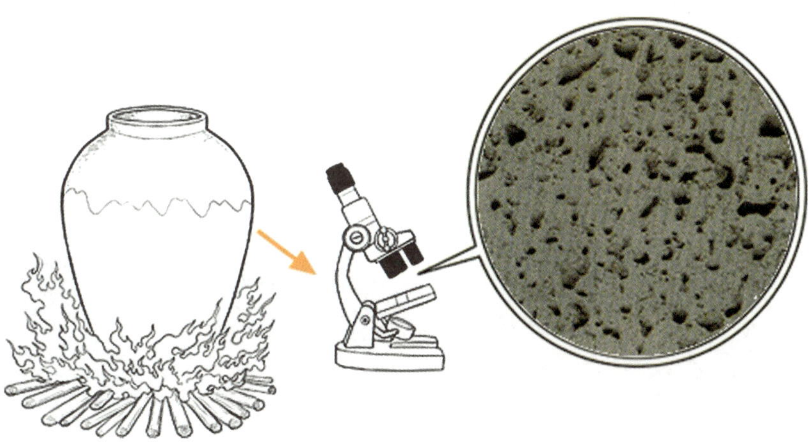

A microscope magnified 100,000 times shows a large number of microscopic pores in the wall of the pottery jar!

The pores are invisible to the naked eye and are the channels through which the liquor breathes with the outside world. Respiration has two functions:

Exhale: Some low boiling point components (aldehydes) and sulfides in new liquor are exhaled through the exchange channels and slowly evaporate.

Inhale: Outside air enters the liquor through the micro-pores, prompting oxidation and esterification.

Aldehydes are continuously oxidized to carboxylic (SUO) acids, while alcohols and aldehydes interact for a long time to generate a small number of esters, producing esters with an aromatic odor, thus mellowing the liquor.

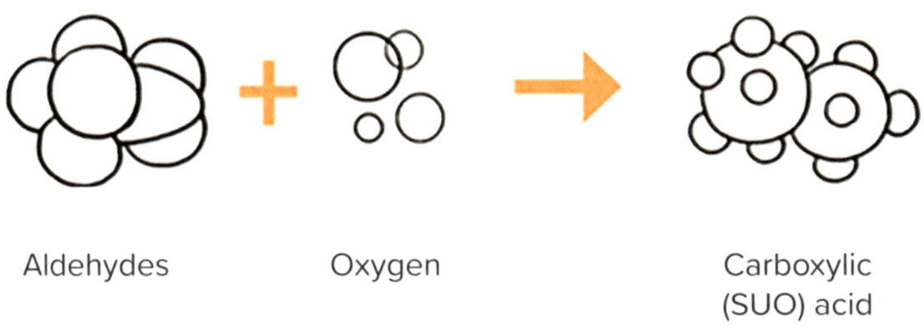

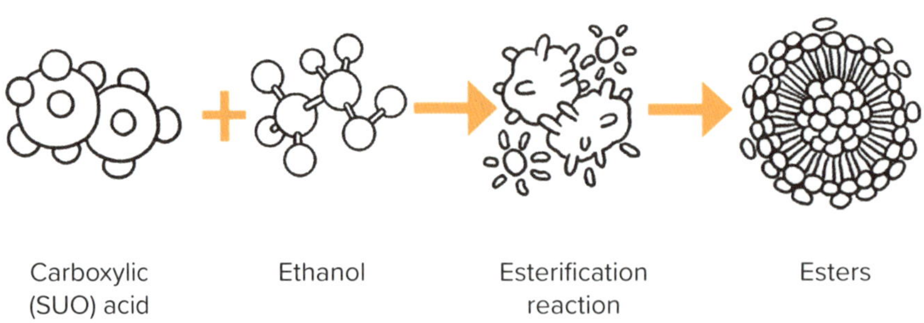

This is the process of how baijiu ages and matures!

Luzhou Laojiao needs to be stored for several years, and the impurities and irritants in the liquor evaporate away. Researchers have done experiments to compare:

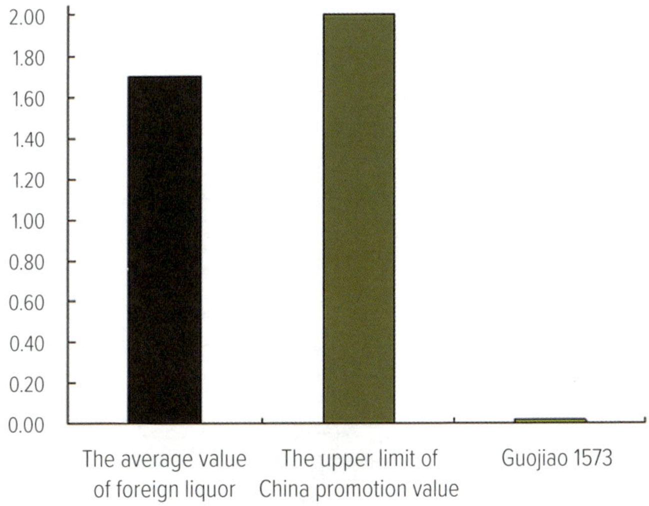

Tips: 0.03 g / 100 ml is the lower limit of the sensitivity of the current instrument. With the current level of technology, we did not detect the content of fusel oil in Guojiao 1573. The content of fusel oil in Guojiao 1573 is six times lower than the average of foreign liquors. This is the fundamental reason why consumers generally perceive that foreign liquors tend to go to the head when they drink too much, while Guojiao 1573 does not go to the head even in excess.

The content of the chart is from Dr. Yuan Han's Postdoctoral Report on Technical Marketing—"Technical Marketing Research Report on Guojiao 1573."

By the way, China's regulations stipulate that the amount of fusel oil in liquor should not exceed 0.2 g / 100 ml. Foreign liquors have an average content close to the upper limit of the regulated value in China, while some even have content of 0.26 g / 100 ml.

Distilled spirits refer to the raw materials containing sugar or starch, distilled by saccharification and fermentation and made from liquor.

Prepared liquor refers to fermented or distilled liquor as the base, prepared by adding edible auxiliary materials.

1. **Sensory indicators:**
   Transparent colorless liquid (prepared liquor can be colored) without precipitation impurities, no odor and taste.
2. **Physicochemical indexes are shown in the following table:**

Item	Indicators
Methanol (g / 100 ml)	
Cereals as raw materials	≤ 0.04
The raw material of the cereals and substitutes	≤ 0.12
Fusel oil g / 100 ml, including isobutanol and isoamyl alcohol	≤ 0.20

The content of the chart is from the national standard of the People's Republic of China.

If you don't have a headache, who would have a headache?

In other words, Chinese baijiu is the distilled spirit with the highest grain consumption rate, the longest distilling cycle, the most complex process, the richest aroma composition, and the fewest impurities in the world. This is precisely why good baijiu doesn't go to the head.

CHAPTER 20

Never Drink More Than You Can Drink—How to Know about the High or Low Tolerance in Drinking?

In the world of adults, there are inevitably various banquets.

A seemingly simple drinking game actually contains a lot of wisdom.

Some people eat meals, and some drink liquor.

Some people make contacts, and some people earn opportunities.

Every glass of liquor you have drunk, every person you have toasted, every sentence after the liquor, is the "naked run" of your character in front of the liquor game.

Zhuge Liang

We can observe people's character through liquor after they get drunk.
—Zhuge Liang, *General Court*

Thus, the boss of wisdom will never let go of such an opportunity to "know people."

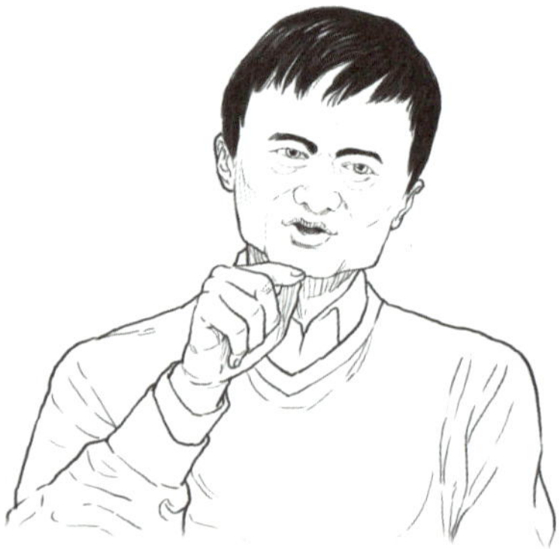

Those who cannot drink but love to show off, and get drunk like mud after three cups, are clowns, so bosses do not use them.

Those who can drink but pretend to be unable to drink, and try to instigate others to drink are insidious and cunning, so bosses do not use them.

Those who can drink, but drink with measure, and do not persuade other people to drink, can be entrusted with important duties.

And as a smart employee, you should cherish the opportunity to participate in a drinking game with the boss.

Have you found that at the same party, some people see the liquor, while some see the party; some people get drunk after a glass, and some are not drunk after a thousand glasses?

The most exquisite thing about baijiu is that it does not disguise itself. Before each drinking game, in addition to the need for a self "liquor test," one also needs to know each other's drinking capacity!

So, what are the factors that determine a person's drinking capacity?

1. Genetic Gene (G)

(Influence index 75%, determines a person's basic alcohol intake)

A glass of liquor enters the body: 5% is discharged through breathing, 5% is discharged through urine, and the remaining 90% has to be disposed of by the liver. The process is as follows:

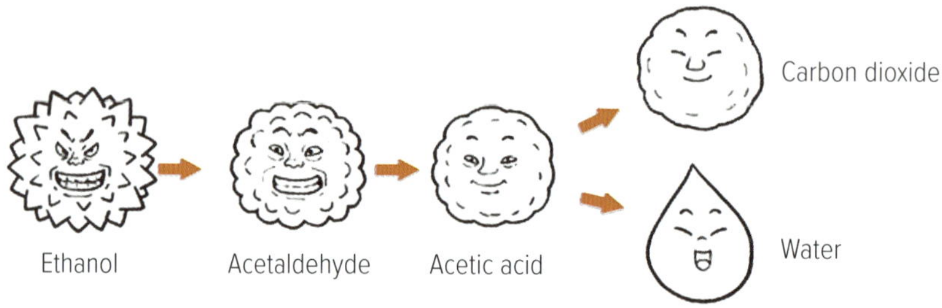

The process of turning ethanol into acetaldehyde, and then acetaldehyde into acetic acid, does not happen for no reason and requires two enzymes.

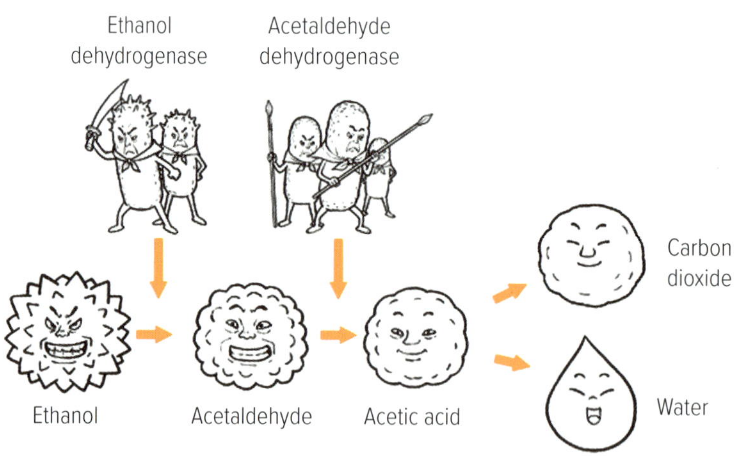

Ethanol dehydrogenase first breaks down the ethanol in liquor into acetaldehyde, broken down by acetaldehyde dehydrogenase into acetic acid, and is finally metabolized and excreted from the body.

Therefore, the amount of these two enzymes determines to a large extent the drinking capacity of a person.

And the content of these two enzymes is mainly determined by genetics.

Therefore, the drinking capacity cannot be practiced, but only the tolerance to "drunkenness" and the control of willpower can be gained in practice.

According to the content of the two enzymes in the body, people can be divided into four categories.

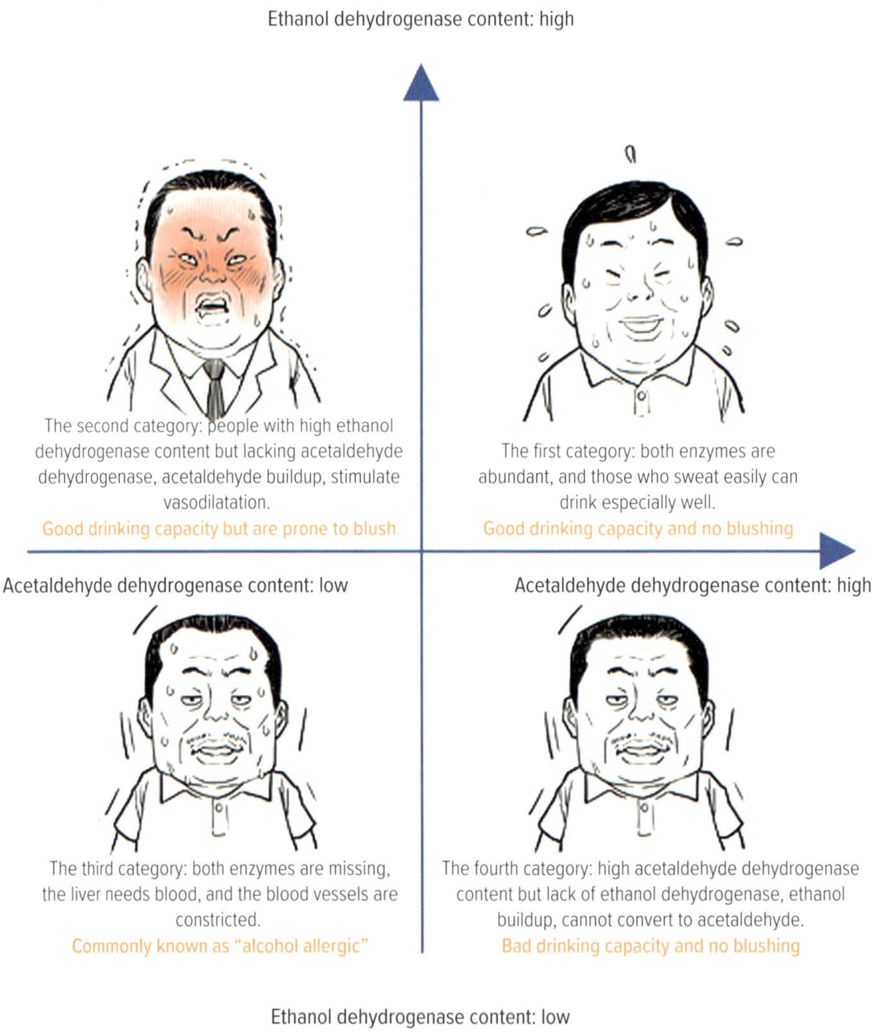

Four-Quadrant Diagram of the Relationship between the Drinking Capacity and Blushing

The first category: Both enzymes are very powerful, these people drink a lot and do not blush (commonly known as "not on the face"), and those particularly prone to sweating are especially good at drinking.

The second category: High content of ethanol dehydrogenase and low content of acetaldehyde dehydrogenase; after drinking alcohol, the ethanol in the body can be quickly decomposed into acetaldehyde, but acetaldehyde cannot be quickly decomposed, resulting in the accumulation of acetaldehyde, stimulating capillary dilation, so the reaction is a red face. This category of people drink "on the face" but have a considerable drinking capacity.

The third category: Both enzymes are missing, and when they drink, they get a red face and even have skin allergies; this group belongs to alcohol allergic body type.

The fourth category: Acetaldehyde dehydrogenase content is high, but there is a lack of ethanol dehydrogenase, so ethanol cannot be quickly and effectively decomposed. Therefore, although these people do not drink to the face, their drinking capacity is bad.

So, people who drink "on their faces" are not necessarily bad drinkers, and people who don't drink on their faces are not necessarily good drinkers.

Therefore, when you meet the fourth category of people, do not persuade them into drinking, neither do that to the first category of people, and you know the consequences!

According to the laws of human genetics, as far as alcohol consumption is concerned, in general:

Southerners < Northerners

Easterners < Westerners

If you encounter a Russian uncle, just surrender!

2. Physical Health (H)

(Influence index 15%)

For the same person, physical fitness and health affect the drinking capacity.

When sick and weak < When healthy

Old age < Young adulthood

Average person < Strong person

3. Liquor Quality (Q)

(Influence index 15%)

The basic requirements for describing a good liquor are no headache, no stinging in the throat, and slow to get drunk and quick to wake up after drinking. Therefore, if good liquor is swallowed smoothly, it will naturally enhance the drinking capacity.

On the other hand, if you drink bad liquor, your body will naturally reduce the amount of alcohol you drink out of self-protection, and it will also ruin the mood of the drinker.

4. Friend (F), Mood, Atmosphere, etc.

(Influence index 15%)

When people are in the mood, every word they say, the poem they recite, song, or dance they do will increase the amount of alcohol they drink.

On the other hand, if we do not have anything in common at the banquet, we will have less fun when we drink.

5. Drinking Time (T)

(Influence index 5%)

The longer the drinking time, the longer the time given to the body to detoxify the alcohol, resulting in a natural increase in alcohol consumption.

Therefore, some people cannot drink in a hurry, but they can drink "mianjiu" (in Sichuan dialect, meaning long drinking time) for thousands of cups of liquor.

Based on the above analysis, we can calculate the formula for one's drinking capacity in a certain drinking game:

Volume Σ = base volume × variation factor R × physical health (1±15%) × quality of the liquor (1±15%) × atmosphere of the drinker (1±15%) × drink time (1±5%)

The formula is simplified as follows:

$\Sigma = Bac \times R \times \{H(1\pm15\%) \times Q(1\pm15\%) \times F(1\pm15\%) \times T(1\pm5\%)\}$

Tips: Bac is the base volume of alcohol, with an index of influence of 75%, and R is the variable coefficient: The factors of the living environment, eating habits, and volitional control over drunkenness, with an index of influence of 25%, and H, Q, F, and T are the variables of physical health, the quality of alcohol, the object of the drinking, the atmosphere of the scene, and the length of time for the drinking.

Depending on how much alcohol we drink, we classify drinking into five states: nourishing, slightly intoxicated, slightly drunk, heavily intoxicated, and dead drunk.

Nourishing: to persevere

Slightly drunk: to feel something

Slightly intoxicated: feeling something great

Heavily intoxicated: needing help

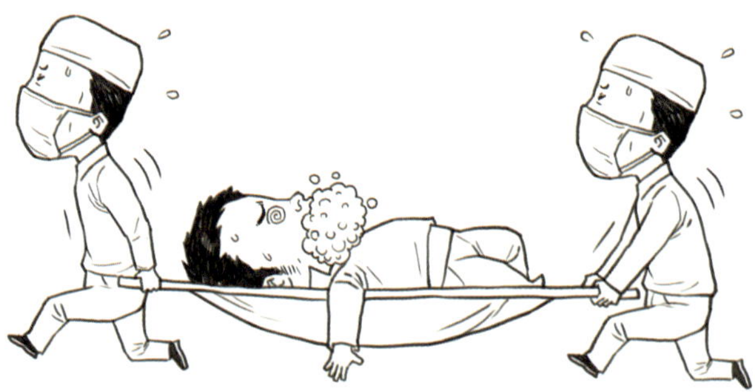

Dead drunk: need to be carried

Tips: Usually, it is good to be slightly drunk; when you have a big drinking game, it is better to control oneself between being slightly intoxicated and heavily intoxicated, but not to be dead drunk. This is not only the upper limit, but also the bottom line.

When socializing, let your leaders and friends drink pleasantly without falling down, and control the time to get drunk and the best degree of drunkenness. This is not only an ability, but also wisdom.

Zhou Henggang, a famous baijiu titan, gave himself the pen name "wuliangjiutu"; when people asked the meaning, Zhou replied:

When I meet my friends and drink freely, "Wuliang" means "large capacity"; when I feel that my health is not good, or really do not have the desire to drink, "Wuliang" means "no capacity."

Zhou Henggang, a master of baijiu

Different levels of ethanol in the blood will present different states!

10 mg / 100 ml: The mood starts to relax and becomes outgoing.

30 mg / 100 ml: Further decrease in vision, the alertness and responsiveness begin to diminish.

50 mg / 100 ml: Vision worsens and hearing starts to be affected to the extent that speed cannot be judged correctly.

80 mg / 100 ml: Inability to concentrate, the vision is only 1/4 of normal, reaction time is 30% to 50% longer than normal, and a loss of balance begins.

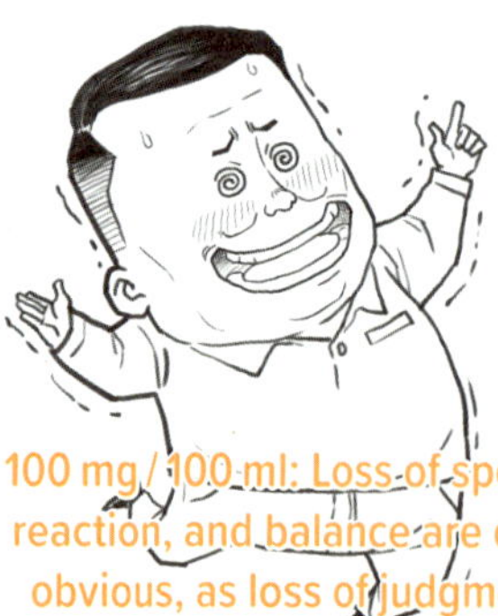

100 mg / 100 ml: Loss of speech, reaction, and balance are quite obvious, as loss of judgment.

200 mg / 100 ml: Loss of ability to move. There may also be an attempt to eliminate alcohol from the stomach by vomiting and muscle relaxation.

Many say they drink to the point of unconsciousness, which is too dangerous. In fact, when you have blurred vision, slow reactions, or even the inability to walk normally, it means that you are already drunk.

According to the "Blood and Breath Alcohol Content Threshold and Test for Vehicle Drivers":

So, the question arises, how do you calculate the blood alcohol content?

According to Swedish chemist Erik M. P. Widmark:

$$\text{Blood alcohol content (mg/100ml)} = \frac{\text{Amount of alcohol consumed (g)}}{\text{Weight of drinker (kg)}\ \ \text{Coefficient r}} \times 100$$

Amount of alcohol consumed (g) = Amount of alcohol consumed (m) × Alcohol content % × 0.8 (g)

Erik M. P. Widmark, a Swedish chemist

The coefficient r is usually set at 0.75, but for more accuracy, the following values can be used:

Men: 0.68 to 0.70

Women or young men: 0.55–0.60

Infants and children: 0.75–0.80

Having said all these, do you know the other person's drinking capacity?

Postscript: Why Is the Strong-Aroma Flavor Baijiu Peerless in Smell?

The birth of the earth and life on earth is a very small probability event, so that some scientists predict that if the average temperature of the earth rises 3.5°C, life on earth will cease to exist. One day, when the light-sensitive substances of plants accidentally infected the genes of animals, the eyes of animals gradually evolved, and so today, humans have eyes to discover light. Similarly, liquor was born from a very small probability event—when a ripe fruit from a tree fell into a puddle. Under the influence of the right temperature, humidity, and microbial enzymes, the first puddle of wine on earth was born. Therefore, Jiang Tong of the Jin Dynasty, who made *Wine Letters*, wrote: "There is rice that is not exhausted, the commission is retained empty mulberry, which is depressed into the taste, with a long-stored gas fragrance, so the original came out of this, not by a strange formula." So, who was the inventor of liquor? It was not Yidi, nor Dukang; it was nature, it was a gift from the heavens. To be precise, it was the man who "discovered" liquor, not "invented" liquor.

1. Revere to the Universe, Distill in Natural Way

Therefore, the really smart liquor makers know how to follow nature, so that "heaven and earth are born with me, and everything is one with me," to achieve the "unity of heaven and earth," the realm of revering to the universe, and distilling in natural way. This is also Luzhou Laojiao's corporate philosophy of "distilling with heaven and earth, coexistence on earth."

The three basic flavors of Chinese baijiu in the solid-state fermentation: light aroma, strong aroma, and soya-sauce aroma, are the result of our ancestors' wisdom and natural climatic conditions in the regions, the unity of heaven, earth, and man, using the natural method. The three flavors (although there are currently twelve flavors of Chinese baijiu, all other flavors are based on these three flavors, just as the colorful world is based on the three primary colors of red, yellow, and blue) processes represent the climatic characteristics of the Yellow River Basin, the Yangtze River Basin and their tributaries, the Chishui River Basin, and the characteristics of farming civilization. This is the optimal choice of the ancestors to make good liquor in response to the local climate.

Fenjiu represents light-aroma flavor baijiu. The process characteristics of "fermenting in the underground vat, steaming grains and distilling liquor separately, and separate steaming in two rounds" is the result of the climatic characteristics of the Yellow River Basin, where there are many droughts in the north, and the ground is prone to water seepage. Therefore, underground vats are used as fermentation containers. In the Yellow River Basin, the winter is cold, making it difficult for some microorganisms to survive in the winter, so the diversity and complexity of microorganisms are less than that of the strong-aroma flavor and soya-sauce-aroma flavor baijius, which creates the taste characteristics of "pure aroma, mellow, sweet and soft, with a clean and crisp finish" of the baijiu body.

Luzhou Laojiao represents strong-aroma flavor baijiu, which is the representative of liquor culture in the Yangtze River Basin. The cellar is built with local unique yellow mud. Because microorganisms can multiply in the cracks of the mud cellar, the longer the time, the more abundant the microorganisms, and the more fragrant the liquor. In Luzhou in 1573, Shu Chengzong, the "ancestor of the Guojiao," appeared to accidentally "use local materials" but instead achieved the legend of "national living cultural relics." At the same time, with the process of "adding more materials to fermented grains," microorganisms and flavor materials exist harmoniously, forming the unique process characteristics of the "thousand-year cellars and ten thousand-year fermented grains" of strong-aroma flavor baijiu and the taste characteristics of "intense aroma, smooth and mellow, and harmonious flavor" of the baijiu body.

Soya-sauce-aroma flavor, represented by Maotai, is the result of the combination of the micro-ecological environment of the Chishui River Basin and the unique high-temperature fermentation process. With the characteristics of twice-feeding grain, nine times steaming, eight times fermenting with qu, and seven times taking liquor, it has created the taste characteristics of "outstanding soya-sauce aroma, elegant and delicate, leaving fragrance in the empty cup, lasting aftertaste, soft and mellow in the mouth."

Because of the hard texture of the underground vat (pottery jar), stone cellar, where there is no space for microorganisms to live, they will not become a breeding ground for microorganisms; therefore, whether in terms of process quality or cultural value, or heritage value, the light-aroma flavor baijiu's underground vat, soya-sauce-aroma flavor baijiu's stone cellar is not as rare and precious as the strong-aroma flavor's mud cellar (especially refers to the old cellars for continuous uninterrupted use more than 30 years old) and is rich in heritage significance, which is the reason why so far the stone cellar has not been rated as a "national treasure of cultural relics."

2. Why Is the Strong-Aroma Flavor Baijiu Peerless in Smell?

Have you ever thought, when we say the three basic flavors, often without thinking out loud "strong aroma, light aroma, soya-sauce aroma" rather than "light aroma, strong aroma, soya-sauce aroma" or "soya-sauce aroma, strong aroma, light aroma" and so on, why?

In 1952, the First National Liquor Evaluation Conference was held in Beijing under the personal supervision of Premier Zhou Enlai in order to promote the recovery and development of the Chinese baijiu industry. Since the theory of baijiu was not mature enough at that time, the organizers required that the liquors to be in the conference must have "a long history, a high reputation at home and abroad, and be not only distributed nationwide but also exported." After fierce competition, Maotai, Luzhou Laojiao, Fenjiu, and Xifeng Liquor eventually emerged as China's earliest "Four Great Baijius." In the 1960s, the industry referred to baijius with similar characteristics and techniques to Maotai as "Mao-aroma" and those with similar characteristics and techniques as Luzhou Laojiao as "Lu-aroma," those with similar flavors and techniques to those of Fenjiu as "Fen-aroma," and Xifeng Liquor as "Feng-aroma."

Note that at this time, the concepts and theories of "strong aroma," "light aroma," and "soya-sauce aroma" had not yet been fully developed until 1979, more than 20 years later, when Zhou Henggang, a leading baijiu expert, presided over the Third National Liquor Evaluation Conference.

After the first selection in 1952, in order to quickly improve the quality and production capacity of liquor, the state organized a group of experts to identify and pilot the three representative baijius' baijiu-distilling processes—Luzhou Laojiao, Maotai, and Fenjiu, respectively, and to summarize them scientifically so that they could be popularized nationwide as soon as possible. According to the Visionary Plan for Scientific and

Technological Development 1956–1967, which was deployed by Premier Zhou Enlai, the distilling process of Luzhou Laojiao Daqu was included as a key topic for research.

From October 1957 to April 1958, 62 technicians from 16 units, including Sichuan Sugar and Wine Industry Research Office (now Sichuan Food Fermentation Industry Research and Design Institute) and Sichuan Monopoly Company, resided at Luzhou Laojiao, led by experts such as Chen Maochun and Xiong Zishu, to conduct a comprehensive review of the baijiu-distilling process of Luzhou Laojiao. This pilot started the prelude to the three major pilots of Chinese baijiu.

The theoretical and practical results of the three pilots were quickly disseminated to baijiu companies nationwide. The three companies sent not only theoretical knowledge, process operation techniques, and expert teams to major national distilleries, but also brands and categories, such as "Laojiao," "Tequ," and "Touqu," which are still used as brand names today. At that time, there was almost no concept of market competition, not to mention the awareness of brand protection.

So, we saw the "Baoshan Maotai" from Dongguan Baoshan, Guangdong, "Mulan Fenjiu" and "Longbin Fenjiu" from Heilongjiang, and "Ningcheng Laojiao" from Liaoning, "Hetao Laojiao" from Inner Mongolia, and so on. I believe that at this time, "Maotai" or "Fenjiu" was not actually a brand concept, but the concept of category or flavor. When some were called "× × Maotai," the "Mao-aroma" process was used, and so on; all named "× × Fenjiu" were made by the "Fen-aroma" process, and all named after "Laojiao" were actually made by the "Lu-aroma" process. The name "Laojiao" is actually short for "Luzhou Laojiao," which is a relatively weak identifier of the place, and some distilleries still continue to use it today.

Of course, Luzhou Laojiao was at the forefront of the process of popularizing the distilling process throughout the country, with the least conservative and studious, and it undoubtedly made the greatest contribution. Looking through history, there is no shortage of similar written accounts.

"In 1953, the Luzhou Laojiao Company, with its strong scientific and technological force, sent Luzhou distilling technicians such as Zhang Fucheng to help rebuild the cellars of Yibin's miscellaneous grain liquor (the predecessor of Wuliangye) and teach Yibin's distilling workers the process of distilling strong-aroma flavor baijiu, thus restoring the production of Wuliangye, which had stopped before the founding of New China. After the 1960s, more than 20 training courses on distilling technology, tasting and blending, flavoring and physical and chemical testing, and factory management were held for the distilling industry, training thousands of people in distilling technology and business management, and spreading the craft of strong-aroma flavor baijiu throughout the country and distilling Luzhou Laojiao Daqu famous throughout the world" ("Contemporary Sichuan Series" Editorial Department, *Luzhou, the City of Baijiu,* Sichuan People's Publishing House, 2000).

Through the efforts of generations of Luzhou Laojiao distillers, the strong-aroma process spread throughout the country and formed the pattern of "world of strong aroma."

In 1963, Luzhou Laojiao, Wuliangye, Quanxing Daqu, and Gujing Gongjiu were selected as "China's Famous Baijius" at the Second National Liquor Evaluation Conference, and half of the "Eight Famous Baijius" was made up of strong-aroma flavor baijiu.

In 1979, at the Third National Liquor Evaluation Conference, Luzhou Laojiao, Wuliangye, Gujing Gongjiu, Yanghe, and Jiannanchun were selected as one of the "Famous Chinese Baijius," and five of the "Eight Famous Baijius" were strong-aroma flavors. It was also at this session that experts formally established the concept of "strong aroma," "light aroma," and "soya-sauce aroma" based on the process and flavor characteristics of several famous baijius, plus the rice-aroma flavor baijiu of rice as a raw material represented by the Guilin Sanhuajiu. The earliest of the "Four Great Flavors" of Chinese baijiu came from this.

As the representative of "strong-aroma flavor," Luzhou Laojiao has thus established the industry position as the "ancestor of strong-aroma flavor, the leader of baijiu" and the "standard of strong-aroma flavor." Ten years later, in 1989, Luzhou Laojiao Tequ was awarded "China's Famous Baijiu" for five consecutive years. In order to reflect on the meaning of "standard," Luzhou Laojiao changed the "square bottle" of the 1980s to a "knife-shaped coin" bottle, expressing the meaning of "standard" through the appearance of the "knife coins and cloth coins" and the label of the Qin and Han Dynasties. In the same year, Zhou Henggang, an expert in the baijiu industry, inscribed the four words "Nong Xiang Zheng Zong" (authentic strong-aroma flavor baijiu) for Luzhou Laojiao to correct some of the industry's communication chaos at the time.

Since then, in 1984 and 1989, the strong-aroma flavor baijiu has gained no less than 50% of the seats in the National Famous Liquor Awards.

Between the 1960s and the 1980s, distilleries from Sichuan, Shaanxi, Yunnan, Henan, Anhui, Hubei, Liaoning, Jiangsu, Guangxi, and Gansu provinces visited Luzhou Laojiao to learn about baijiu-distilling techniques. Luzhou Laojiao held 27 distilling technology training courses and trained thousands of distilling technicians, blenders and core technical cadres for distilleries in more than 20 provinces and cities, which promoted the technological progress of Chinese baijiu and the development of strong-aroma flavor baijiu, and the pattern of "world of strong aroma" of Chinese baijiu took shape quietly.

Lai Gaohuai, the former chief engineer of Luzhou Laojiao and the first Chinese master distiller, wrote in his book *60 Years of China's Baijiu Review and Prospects (1951–2011)*:

> "During the period from 1978 to 1984, training courses for distilling technical personnel were held in Luzhou, with more than 50 times training of more than 4,000 trainees, training a large number of talents for liquor enterprises and scientific research units across the country!
>
> Among the famous distilleries in and outside of Sichuan Province, the trainees include: Sun Songhua, General Foreman of the Gujing Gong Distillery, Guo Yonghong, General Foreman of the Yanghe Distillery, Huang Derun, General Foreman of the Shuanggou Distillery, Zhang Guoqiang, General Foreman of the Anhui Kouzi Distillery, Hao Pingjiao, General Foreman of the Hunan Shaoyang Distillery, Zhang Wuju, General Foreman of the Jilin Yushu Distillery, Xu Zengjia, General Foreman of the Dehui Distillery, Zhang Baoxin, General Foreman of the Liaoyuan Distillery, Han Sufen and Wang Weiping, General Foremen of Hebei Congtai Distillery, Li Yongqing, President of the Heilongjiang Distillery Association, Cao Shufang, General Foreman of the Shenyang Laolongkou Distillery, Jiang Hongxing, President and Shi Weiping, General Foreman of the Hubei Zhijiang Distillery, Tan Huiqing, General Foreman of the Jianshi Distillery, Zou Xianhong, President of the Huangshantou Distillery, Chen Jiajian, General Foreman of the Xiangfan Distillery, Wang Jianxin, General Foreman of the Chongyang Distillery, Zeng Qiande, General Foreman of the Guizhou Xishui Distillery, and Cheng Guoxi, General Foreman of the Henan Dukang Distillery. Technical backbones of distilleries of the Yili Distillery in Xinjiang and the Hetao in Inner Mongolia are also among trainees."

In 2019, China's total baijiu production was 7.985 million kiloliters, of which about 5.527 million kiloliters, or more than 70 percent, were strong-aroma flavors. Among the three mainstream Chinese baijiu flavors of "strong aroma, light aroma, and soya-sauce aroma," the market share of strong-aroma flavor baijiu was more than twice as high as the sum of light-aroma flavor and soya-sauce-aroma flavor baijius.

At this point, you should understand why "strong aroma, light aroma, and soya-sauce aroma" are the order of the day.

Meanwhile, in 2006, Luzhou Laojiao was selected as the first batch of national intangible cultural heritage for the traditional distilling techniques of strong-aroma flavor baijiu, which Fenjiu represents light-aroma flavor baijiu, and Maotai for soya-sauce-aroma flavor baijiu, each with its own "Intangible Cultural Heritage" project number. In 2008, the three companies were selected to the United Nations "Oral and Intangible Cultural Heritage of Humanity" reserve list.

3. 70 Years of Chinese Baijius

From the founding of the People's Republic of China in 1949 to today, more than 70 years have passed since then. We have gone from being a poor and weak country to becoming the second-largest economy in the world and achieving prosperity for all. The Chinese baijiu industry has also gone through a stage of development from a planned quota system to full liberalization of market competition, from expanding production capacity and quality to pursuing high-quality development, and from quality marketing to cultural marketing.

From the 1950s until the late 1980s, Luzhou Laojiao was undoubtedly the first generation of Chinese baijiu domination. In terms of process popularity, as mentioned above, Luzhou Laojiao was known as the "Huangpu of the liquor world" with its thousands of trainees; in terms of production capacity, in 1988, Luzhou Laojiao built the first domestic Luohan distilling ecological park with an annual production capacity of 10,000 tons, while four years later, in 1992, Maotai's production only exceeded 2,000 tons. In terms of sales and profit tax generation, in 1988, Luzhou Laojiao achieved profits and taxes of RMB 100 million yuan, the highest in the country, which was over 30 million more than the sum of the other five golden flowers of Sichuan liquor (including Tuopai Qujiu, which was selected as a famous spirit in 1989 [author's note]). This year, Wuliangye achieved profits and taxes of RMB 22.088 million yuan, and Maotai achieved profits and taxes of RMB 13.91 million yuan.

At the beginning of 1988, the state officially liberalized the price of baijiu, and the price of the famous baijiu went up, but only for less than a year. By the end of the same year, the state issued a policy to limit government consumption and made a "unified price reduction" for 13 kinds of famous liquors. Luzhou Laojiao took the initiative to reduce the prices of its products. The price of Luzhou Laojiao products during this period can be said to have seriously deviated from the height of its quality and brand, thus missing out on the golden decade of "consumer upgrading" in the 1990s.

Each age brings forth new genius from this noble land, and each will rule its own domain for years to come. After that, in 1989, Fenjiu rose to the top of the industry with its production capacity, and was known as "Fen Boss" until 1994, when Wuliangye overtook it, and the Shanxi Shuozhou counterfeit baijiu case gave a fatal blow to Fenjiu in 1998.

In 1994, Wuliangye took over the baton of "industry leader" from Fenjiu and became the third generation of domination. For the Chinese baijiu industry, the 1990s should be said to have been Wuliangye's time, with Wuliangye's revenue and net profit more than four times that of Maotai's in 1998, and Wuliangye's volume still more than twice that of Maotai's in 2005, but Maotai's net profit had taken the lead in 2005. It was not until 2012 that Maotai surpassed Wuliangye in terms of revenue and net profit, and the dominance of the Chinese baijiu industry changed hands again. After a brief adjustment in 2012 and 2013, Maotai took the lead in both stock price and market value, as well as in sales revenue.

List of the Development Paths of Baijiu Companies over the Past 20 Years

Development stage	Status	Industry policy	The situation of baijiu enterprises
Before 1989	Steady development	Emphasis on craftsmanship and baijiu quality, five "National Famous Baijiu" selections	Luzhou Laojiao, Fenjiu, and Wuliangye, expanded production capacity, gained competitive advantage one after another, and price control liberalized.
1989–1992	Industry adjustment, the production growth rate declined.	Restrictions on government consumption and price suppression of famous liquors	Baijiu companies cut prices, with Maotai prices once dropping by more than 50%.
1992–1997	Baijiu companies focused on advertising and marketing developed rapidly.	The industry expanded rapidly as advertising and marketing took hold.	Kongfujiajiu became famous as the CCTV top bidder, and Qinchi became the top bidder twice, but due to the undesirable quality, the top bidder subsequently fell.

Development stage	Status	Industry policy	The situation of baijiu enterprises
1997–2003	The industry went into a winter period, and production dropped sharply.	Industrial policies restricted the development of the baijiu industry.	The Shanxi counterfeit baijiu incident and the Qinchi crude baijiu incident led to an industry crisis; however, at the same time, Quanxing launched Shuijingfang, Luzhou Laojiao launched Guojiao 1573, and Yanghe launched Blue Classic, starting the next golden decade.
2003–2012	During the golden decade, the volume and price of baijiu rose.	The rise in the price of mid-end to high-end baijiu is due to the increase in business and political activities driven by economic activities.	Emerging brands such as Shuijingfang, Guojiao 1573, and Blue Classic were successful and led the revival of the baijiu companies. Maotai overtook Wuliangye as the fourth generation dominant brand after Luzhou Laojiao, Fenjiu, and Wuliangye.
2012–2015	Deep adjustment period, the price decline	Restrictions on public spending on government cars, overseas trips and official receptions, prohibition of alcoholic beverages around the world, overcapacity	The decline in baijiu prices and polarization of baijiu companies.
2015–present	Rapid recovery of the industry, with concentration and differentiation.	Business consumption leads the industry's revival, and the Development and Reform Commission cancels restrictive policies on baijiu, ushering in a period of policy dividends for baijiu.	Brand concentration is rapidly increasing, manifesting itself in the concentration of origins, famous baijius, brands and culture. Maotai, Wulangliu and Guojiao 1573 have been certified as the top three high-end baijius, gaining relative advantages in this round of concentration.

4. The Rediscovery of the Value of Strong Aroma

Due to the benchmarking effect of Maotai, there has been a bit of "soya-sauce-aroma fever" in recent years, but some untrue, even distorted and alienated propaganda for baijiu flavors has also misled consumers. As said in the first part of this book, the three basic flavors of Chinese baijiu are the result of local geography and climate and natural distilling methods, and there are only style differences between them, not high and low; just as "some people love carrots while others love green vegetables," consumers have the right to choose freely after knowing the truth about the process and flavors.

However, as a famous baijiu enterprise of strong-aroma flavor baijiu, it should also reflect on itself. Is the explanation of the complexity inadequate in the public communication of the strong-aroma flavor distilling process? Is its historical value not explored enough? Has its health value not been explored enough?

Because of its unique process of "mud cellar producing fragrance, adding more materials to fermented grains," strong-aroma flavor baijiu requires "thousand-year cellars and ten thousand-year fermented grains," the older the mud cellar, the more microorganisms, the richer the variety, the more fragrant the baijiu made. This is a typical characteristic that distinguishes it from others. Therefore, we have found that among the eleven important heritage sites under state protection in the baijiu industry announced by the State Administration of Cultural Heritage, eight are strong-aroma flavor baijiu enterprises, one is a soya-sauce-aroma flavor enterprise, one is a light-aroma flavor enterprise, and one is qingkejiu (the process is close to light-aroma flavor baijiu). The mud cellar of strong-aroma flavor is the only one that has the economic and historical value of a "living cultural relic."

Compared with the **12987** processes of soya-sauce-aroma flavor (one-year production cycle, two cycles of feeding, nine cycles of steaming, eight cycles of fermentation and addition of qu, and seven cycles of liquor extraction and blending), strong-aroma flavor has a more complex process and more scarce quality baijiu output. In order to summarize the essence of the strong-aroma flavor process and tell the story of strong-aroma flavor baijiu well, we have tried to distill the distilling process characteristics common to all strong-aroma flavor baijiu enterprises into the "516" strong-aroma flavor process recipe. That is:

(1) 5 "fours": four times a year for grain, four times for steaming, four times for bending, four seasons of fermentation (spring, summer, autumn, winter), four times for taking liquor, year after year, week after week.

(2) 1 "infinite cycle," expressed by the symbol "3/4 ∞" (∞ means an infinite cycle, which can be read as "infinite"): the unique process of "adding more materials to fermented grains" of the strong-aroma flavor baijiu, that is, 1/4 of the old fermented grains are discarded each time, and 3/4 of the remaining distilled fermented grains are added to 1/4 of the new grain, which is an infinite cycle of new grain and old fermented grains, year after year. As Zhuangzi said in the chapter of *Zhuangzi · The World*, "One foot-long whip, take half of it every day, inexhaustible for ten thousand years" is a principle. This is the core mystery of strong-aroma flavor baijiu, because no matter light-aroma flavor or soya-sauce-aroma flavor, before starting the next round of fermentation, the distilled fermented grains of the previous round will all be discarded, so there is no aroma inoculation, and the cycle is transmitted from generation to generation.

(3) 6 division process: "6 divisions" means "grain feeding in layers, fermentation in layers, stacking fermented grains in layers, distillation in layers, liquor picking in sections, and jar dividing according to quality." The fermented grains in the mud cellar are divided into top-layer fermented grains and upper-layer, middle layer, and lower-layer fermented grains. Since each layer of fermented grains has a different fermentation state and is treated differently for the next round, workers have to carry out more complicated "layering" operations in grain feeding, stacking fermented grains, fermentation and distillation to ensure fermentation quality. At the same time, it is more important to adopt the principle of "picking the liquor by stage" in the distillation process, the principle of "separate quality and jars" in the storage process, and finally, graded storage and pricing (these operations are more complicated, more precise and more elaborate than those of the soya-sauce-aroma flavor baijiu). Therefore, in the 1960s, Luzhou Laojiao first adopted the term "Tequ," which refers to "Special Grade Baijiu," the equivalent of the "National Quality" quality standard. The term "Touqu" refers to "first-class good qu baijiu" and "Erqu" refers to "second-class good qu baijiu," which is equivalent to the "provincial excellent" standard. We use the letter "P" (abbreviation of the English word "picked") to refer to liquor picking; "x%" refers to the picking rate of high-quality baijiu, and the "x" value depends on the quality level of the crude baijiu, the age of the old cellar and the amount of the workers' operation. The higher the quality level of the crude baijiu, the smaller the "x" value; the older the age of the old cellar, the larger the "x" value, conversely, the younger the cellar age. As Xiong Zishu, a famous liquor expert, wrote in his article "The Origin and Development of China's First Cellar," "Baijiu cellars over 30 years old produce 20% (the crude baijiu that can reach the quality standard of famous baijiu [author's note]), baijiu cellars over 50 years old produce 40%, and baijiu

cellars over 100 years old have a famous liquor rate of 60%; this is the reason why the 'Three Hundred Years Old Cellar' Daqu is particularly famous." (*Liquor-Making Science and Technology*, no. 2, 2001)

Therefore, compared to other-flavor baijius, strong-aroma flavor baijiu's quality liquor rate is lower, and the output of high-end baijiu is also scarce.

The above are the author's thoughts about strong-aroma flavor baijiu: Chinese strong aroma, shared by the world. Chinese baijiu is the essence of China's agricultural civilization, and strong-aroma flavor baijiu can be called the pearl on this crown. It is the gift of heaven and earth, the wisdom of the ancestors, the essence of grain, and the aging of time that makes a cup of strong-aroma flavor baijiu. However, today we do not really tell the story of strong-aroma flavor well, perhaps because we do not really understand it; for example, the "three medial" processes (medium-temperature daqu, medium-temperature fermentation, medium-temperature flow of baijiu) of strong-aroma flavor is precisely the Chinese wisdom of taking the middle ground, and the "six-part" process is the simple dialectic practice and simple marketing philosophy of dividing one into two and turning the whole into parts; for another example, the process of "adding more materials to fermented grains," in which 1/4 of the old fermented grains are removed each time, and 3/4 of the old fermented grains are kept in an infinite cycle, is this not the Chinese philosophy of "leaving some room"? Or maybe we are not broad-minded enough, strong-aroma flavor baijiu famous enterprises are too many, and they are each in their own way, each spreading their own "personality," rather than uniting together to speak of the "commonality" of strong-aroma flavor baijiu; if strong-aroma flavor baijiu needs a pioneer, then start with Luzhou Laojiao.

As the first popular science book in the liquor industry that relates baijiu culture and baijiu knowledge in the form of "cartoon + text," *The Cellar Master Speaks* has been well received by readers for its "easy-to-understand language, witty and humorous cartoons, and serious science" style since the first series was published. The style has been welcomed by the majority of readers. Now, *The Cellar Master Speaks* has been written and drawn picture by picture, and has already been published in its third series. We have assembled the key chapters of the first three series into this book, *Luzhou Laojiao: Chinese Baijiu in Comics (Deluxe Edition)*, which is actually a classic version of "Twenty Lectures on the Baijiu Culture of Luzhou Laojiao," including topics concerned by many readers: the history of Luzhou Laojiao, the history of strong-aroma flavor baijiu, the interpretation of the seven resources of Luzhou Laojiao: land, cellar, art, fermentation, water, grain and storage, as well as "Why does strong-aroma flavor baijiu have a better aftertaste?"

"Why is aged liquor more fragrant?" "Why do more drinkers live longer since ancient times?" "Why can you drink liquor on ice in summer, and why not all liquor is suitable for drinking on ice?" "How can you tell other people's drinking capacity?" "Why do some foreign liquors more easily go to the head than baijius?" We hope that readers will benefit from this book.

For the successful publication of *The Cellar Master Speaks* series and this book, first of all, we must especially thank the chairman of Luzhou Laojiao, China Distilling Master Liu Miao, General Manager Lin Feng, and Executive Vice President Wang Hongbo, as well as Chief Engineer and China Distilling Master Shen Caihong, and China Distilling Master and Chief Quality Officer He Cheng, for their strong support; as a popular science series, we will continue to work hard to create more; of course, also with the strong support of the company's leadership, we have opened a second track, the popular science animation number "Jiao Xiao Er Bu Er," and the fan base has exceeded 3 million after less than one year's operation, with 150 million plays. At the same time, we would like to express our special thanks to Mr. Sun Baoguo, President of Beijing Technology and Business University and Academician of the Chinese Academy of Engineering; Mr. Song Shuyu, Chinese Distilling Master and Chairman of the China Alcoholic Drink Association, for their prefaces to this book; Dr. Zhang Suyi, Chinese Distilling Master and China's Chief Spirits Taster; Mr. Xu Defu, a professor-level senior engineer and distilling master of Sichuan Province, as well as our team of distilling masters: Yang Ping, a great craftsman, Zhou Jun, a national spirits taster, Dr. Qin Hui, Dr. Wang Songtao, and others for their precious advice about their profession. Finally, we would like to thank our team members Mou Xueying, Zhao Mingli, Xiao Guilan, Fu Han, Wen Jialu, Chen Keyue, Xie Ruolan, Li Yunfeng, and Zhang Lan for their meticulous editing and proofreading of the entire book with great responsibility and dedication.

Liquor is the crystallization of human civilization, the water of life, and the source of art given by God to humankind. We hope that when we enjoy all the beauty of liquor, we can know more about it, appreciate it, and know how to tame it instead of being tamed by it.

LI BIN
July 9, 2021

References

Ai, Jinzhong, Zhang Kun, Du Yanhong, Nie Jianguang, and Wang Chao. "Research on the Nano-morphology of Hongxing Erguotou Liquor by Atomic Force Microscope" *Liquor-Making Science and Technology*, no. 4 (2010).

Chen, Maochun, et al. *Luzhou Laojiao Daqu Liquor*. Beijing: Light Industry Publishing House, 1959.

Chen, Maochun, et al. *Luzhou Laojiao Daqu Liquor*. Beijing: China Light Industry Press, 1959.

Cui, Li. "Nutrition Component of Chinese Liquor and Its Benefit to Human Health." *Liquor Making*, no. 1 (2008).

"Contemporary Sichuan Series" Editorial Department. *Luzhou, the City of Baijiu*. Chengdu: Sichuan People's Publishing House, 2000.

Editorial Committee. *Luzhou, the City of Baijiu*. Chengdu: Sichuan People's Publishing House, 1999.

Fu, Jinquan, ed. *Research and Application of Chinese Liquor-Making Microorganisms*. Beijing: China Light Industry Press, 2008.

Han, Xinglin, Wang Yong, Wei Jinwang, Wang Deliang, Tang Kuntian, and Zhao Caiyun. "Analysis of Polyhydric Alcohols in Qing-flavor Liquor." *Liquor-Making Science and Technology*, no. 8 (2013).

Han, Xinglin, Yao Yiping, Ni Yongpei, Xiang Xingben, Wang Shaolei, Chen Bin, and Huangfu Jie. "Analysis of the Flavor Composition for Ying Jiagong Baijiu's Sweet Feeling." *Liquor-Making Science and Technology*.

He, Manzi. *Chinese Liquor Culture*. Shanghai: Shanghai Chinese Classics Publishing House, 2001.

Hu, Jiyang. "Investigation on the Contributing Factors of Sweetness of Luzhou-flavor Liquor." *Liquor-Making Science and Technology*.

Hu, Yonghe. "Significance of Pits for the Production of Luzhou-flavor Liquor." *Liquor-Making Science and Technology*, no. 4 (2006).

Lai, Gaohuai. *60 Years of China's Baijiu Review and Prospects (1951–2011)*. Chengdu: Sichuan University Press, 2012.

Lan, Yong. *Historical and Cultural Geography of Southwest*. Chongqing: Southwest Normal University Press, 1997.